IDEOLOGY AND POLITICAL LIFE

THIRD EDITION

IDEOLOGY AND POLITICAL LIFE

Kenneth Hoover
with
Vernon Johnson
John Miles
Sara Weir
Western Washington University

Harcourt College Publishers
Fort Worth   Philadelphia   San Diego   New York   Orlando   Austin   San Antonio
Toronto   Montreal   London   Sydney   Tokyo

Publisher	Earl McPeek
Executive Editor	David Tatom
Market Strategist	Laura Brennan
Project Manager	Barrett Lackey

Cover and Interior Design—Candice Carta, York Production Services

ISBN: 0-15-507498-9
Library of Congress Catalog Card Number: 00-106592

Address for Domestic Orders
Harcourt College Publishers, 6277 Sea Harbor Drive, Orlando, FL 32887-6777
800-782-4479

Address for International Orders
International Customer Service
Harcourt College Publishers, 6277 Sea Harbor Drive, Orlando, FL 32887-6777
407-345-3800
(fax) 407-345-4060
(e-mail) hbintl@harcourtbrace.com

Address for Editorial Correspondence
Harcourt College Publishers, 301 Commerce Street, Suite 3700, Fort Worth, TX 76102

Web Site Address
http://www.harcourtcollege.com

Printed in the United States of America

0 1 2 3 4 5 6 7 8 9   039   9 8 7 6 5 4 3 2 1

Harcourt College Publishers

To Our Students

TABLE OF CONTENTS

PREFACE

This book presents the ideologies essential to the understanding of contemporary American politics. For the student of politics, it will serve as a basic text on the meanings of these ideologies. The reader will have the chance to confront each ideology in its own terms and then to understand its origins, development, and current political significance. In the final chapter, we summarize some important characteristics of ideologies and comment on how they influence politics.

An awareness of the organizational pattern of the chapters will help the reader greatly. There is a pattern to the chapters. Each chapter begins with a simplified description of the *image* of political life that can be derived from one ideology. The second part of the chapter is an *analysis* designed to unfold the assumptions, shifts of meaning, and experimentation that went into the development of the image. The images of political life are, in a sense, utopias written from the point of view of a specific ideology. Some ideologies can't be reduced to a single image. For example, contrasting images are developed to illustrate two different versions of conservatism: libertarian and traditionalist.

The analytical part of each chapter explores how the ideas emerged, how they are applied to contemporary political issues, and how they have been criticized. The history of each ideology is organized primarily in terms of introducing themes rather than concentrating on dates, names of theorists, or historical epochs, which are mentioned only as they become relevant to the development of the ideas.

The chapters are grouped into Part One, "The Roots of the Present," and Part Two, "Contemporary Ideologies." The first part of the book is thematically integrated through the development of a two-dimensional left-right ideological spectrum. This spectrum forms a common framework for understanding the variations found in the basic ideologies of our time. Although it is intuitively familiar to those interested in ideology, the spectrum developed in the text incorporates a fresh analysis of the underlying issues that separate left from right.

The revisions to Part One mainly involve a concerted effort to get closer to the original sources so that the proponents speak for themselves, rather than through the voices of interpreters with various ideological agendas. The history of political thought is steeped in controversy, and the scholar's job is to ensure fairness—if not objectivity. No one comes to these ideas as a neutral, but there is such a thing as due consideration for accuracy. A sabbatical at the London School of Economics; St. Catherine's College, Oxford; and the University of Washington has provided the time and the ideal places to pursue such inquiries.

In this third edition, Part Two is nearly all new. The original author is joined by three colleagues at Western Washington University, each of whom presents a distinctive voice in discussing the politics of gender, race, and the environment. Sara Weir, who teaches and does community work in public policy and feminist theory, writes of the several feminisms in contemporary thought. She discusses the ways that feminists have critiqued classical ideologies and developed new ways of exploring the meaning of liberation. Vernon Johnson, a specialist in comparative politics, draws upon his research in Africa and the U.S. on post-settler colonies to illuminate the struggle to define black nationalism. Johnson's work with the Northwest Coalition for Human Dignity and other organizations figures in his perspective on these themes. John Miles, Director of Western's Center for Geography and Environmental Social Sciences, reflects on the long effort to bring the environment to the center of political discourse. As a mountaineer and former member of the Washington State Forest Practices Board, he, too, speaks from experience as well as scholarly insight.

The purpose of Part Two is to give students the chance to think about the ideological forces that are changing contemporary politics. The conclusion to Part Two makes use of research done by Kenneth Hoover on the connections between ideology and identity.

ACKNOWLEDGMENTS

A book of this kind grows out of the summation of many influences, not least the kind of collegial interaction represented in Part Two. So many others have been involved in three editions that it is better to simply salute the community of scholars and students who make these books possible than to risk missing someone of importance. Specific research assistance for this edition was provided by two fine students, Diego Bartholomew and Johnny Peel. Western Washington University's sabbatical program and the support of Dean Peter Elich, Dean Mohab Ghali and Provost Larry DeLorme were essential in this effort, as was the most welcome assistance provided by Sue Scally and Director Geri Walker of Western's Bureau for Faculty Research.

Kenneth Hoover
Western Washington University

THE ROOTS OF THE PRESENT

PART ONE

CHAPTER ONE

INTRODUCTION TO PART ONE: THE IDEOLOGICAL SPECTRUM

What persuades men and women to mistake each other from time to time for gods or vermin is ideology. One can understand well enough how human beings may struggle and murder for good material reasons—reasons connected, for instance, with their physical survival. It is much harder to grasp how they may come to do so in the name of something as apparently abstract as ideas. Yet ideas are what men and women live by, and will occasionally die for.

TERRY EAGLETON
Ideology: An Introduction (1991)

Ideas provide images of the world, images that give shape to our thoughts and feelings. To the extent that they are held in common, these images open up the possibility of shared insights and action. This book is about shared images of a particularly powerful kind: political ideologies.

What are ideologies? Many people think that other people's beliefs are ideological, but not their own. It is true that not all political beliefs are ideological, but you can better judge whether you yourself have an ideology once the examples of ideology in this book are understood and you have a general definition of ideology in hand. In the scholarship of ideology, there are many definitions distinguishing ideology from philosophy, theory, and personal predisposition. To make the concept as accessible as possible, this book will present a broad view of ideology.

In working toward a definition of ideology, we will follow the path taken by Michael Freeden in his comprehensive study of the connections between politics, concepts, and ideologies. Freeden observes that:

> In concrete terms, an ideology will link together a particular conception of human nature, a particular conception of social structure, of justice, of liberty, of authority, etc. '*This* is what liberty means, and *that* is what justice means,' it asserts.

Each ideology discussed in this book will assert specific meanings for such contentious concepts as equality, justice, freedom, etc. The act of settling the conflict over these meanings leads directly to decisions about political action. Freeden continues:

> Ideologies need, after all, to straddle the worlds of political thought and political action, for one of their central functions is to link the two. The political sphere is primarily characterized by political decision-making, and decision-making is an important form of de-contesting a range of potential alternatives.[1]

Ideologies help people to "make up their minds" by resolving confusion and ambiguity about politics.[2] This leads us to a definition: *Ideologies link underlying beliefs about the human condition to political ideas that contain a plan of action.*

As an example, to believe that justice *means* that every human being is entitled to basic human rights is to be oriented toward actions to establish and protect those rights. Why would we believe such a thing? Because some underlying philosophical or religious view tells us that "all [people] are created equal, and endowed by their Creator with certain inalienable rights." The American Declaration of Independence was a profound exercise in ideology that rallied thousands of colonists to act against the enormous power of the British empire.

In the course of deciding how to act, we also establish an element of our identity as a person. Michael Freeden concludes:

> . . . Ideologies serve as the bridging mechanism between contestability and determinacy, converting the inevitable variety of options into the monolithic certainty which is the unavoidable feature of a political *decision,* and which is the basis for the forging of a political identity.

---

1. Freeden, *Ideologies and Political Theory: A Conceptual Approach* (Oxford: Oxford University Press, 1996), 76–77.

2. For a discussion of how ideologies and identities are intertwined, see Kenneth Hoover, James Marcia, and Kristen Parris, *The Power of Identity: Politics in a New Key* (New York: Seven Bridges/Chatham House, 1997). For an illustration, see Kenneth Hoover, "Ideologizing Institutions: Laski, Hayek, Keynes, and the Creation of Contemporary Politics," *Journal of Political Ideologies,* 4 (1999) 1, 87–115.

The Declaration of Independence held out a new vision of justice and, in the process, created a new political identity: *the American*. The English were surprised to discover such people where there had mainly been "colonists" before.

The sources of the Declaration's vision were in centuries of European political philosophy going back to the Greeks and Romans, along with some thoughts borrowed from the Iroquois and other Native Americans.[3] The Declaration of Independence *de-contested* the competing elements of these ideas and brought coherence to a chaotic era of politics. From this example, we can sense the power, the possibilities, and the great dangers inherent in ideology, as well as the uses ideologies make of ideas, and the identities that ideologies help to form. All ideologies have some characterization of the human condition at their core, even if it is the denial that all people share a common human nature.[4] These characterizations of life all employ *images* of power relationships between individuals and society. Images of power relationships provide the starting point for each chapter in this book. They are the inspiration for each ideology's plan of action.

In the name of conservatism, liberalism, Marxism, fascism, and the other ideologies discussed here, societies have been reshaped, great sacrifices have been made, and wars have been fought. Yet the public understanding of these ideologies has been confused by historical changes, competing interpretations, sloganizing, and deceptive advertising by candidates and political parties. The plan of this book is to describe each *image* as vividly as possible and then to *analyze* its origins and meaning.

We will see in each image the visions of theorists who have shaped the main ideas. You need to ask questions such as these: What assumptions lie behind the theories? Which assumptions might be open to evaluation based on observation and experience? What distribution of power and privilege follows from each image?

Most of us can't conceive of living in a society that fits precisely with one or another of these images. Instead, we would find that elements of each ideology are represented among the citizens of most nations and communities. The conflicts within a society are often shaped by people acting on contrasting ideological assumptions. The assumptions may not be clear to the user, and they are often the more potent for being unanalyzed. The analysis in this text is directed toward untangling these various threads of assumption and argument.

Ideology is a crucial part of political life. Few people will obey (or defy) authority without some kind of justification. Modern societies build huge struc-

---

3. Cf. Harold Hellenbrand, "Not 'To Destroy But to Fulfil': Jefferson, Indians, and Republican Dispensation," *Eighteenth-Century Studies,* 18 (Autumn, 1985) 4: 523–549.

4. On the history of disputes over the meaning of ideology, see David McLellan, *Ideology* (Minneapolis: University of Minnesota Press, 1986).

tures of authority and power on concepts of power that are derived from ideologies. As we will see, the revolution that established the U.S. Constitution was deeply influenced by ideologies imported from Western Europe. Karl Marx's ideological conceptions provided a justification for revolutions in Russia and China, two of the largest nations in the world. Contemporary American political discussion centers on the rival claims of liberals and conservatives.

Ideological systems embracing ideas from economics, sociology, politics, and philosophy supply the integrating intellectual themes of a culture. They form a language of justification for myriad decisions affecting people's lives together. Whether such ideas really do govern our actions cannot be conclusively determined, but there is no doubt that action is linked to ideas.

To understand an ideology is to see what its ideas about power involve and how these ideas are related to assumptions about individual and community life. To evaluate an ideology, one must add to this understanding an analysis of whether its assumptions are correct, its ideas about power are reasonable, and its recipes for governing are workable. This is a tall order. Our purpose here is to enable you to recognize ideology and evaluate its claims.

This book is not a comprehensive history of ideologies. Spokespeople for the various ideologies have been selected from the point of view of teacher-scholars trained in political philosophy. We have tried to single out the most important figures, not necessarily as they were viewed in their own time but, rather, as they appear from a contemporary perspective. Who contributed most significantly to the ideologies we live with today? As a consequence of this focus, the history will not always be chronological and will certainly not be encyclopedic, and it will omit mention of many who are important in favor of concentrating on those who crystallized the essential changes.

The approach taken to ideology in these chapters involves rejecting one commonly made distinction: that between politics and economics. The title of the book is *Ideology and Political Life*. The phrase *political ideology* does not appear in the title because politics and economics can't be separated from each other at the level of ideology. Historically, these two fields were combined as "political economy." As succeeding chapters will illustrate, conceptions about power concern economics in a very fundamental sense.

THE IDEOLOGICAL SPECTRUM

Ideology usually enters into conventional political talk through images such as "Margery is a real right-winger" or "José is a leftist." The notion that ideologies can be arrayed along a line from left to right, and that these directions are broadly associated with socialism on the left and conservatism on the right, has a powerful hold on the public imagination. But how is this spectrum put together? Is it of any real use in understanding ideology?

The answers given in this book to the first question suggest that the spectrum needs to be seen in a slightly different way than is conventional. We will also see that the spectrum helps us more with the *history* of ideology than with *contemporary* ideologies, though it does shed some light on the roots of feminism and of racial politics. Toward the end of this chapter, it will become apparent that feminists are raising issues different from those that divided classical liberals from traditional conservatives, for example. The reason for this disjunction between the past and the present is that the issues of central concern in our politics appear to be changing—but first it is important to understand what the spectrum represents.

It is conventional to argue that the principal issue involved in the spectrum is equality: those on the "left" believe in equality; those on the "right" don't. This is a valid distinction and one that works, up to a point. It helps in separating the advocates of equality, such as reform liberals and socialists, from the critics of equality, such as monarchists and Fascists.

Any image as simple as a spectrum for something as complex as ideologies inevitably distorts the subject. One distortion is that no one believes in absolute equality, nor does anyone really believe that people have absolutely nothing in common. If the distinction between left and right is phrased in this extreme way, it becomes easy to dismiss the extremes, or to stereotype all leftists as dreamers and all rightists as snobs. The crudeness of the distinction gets in the way of serious analysis.

So it is important to restate this key distinction. In this presentation of the spectrum, those on the *left* are associated with the belief that *similarities between people are more important than differences,* and those on the *right* are associated with the conviction that *differences are more important than similarities* (see Figure 1.1). If the distinction is phrased in this way, it becomes apparent that a serious issue is at stake.

As examples of how ideologies would be placed on the conventional spectrum, see Figure 1.1. Placement is based on approaches to issues of similarities and differences. Classical liberals, acting on the conviction that every person

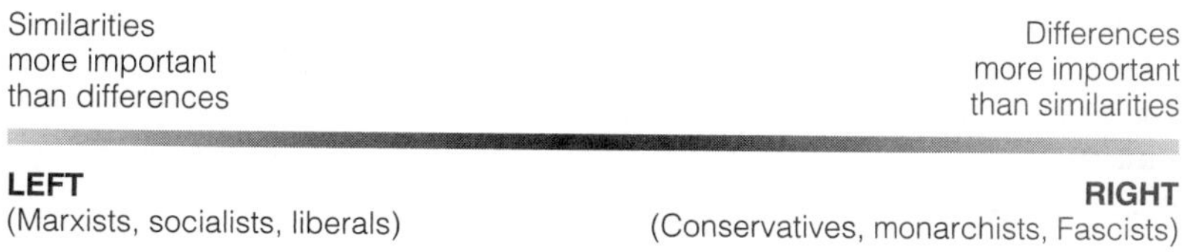

Similarities more important than differences	Differences more important than similarities
LEFT (Marxists, socialists, liberals)	**RIGHT** (Conservatives, monarchists, Fascists)

FIGURE 1.1   A One-Issue Ideological Spectrum

(handwritten margin note: Valid but up to a point)

shares the capacity to reason, assert the right of individuals to freedom of expression. Each person is capable of reason, and no one is by nature more suited to rule than any other. Thus, representative government can be justified.

Socialists carry the point further, arguing that our common needs would best be served by shared labor and an equitable division of the results of labor. They add the notion of economic sharing to the concept of equal political rights, placing them further to the left on the conventional spectrum.

Traditional conservatives, on the other hand, base their views on the presumption that people have different abilities, characters, and qualities. For them, these differences are the critical factor in approaching questions of order, the limits of freedom, and justice. Arranging the world so that there is a suitable place for each person to work within his or her limits is the objective of conservative institutions. The military, the church, the family, and, in the current context, the corporation are institutions that reflect traditional conceptions of role differentiation and hierarchy.

The controversy over human similarities and differences is at the core of much of the history of ideology. The French Revolution was fought in the name of Liberty, Equality, Fraternity. All three were values that asserted the solidarity of the ordinary people of France against their privileged masters. In fact, the image of left versus right originated in the customary seating in the Estates General, which advised the king of France prior to the revolution. Those who favored reform sat to the King's left, his allies, the friends of the old order, sat to his right.

There is, however, a second issue that divides the ideologies: the question of *freedom and power*. Some ideologies are oriented to a powerful state, for example, as the key to attaining the values central to the ideology. Fascists place the state at the heart of the ideology, arguing that it is the means for the realization of racial supremacy. Marxist-Leninists, as we will see, also see state power as essential to the revolutionary struggle. The state is the vehicle for the party of the proletariat and the means by which revolutionary priorities can be achieved.

On the other hand, classical liberals and libertarian conservatives, who *disagree* on the question of the relative importance of similarities and differences, *agree* on the primacy of individual freedom with respect to concentrations of power. Classical liberals (see Chapter 2) are the major proponents of the idea that individuals have rights that should be protected from interference by the state. Individualist conservatives (see Chapter 4) argue that the freedom to pursue one's own material self-interest in the marketplace is the most important aspect of liberty and that the power of the state to interfere in the market should be minimized. Both of these groups set important limits on the power of government and view politics from the perspective of a need to ensure individual freedom to the maximum possible extent.

As a way of capturing this image, it is important to introduce a second dimension to the spectrum, as shown in Figure 1.2. In this image, the familiar

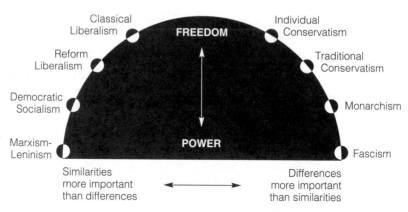

 FIGURE 1.2   A Two-Issue Ideological Spectrum

left-right spectrum is preserved. Socialists are on the left, conservatives on the right. But the vertical dimension reveals the contrasting positions of each ideology on the issue of freedom versus power. On this second dimension, Marxism-Leninism is in the same position as fascism: both focus on the state as the means of achieving their most essential purposes.

In the same fashion, reform liberalism and traditional conservatism have similar views about the importance of an active state, though for dissimilar purposes. Reform liberals want the active state to regulate the economy as a way of increasing equality, and traditional conservatives argue that the state should be active in maintaining order and in supporting other authoritative institutions of the society, such as the family, the church, and the military. *same but different reasons*

This two-issue spectrum establishes a perspective on the major ideologies. We can begin to see how they differ, as well as how they developed in relation to one another. An alternating pattern of reform followed by reaction characterizes this history and helps make sense out of it. Classical liberalism emerged from the struggle against monarchy. Classical liberalism, in turn, was challenged from the right by traditional conservatives and from the left by democratic socialists as well as Marxists. Fascism was a reaction against democratic socialism and Marxism. The successor to classical liberalism was reform liberalism, which incorporated some elements of socialism but retained the basic commitments of liberal political philosophy. In the last two decades, reform liberalism has met with a highly effective critique from individualist conservatives.

The story to be told here, then, is of a struggle over ideas that shape political movements, parties, policies, and even revolutions. The issues in that struggle center on the significance of human similarities and differences, as well as differing perspectives on individual freedom and the power of the state.

As this book's table of contents makes evident, the sequence of chapters proceeds in such a way as to reconstruct this historic struggle. Classical liberalism is the protagonist in the discussion, because our political institutions are steeped in it. After considering the image of political life sponsored by liberalism, we move to its historical rival, traditional conservatism. The subsequent chapter shows how modern conservatism has been influenced by the classical liberal tradition in the form of libertarian ideology and has produced libertarian conservatism, which is contrasted with anarchism. We move on to examine "reform" liberalism, the modern face of liberalism. From there, we shift consideration to the major alternatives to liberalism and conservatism, Marxism and socialism. The concluding chapters deal with fascism, liberation ideologies, and the emergence of a "third way."

Having established the differences, and perhaps even exploited the distinctions to increase the contrasts, we will try to find in the concluding chapter common characteristics of ideologies and a perspective for working out a personal view of ideology.

THE USES OF IDEOLOGICAL ANALYSIS

After a generation of political analysis that has deemphasized and even disregarded ideology as a factor in political behavior, we find ourselves at the beginning of a new millenium with a political situation that has apparently been transformed by ideology. Consequently, it is not surprising that political scientists have begun to reevaluate the role of ideology. Although it is by no means clear that ideology operates independently of considerations of class, self-interest, and the dynamics of bureaucracy, to name a few of the rival explanations of political behavior, there is at the very least sufficient cause for uncertainty about the precise role that it does play.

Recent research has begun to challenge the generalization, made on the basis of early behavioral studies, that the public knows or cares little about ideology. It is becoming apparent that at least a third of the U.S. population has a general grasp of ideological distinctions, another third has a rather confusing picture, and the remaining third hasn't given it much thought—or won't respond to the questionnaire. Given the difficulties of eliciting responses to complex phenomena such as ideologies, it may be that such surveys understate the extent to which ideological beliefs are present.[5] Suffice it to say that ideologies do appear to con-

---

5. See Norman Luttbeg and Michael Gant, "The Failure of Liberal/Conservative Ideology as a Cognitive Structure," *Public Opinion Quarterly* 49 (Spring 1985): 80–93, specifically 91.

strain the views of many people on specific issues and to influence voting deci-sions.[6]

Ideology does not have to be clearly articulated or consistent to be powerful. It is likely that most people have a *set* of ideologies rather than a single ideology and that elements of this set are mobilized in response to particular cues.[7] We know, for example, that many people believe *both* that poor people are the victims of exploitation *and* that poor people are lazy and undeserving. It is possible to mobilize one or the other ideological framework depending on the cues that are present in the situation. A hungry family searching through a dumpster full of garbage may evoke one framework, and a welfare recipient buying steak with food stamps may evoke the other. The point is that only by disentangling the threads of ideology can we understand the impact of these ideas on behavior; to fail to do so is to misunderstand the sources of much of our politics.

Few political scientists predicted the fall of the Wall in 1989, or the resur-gence of conservatism or, for that matter, the rise of the counterculture in the late 1960s. Perhaps it was because they had become inattentive to the significance of ideology. So we have some reason for seeing ideology as pervasive. Ideology, to reiterate, is a crucial part of political life. Few people will obey or defy their gov-ernment without some kind of justification.

CONCLUSION

Some potent ideological terms have not been dealt with thus far: democracy, nationalism, anarchism, populism, and progressivism, to name several. These concepts will appear in the discussion that follows as they enter into the forma-tion of the major ideologies. Nearly all modern ideologies endorse democracy, but in each of them democracy is hedged with various limits on institutions and processes that are fairly predictable once the underlying issues of equality and freedom are clearly understood. Similarly, nationalism plays a role in several ide-ologies on the right, though it means different things to traditional conservatives, monarchists, and Fascists.

Populism and progressivism will be discussed in the context of contempo-rary splits within the two major political formations of our time, reform liberal-

---

6. This revisionist line of research is in response to Philip Converse's earlier and very influential work reported in Angus Campbell et al., *The American Voter* (Chicago: University of Chicago Press, 1980). See Mark Peffley and Jon Hurwitz, "A Hierarchical Model of Attitude Constraint," *American Journal of Political Science* 29 (1985): 885. Cf. William Jacoby, "Levels of Conceptualization and Reliance on the Liberal-Conservative Continuum," *Journal of Politics* 48 (1986): 423–432.

7. See Murray Edelman, *The Symbolic Uses of Politics* (Urbana: University of Illinois Press, 1964).

ism and conservative capitalism (see Chapters 3 and 4). These are important distinctions, particularly in American politics, and they will be seen as guides to understanding how ideology enters into the current political scene.

Finally, anarchism will be examined as a way of gaining perspective on libertarian, conservatism, with which it shares some key arguments (Chapter 4). Anarchism does not fit neatly within the spectrum we have developed. Although it is the most libertarian of all the ideologies, anarchism of the left differs on questions of equality and human cooperation from anarchism of the right. The latter is where the connection to libertarian conservatism can be made. By considering various anarchist points of view, we can grasp the distinctive character of libertarian conservatism.

This book considers the most sweeping questions of human association. If these ideas meet with your individual experience in revealing ways, and if there is guidance here for well-informed action, then we have accomplished our main purpose.

CHAPTER TWO

CLASSICAL LIBERALISM

*To deserve, to acquire, and to
enjoy the respect and admiration of
mankind, are the great objects of ambition and emulation.*

ADAM SMITH

(1776)

*The community is a fictitious body, composed of the individual persons who are considered
as constituting as it were its members. The interest of the community then is, what?—the
sum of the interests of the several members who compose it.*

JEREMY BENTHAM

(1789)

The liberal image of political life has had a powerful impact. Classical liberalism has permeated Western society and now, at the millenium, it is one of the driving forces in the globalization of political culture. Movements for representative government and open markets owe their inspiration to the ideas we will examine in this chapter.

Classical liberalism, as a political ideology, is the protagonist of Western intellectual history in the modern era. As such, it has been the focal point of major critiques from socialists on the left and conservatives on the right. At the same time, classical liberal ideas have been borrowed for the purposes of the left, as well as the right, in order to make their agendas more appealing to a broader public. Although the victim of criticism by the left. Many ideas have been borrowed by both wing

13

What is confusing for many students is that contemporary *reform* liberalism is not the same as the *classical* liberalism that is the focus of this chapter. We will find that classical liberals of the eighteenth and nineteenth centuries believed in limited government, whereas reform liberals believe in more extensive uses of political power (see Chapter 5). Before we can understand the meanings of the term *liberal* today, it is necessary to see how classical liberalism originated. With that in mind, we can identify the historical reasons for the shift from classical to reform liberal attitudes concerning the role of government.

Ideologies originate in struggles to solve problems of power and authority. The problem that classical liberalism set out to solve was the arbitrary use of power by monarchs in medieval Europe while, at the same time, preserving the nation-state as a means of dealing with common needs for peace, security, and personal development. Developed in the struggle against divine right monarchy, liberal ideas became a loosely organized system of political thought that affected every dimension of power relationships in society.

The story of classical liberalism, as we will see in this chapter, is a tale of exploration. Liberal political theorists explored the various possibilities for bringing the individual and the state into some sort of workable arrangement where the best attributes of each would be combined for the purpose of advancing civilization. While partisans of the left and right would have us believe that liberalism is all about individualism, at one extreme, or about rationalizing the use of coercive power through the state, at the other, the truth lies in the tension between these poles.[1]

Classical liberals feared anarchy at least as much as tyranny. In the formative struggle of the English Civil War and its aftermath, seventeenth-century theorists such as Hobbes and Locke had witnessed both extremes. They had seen excesses of power in the reign of Charles I and in the dictatorship of Oliver Cromwell, and they were witnesses to the brutalities of a Civil War where, in the name of their God, Protestants and Catholics murdered each other. Divided as well by urban and rural economic interests, and loyalties to a variety of leaders, the people of England had descended into a world where life was, as Hobbes observed, "solitary, poor, nasty, brutish and short." The tension between state power and individual freedom has rarely been so sharply evident.

The device that classical liberals used to resolve this tension was to substitute legitimate authority for coercive power. The distinction between authority

---

1. See, for example, C. B. Macpherson, *The Political Theory of Possessive Individualism* (New York: Oxford University Press, 1962), and the origins of his Marxist view of liberalism in Harold Laski, *The Rise of European Liberalism* (London: Transaction, 1997 [1936]), pp. xxiv–xxiv, 24; Friedrich Hayek, "The Principles of a Liberal Social Order," in Chiaki Nishiyama and Kurt Leube, *The Essence of Hayek* (Stanford, Calif.: The Hoover Institution, 1984), 31.

and power is one of the most fundamental in the study of politics. As described in *The Power of Identity: Politics in a New Key,* the distinction may be understood as follows:

> *Power* involves the ability to coerce compliance, *authority* rests on the capacity to enlist compliance voluntarily. Political systems that rely on a high level of authority have little need for exercises of power. The respected coach, the natural team leader, the dissident with integrity—all command a following that no amount of power can compel. On the other hand, totalitarian systems use power and the threat of coercion to produce conformity with regime goals, and work hard at producing the illusion of voluntary compliance.[2]

Classical liberals thought they could legitimize government by making it accountable to the people through constitutions and, later, elections. By substituting legitimate *authority* for the *power* of the monarch, the essential functions of government could be performed with a minimum amount of coercion.

The Declaration of Independence contains a long list of grievances about the arbitrary and vindictive use of power by the English monarch. This list comprised the evidence for the claim that British rule was unjust. The colonists therefore asserted the right of the people to abolish colonial rule and establish a new government founded on constitutional principles. This illustration is meant to convey the critical importance of the distinction between authority and power. In the discussion below, you will see how classical liberals tried to work out the meaning of this distinction in the practice of politics.

Before proceeding to evoke the image of a classical liberal utopia, there is one final difficulty that needs to be recognized. The hallmark of all truly powerful ideological systems is that they come to be seen as sacred in a religious sense or, in our secular age, as "natural."[3] From this characteristic arises another problem in understanding liberalism: it is so rooted in our culture as to be nearly unconscious. To retrieve its ideas for analysis requires, first, that we create a simplified and idealized model of the classical liberal polity. Using that image as a beginning point, we can explore the history and implications of the liberal view of political life.

It is easiest to see the liberal image by the use of an illustration. We will construct a liberal utopia: a community with a representative government, constitu-

---

2. Kenneth Hoover, James Marcia, and Kristen Parris, *The Power of Identity: Politics in a New Key* (New York: Seven Bridges/Chatham House, 1997), p. 75.

3. For detailed interpretations of the rise of classical liberalism, see Karl Polanyi, *The Great Transformation: The Political and Economic Origins of Our Time* (Boston: Beacon Press, 1957), and Louis Dumont, *From Mandeville to Marx: The Genesis and Triumph of Economic Ideology* (Chicago: University of Chicago Press, 1977).

tional limits on power, and rights of free expression, private property, and association. As we examine the implications of this illustration, the liberal concept of politics will become clear. For the moment, we will set aside current meanings of the term *liberal*. The first task is to develop the classical liberal position and, later, its connection to contemporary liberalism and the "welfare state."

THE CLASSICAL LIBERAL IMAGE OF POLITICAL LIFE

At the core of the liberal image of political life lies the notion of a community organized around a limited, representative government where individuals are free to earn a living and express themselves so long as others are not harmed in the process. It is a community of people who are able to develop their abilities and to join together to achieve a more civilized way of life. The structure of power, both political and economic, is tied to the service of these ends.

The most important institution is government-based on consent. While there are considerable variations in how this consent is obtained in practice, the essential point is that the authority to govern is accountable to the people. The modern version of the classical liberal utopia would base the rationale for government in universal ideals of the protection of human rights. A constitution would establish mechanisms of representative government charged with the protection of these rights. The constitution would also limit the power of government to interfere with the ability of individuals to work, trade, and express their beliefs. At the same time, the constitution would empower government to use force in defending these arrangements and enable common action on behalf of agreed-upon social goals.

The protection of private property, and the formulation of laws governing its use and exchange, occupy the major part of the law-making function. Contracts enforced by the state provide a legal means for conducting property relationships without having to resort to individual coercion. Proposing and enforcing those laws is the business of the executive. Disputes between property owners are generally settled by the judiciary. Through representative government, individuals and organized interests compete for power by influencing elections and political appointments, pressuring for legislation, and shaping law enforcement practices.

A principal function of representative government is to establish a framework of law within which exchange relations can take place efficiently. The marketplace is where one's labor and capital, and the goods and services that are produced, can be bought and sold through voluntary exchanges. Access to goods and services would be determined by each individual's resources rather than by the use of force or fraud. Without the right to own property and to lay claim to the results of labor and of capital investment, there would only be, so the classical liberal thinks, theft, coercion, and even, as Thomas Hobbes put it, "a war of all against all."

Theoretically, in the perfect market, the jobs would be performed by those most expert in each specialization. Merit replaces aristocratic birth and, over time, other distinctions such as race and gender, as the means of determining who is chosen for positions of responsibility. To the extent that an individual is ambitious and works hard, he or she can prosper or languish according to effort. The rise and fall of prices in response to supply and demand sets the framework for consumption and production. Everyone would presumably benefit from this efficient application of energy and talent to the satisfying of people's wants. Rational procedures for conducting competition become the objective of legislation and the centerpiece of hiring and advancement policies.

The intellectual justification for classical liberalism grows out of an image of freedom disciplined by the recognition of mutual rights and responsibilities. It is through the ideal of freedom of expression that the dignity of the individual is upheld. Classical liberals view freedom as maximizing personal choice over the widest possible range of activities, including working together for the purposes of "life, liberty, and the pursuit of happiness."

Restrictions on freedom emerge from the need to limit one particular sort of behavior: interference by one individual with the rights and property of another. Denying another person the same freedom of expression and material accumulation we wish to have for ourselves is contrary to the good of the community. Similarly, using government to foreclose people's choices of religion, occupation, beliefs, or interests is considered to be wrong if it cannot be justified by identifying some overriding threat to public safety.[4]

The role of government with respect to the use of coercion is defined by the dual task of acting to protect rights, and of refraining from actions that threaten rights. The government adjudicates disputes about the practical meaning of rights, uses its police powers to enforce limits on behavior that threatens rights, and takes action to give meaning and effect to assertions of rights by citizens. In the course of the civil rights struggle in the U.S., the Supreme Court decided landmark cases that greatly extended the reach of the right to vote, to live and work where one chooses, and to be free from private and public forms of discrimination. At the same time, some of the most significant victories of the civil rights struggle involved laws that limited the ability of state and local governments to interfere with federally protected rights. Finally, the "War on Poverty"

---

4. For a summary of some of the nuances in the discussion of "Kantian" and "Millsian" approaches to classical liberalism, see Michael Sandel, *Liberalism and the Limits of Justice* (Cambridge: Cambridge University Press, 1982), pp. 1–14.

was justified, in part, as a way of giving victims of discrimination the means of exercising their rights by entitling all citizens to minimum levels of income, nutrition, and housing assistance.

The affirmative role of government is less clearly defined in classical liberalism. The *authority* of government, as opposed to the power, is a matter of legitimacy established through appeals to the electorate and the persuasiveness of rationales for public policy. There is no clearcut principle that defines what government can do in the name of seeking "the greatest happiness for the greatest number." If a public program can improve people's lives, secure the consent of the governed or their representatives, and do this without violating people's rights, then classical liberalism offers no clear stricture to prevent such action.

While the U.S. Constitution sets out a list of "delegated" powers (and reserves to the people those powers not delegated to the federal government), it also leaves open the possibility of action in areas "implied" by the delegations of power. Furthermore, "the people" are left free to place other powers in the hands of state or local governments. Various state constitutions define these powers broadly.

If we had been designing the government of a liberal utopia at the end of the eighteenth century, we would have reproduced many elements of the U.S. Constitution. There would be executive, legislative, and judicial branches of government and the familiar ritual of elections, fixed terms of office, and legal restraints on the power of officials. There would also be invitations to the use of government resources for building up systems of education, transportation, and commerce. very similar to American 1900

Less familiar would be the restrictions on who could vote for and serve in public office. In 1789, suffrage was limited largely to white male property owners over the age of twenty-one. Slaves were counted as inferior beings, and their status as property was acknowledged temporarily in the Constitution. Because government existed to protect property and the framework of the marketplace, there was thought to be no point in enfranchising or empowering people who did not have a settled economic interest in the system.

Classical liberalism is distinct from democracy *per se* in that rule by the majority can result in the violation of rights of minorities. Little by little through the last two centuries, however, liberal societies have become more democratic. The system was democratized because of the struggles of those previously excluded from participating. It was the development of political power by the working class, by minority groups, and by women that forced the issue of participation against the resistance of entrenched interests based on property and white male preeminence. More recently, democratization has resulted from crises in the system that made demands on all sectors of the population: women in the era of the First World War, blacks in the Second World War, and eighteen-year-olds in the Vietnam War.

C.L. ≠ democracy

Having been called upon to help the nation in a time of crisis, they were not interested in being excluded from representative institutions.

Throughout these struggles, the proposition that "all *men* are created equal" came to be translated into "all *people* are created equal." This justification was based on faith in the creator rather than in any observation of the real distribution of power or wealth. The point of the classical liberal society was to establish the conditions for the reality to approximate the ideal without undue coercion or favoritism. We now have a version of liberalism that combines the marketplace with representative government on the basis of nearly universal suffrage.

This powerful image of free persons interacting through representative institutions, while perfecting individual talents, is at the heart of the classical liberal view of political life. A contemporary liberal theorist, John Rawls, has modernized this imagery by using the metaphor of a game, rather than a marketplace. Organized games allow each person to make the most of his or her position within a framework that will assign results to people's behavior. That's why games have rules, referees, and scores. If everyone plays his or her part well, a good play of the game is achieved, and rewards are distributed in accordance with some worthy principle such as effort or the best exercise of a talent.[5]

The image of the liberal polity revolves around the notion that each person will, by developing his or her own interests and abilities, provide necessities and amenities for others that will make their lives better. The function of government is mainly to ensure that people have the freedom to engage in this pursuit.[6] The rhetoric of liberalism, with its emphasis on individual and social development, is very attractive to the modern mind. In order to analyze the implications of this view of political life, we need to understand its history.

ANALYZING THE ORIGINS OF LIBERALISM

The fundamental theme of liberalism concerns the freedom of the individual to develop her/his talents and use them productively.[7] To understand this ideology, we can follow a sequence of three ways in which individual freedom has been jus-

---

5. John Rawls, *A Theory of Justice* (Cambridge, Mass.: Harvard University Press, 1971), pp. 525–526. What separates games from life is that chance is often used, as in a card game, to randomize the starting position of all players so that everyone has the possibility of winning.

6. For a contemporary defense of liberalism, see David Spitz, *The Real World of Liberalism* (Chicago: University of Chicago Press, 1982), especially his liberal "credo," pp. 213–216.

7. According to the *Oxford English Dictionary*, the term *liberal* was "originally the distinctive epithet [name] of those 'arts' or 'sciences' that were considered 'worthy of a free man'; opposed to *servile* or *mechanical*." (Oxford: Oxford University Press, 1971), p. 237.

tified. There is a rough progression from one mode of justification to the next. The first mode rests on the tradition of *natural law,* the second on the concept of *individual rights,* and the third on a theory of *developmental freedom.* Each set of justifications will be considered as we develop an understanding of classical liberalism.

Liberalism and Natural Law

The history of conceptions of natural law is rich and tangled. Our plan is to make sense of it by concentrating on an emerging theme: the notion that the individual person is at the center of God's order and that this order can be known through reason. This justification, which we can call *natural law individualism,* constitutes the earliest version of liberalism. After exploring this idea, we will look briefly at how it evolved into the more modern liberal notion of self-development as a basis for political life.

What is natural law? This question dominates Judeo-Christian political thought. The argument is that there is an inherent moral structure in society, which is organized around certain general principles. Theologians study these principles as a means of understanding the will of God. The conviction that natural law structures morality makes it possible to argue that sin has consequences, either in this world or the next. Similarly, virtue is rewarded, if not in a sinful world then in the afterlife. The point is that our moral decisions take place in the context of patterns of behavior with moral consequences.

It is the conception of natural order that gives religion its power to resolve the doubts and uncertainties of the faithful. The political theory of Christianity from its beginning to the present is little else than an exploration of the relationship between individual persons and a divinely created natural order. The major issue in Christian political philosophy is not *whether* there is order or chaos but, rather, *how* the order can be understood.

Medieval Christians thought that natural law could be known only through devotion, prayer, and self-purification. Monasteries and nunneries were designed to encourage these practices. In the deceptively mild words of St. Augustine (354–430), we can understand God's natural order only by entering into His "community of love." But what Augustine means by love is the simple recognition that order can be achieved only in heaven and that our best course of action on earth is submission to the authority of church and state. The "city of man," in Augustine's words, is sinful and therefore in need of earthly authority. Only in the "city of God" will justice prevail.

In the search for a more humanly oriented way of understanding God's natural order, Christian theologians finally came to examine reason as a means of finding moral truths. In the thirteenth century, Thomas Aquinas (1225–1274), borrowing from Aristotle, put forward reason as the tool that could be used to reveal God's moral principle. The alliance of reason with religion was an extraordinarily bold stroke. Aquinas legitimized reason and, with that move, allowed humans to participate in the method of God's creation. Where Augustinian thought relied almost entirely on faith and tradition as a guide for behavior, Aquinas took a turn toward *humanism* and opened the way to the European Renaissance.

Rationalism was the liberal element in Aquinas's thought. It is not far from baptizing reason to confirming individualism. If reason can unlock the secrets of the natural order, and if reason is found in all individuals, the possibility exists of placing human judgment at the center of political life. This argument permits the construction of a political order around the exercise of individual reason.

Nevertheless, Aquinas's theory of politics was hardly liberal. He quotes approvingly the traditional maxim that "the good of the nation is more godlike than the good of one man."[8] The function of human law is not to express human perceptions, but to approximate natural and divine laws. We can learn something about what those laws are through reason, but we must not, either as individuals or as nations of people, challenge those laws or the authorities who maintain them.

What was riding on the outcome of the debate about the intelligibility of natural law was, quite simply, power. Augustinian theory supported traditional forms of power and authority. If natural law is sacred and mysterious and human beings are the helpless creatures of a divine master, there can be no politics in the conscious sense, for there are no real choices to be made. Power then belongs to religiously sanctioned authority and is not accountable to human judgment.

If, on the other hand, every citizen can potentially understand and interpret natural law, the construction of a political community becomes a most absorbing and demanding task. The exercise of power begins to become accountable to human judgment. If the sovereign is *immoral* by the standard of reasonable interpretations of natural law, there comes to be a basis for criticism of the sovereign. It is even possible to argue that power can be shared among the members of the community who understand the natural order.

From Natural Law to Individual Rights

Two steps lay between medieval Christian conceptions of natural law and the emergence of a form of liberalism based on individual rights. First, the individual had to acquire a significance equal to or greater than that of the society as a whole.

---

8. Dino Bigongiari, ed., *Political Ideas of St. Thomas Aquinas* (New York: W. W. Norton, 1953), p. 84.

Individual will and purpose had to be recognized as having dignity and independence. Second, an argument had to be developed that would endow this newly discovered individual with a unique role to play in the natural order of things.

The first of these tasks was performed with revolutionary consequences by Martin Luther (1483–1546), John Calvin (1509–1564), and the other Protestant reformers. Luther and Calvin challenged the spiritual and secular order dominated by the Roman Catholic Church. Luther believed in a powerful deity, but he also believed that individuals had to construct their own relationship with God. The church can assist through its teachings and guidance, but ultimately each person faces God alone. The Protestant Reformation put the individual into a private relationship with God and greatly depreciated the mediating role of the institutional church. The individual, having been recognized as the center of religious concern, soon became the focus of political thought.

The Protestant reformers fueled the revolt, but the second phase of the struggle against the traditional order was carried, in the end, by an audacious band of eighteenth-century French political theorists. It was their ambitious project to make human reason itself divine.[9] Rather than seeing human attempts at rationality as poor imitations of the mind of God, the Enlightenment theorists located the divine principle specifically in the mind of the rational individual. Once they had done so, religion became irrelevant to politics.

As reason replaced religion as a basis for authority, the Baron de Montesquieu (1689–1755) argued that government could be based on secular authority and could be controlled through balancing powers among different branches, an idea that found its way directly into the U.S. Constitution. The celebration of reason also had its critical uses. In the French Revolution of 1789, the notion of a natural order based on reason was turned around and used against the clergy and the authority of the church. They were consigned to the dustheap of archaic institutions whose basis in tradition and custom was ridiculed as irrational and authoritarian.

The building of a polity became an exercise in deduction from the universal principles of a rational human nature. Philosophers rather than theologians became the arbiters of the definitions of these principles. As Carl Becker remarks in *The Heavenly City of the Eighteenth Century Philosophers:*

> What these "universal principles" were the Philosophers, therefore, understood before they went in search of them, and with "man in general" they were well acquainted, having created him in their own image. They knew instinctively that "man in general" is natively good, easily enlightened, disposed to follow reason and common sense; generous and humane and tolerant, more easily led by persuasion than compelled by force; above all a good citizen and a man of virtue,

---

9. Kingsley Martin, *The Rise of French Liberal Thought: A Study of Political Ideas from Bayle to Condorcet,* 2nd ed., ed. J. P. Mayer (Westport, Conn.: Greenwood Press, 1980 [1954]).

being well aware that, since the rights claimed by himself are only the natural and imprescriptible rights of all men, it is necessary voluntarily for him to assume the obligations and to submit to the restraints imposed by a just government for the commonweal.[10]

Given this principled citizen, statecraft was no great mystery. The political machinery could be designed as if it were clockwork. Differing classes and interests could be brought into balance through representation in a legislative process. The executive would administer and enforce the law resulting from this process, and the courts would adjudicate disputes arising under the law. In the extreme circumstances of the French Revolution, however, the machinery of the state moved more frequently to the rhythm of the guillotine as real and suspected enemies of the new order were publicly beheaded.

When seen in political terms, Luther's personal rebellion against the institutional authority of the Roman Catholic Church gave practical meaning to a theology that emphasized the role of individual conscience. The Protestant Reformation brought with it the justification for a new individualism. This newly significant individual was, in the course of the next century, endowed with reason. Rationalism was the work of the French *philosophes* and their English liberal allies, whom we will meet after considering the distinctive contribution of an American theorist, Thomas Jefferson (1743–1826).

The argument that individualism is *natural* was to receive a powerful assist from Jefferson, a student of the French and English rationalists. As befits someone who made his living on the land working with nature, Jefferson based his assertion of the primacy of the individual on the individual's ability to play a particular role in the divine order of things—a role that can be acted out only by the assertion of our individual talents and abilities. Jefferson was impressed with the natural order he saw around him, and wanted to make human institutions in the image of that natural order.

Jefferson saw himself as a "natural scientist" of society. If the divine creator intends each person to be unique, then to carry through on that distinctiveness is the sacred mission of each individual. As Daniel Boorstin suggests,

> The proper test, the Jeffersonian declared, was not what a man believed, but how accurately and honestly he avowed whatever the Creator had destined him to believe. The ideas which a man professed were less important than whether those ideas were the characteristic expression of the mind which the Creator had given him.[11]

To put it simply, in diversity there is divinity.

---

10. Carl Becker, *The Heavenly City of the Eighteenth Century Philosophers* (New Haven, Conn.: Yale University Press, 1932), p. 103.

11. Daniel Boorstin, *The Lost World of Thomas Jefferson* (Boston: Beacon Press, 1948), p. 122.

Just as people derive their equality from an "equal creation," so is our unique individuality derived from the same source. To be equal, therefore, is *not* to be *the same* as someone else. Equality doesn't imply similarity. Equality, for Jefferson, means that we have something within us that entitles us to be thought of as equally entitled to human dignity. We are entitled to this dignity even while we go about living our lives in different and distinctive ways.

How can one believe in equality and difference at the same time? Jefferson was, in fact, fascinated by the differences between various kinds of Indian tribes, ethnicities, and races. What Jefferson did believe was that God *intended* these differences. The expression of differences in a free society was in accord with God's plan. Thus the free expression of one's individuality is not a privilege to be granted by the polity, but a right based in nature. In Jefferson's hands, liberalism became a theory dedicated simultaneously to the guarantee of equal rights *and* the freedom to be different.

Jefferson inverted the relationship between religious institutions and individual virtue. Prior to the Reformation, the Church was thought to be the guarantor of moral order.[12] For Jefferson, moral behavior emanates from free individuals living in a liberal republic. In a community of free people, God's intentions would be realized more surely than in a religiously imposed order. These are the conditions by which the divinity in people could become apparent.

This view may sound like a recipe for anarchism, with individuals heading off in all sorts of contrary directions and political community left stranded at the crossroads. Yet Jefferson also believed in a kind of discipline that links individuals to a larger order.

The connection between individuality and polity, Jefferson thought, could be explained only by God's design, for, after all, "the Creator would indeed have been a bungling artist, had he intended man for a social animal, without planting in him social dispositions."[13] Because we are created beings, in Jefferson's view, our interpersonal variations are the measure not of our distance from others but of our complementarity in a larger natural cosmos. In this essential political sense, creaturehood is a concept that combines individuality with the shared aspects of our basic human nature.

The Jeffersonian conception of natural liberty as both the design of God and the fulfillment of an enlightened view of human nature united two powerful

---

12. The church imposed this order in the monasteries through a discipline that made all the monks and nuns *equal and the same*. Uniformity of dress, denial of individual desires and ambitions, rituals of obedience, and expressions of commmunity solidarity are all part of the monastic order. Reflections of this design were found in the religious colonies that brought Europeans to America.

13. Cited in Garry Wills, *Inventing America: Jefferson's Declaration of Independence* (New York: Vintage, 1978), p. 187.

streams of thought, the sacred and the secular versions of individualism. God is responsible for our individual differences, but it is up to each of us to act out our particular role in the social order.

How can we reconcile what Jefferson believed about equality with his involvement in slavery and his view that political participation should be restricted to men? The best that can be done is to see how he might have justified this to himself. In the practical circumstances of his life and times, he believed that slavery should be ended through the gradual repatriation of Africans to their homeland. He thought they would have a better chance there than in a society that had grown accustomed to racially based slavery. As for women, he thought that the tasks of governance required the distinctive abilities of men, and that women's unique qualities were best deployed in other areas of life.[14] Whatever one may think of Jefferson's justifications for these views, the general principles he enunciated were used to go far beyond his own practices of racism and sexism. Advocates for equal rights could appeal to his imagery in subsequent struggles to complete in practice the full program of his theory: a society of equal, independent, yet cooperative citizens whose differences are a source of strength rather than division.

Jefferson's view of liberty is embedded in America's vocabulary and rhetoric, and occasionally in its jurisprudence. The Jeffersonian citizen remains a powerful image in American political thought. Indeed, Jefferson's legacy may be one of the few effective intellectual barriers to the total domination of U.S. culture by the structure of power emanating from the marketplace. He understood the relationship between dispersed economic power and liberty. He advocated giving fifty acres of land to every male citizen who did not own property, and he was a strong proponent of public education based on merit.

Jefferson envisioned a democracy grounded in small landowners and governed by educated citizens. He saw the link between citizenship and productivity as essential. For Jefferson, the liberalism of individual rights led directly to a society of dispersed economic power. As we will see, it is the other institution of classical liberalism, the market, with its roots in a quite different conception of the distribution of property, that has more directly shaped the relationship between citizenship and productivity in classical liberalism.

---

14. Jefferson seems to have thought of the Indians as a noble people whose understanding of natural law was uncorrupted by the influences of European civilization. However, they needed to be brought out of the primitive economy of hunting and gathering into the world of Jefferson's yeoman farmer, and Christianized, so they could become citizens of the new society. See Harold Hellenbrand, "Not 'To Destroy But to Fulfil': Jefferson, Indians and Republican Dispensation," in *Eighteenth Century Studies,* 1984–1985, pp. 524–525. Cf. Joseph Ellis, *American Sphinx: The Character of Thomas Jefferson* (New York: Vintage, 1976), pp. 101–103. 238–239.

The Liberalism of Self-Interest

The notion of liberty as natural was superseded by an even more powerful rival: the idea that liberty is based on a conception of self-interest. Jefferson justified liberty as a natural endowment from the creator. If liberty is justified instead as an accommodation of individual appetites and interests, the recommended political norms and institutions are very different indeed.

For political theory, the debate over interest versus nature is exceedingly consequential. If the political community is no more than the sum of the property relations of individuals, all we need to know about politics can be studied in the form of zoning arrangements, tax rates, and police services. Many people have this conception of political life. But if a polity is something more, if it fulfills a need in human life through a complex set of sociological, psychological, and cultural functions, then politics is far more diverse and varied.

To better understand this debate between nature and self-interest, it is important to consider how it began. In the beginning, the concept of interest was the child of natural law, and the child grew to overwhelm the parent. Let us see how this happened.[15]

The concept of interest originated as the idea that the society has an interest paramount to that of the individual. Niccolò Machiavelli (1469–1527) defined the *interest of the society* quite simply as order. Drawing on the medieval Christian fear of the anarchy that uncontrolled passion releases, and using the evidence of the brutalities of politics in the age of the Borgias and the Medicis, Machiavelli could make the establishment of order the paramount political value without having to argue very hard for it. If, as seemed to be the case, order could be produced only in a well-led state, it was easy to justify any means necessary to achieve that end. In such a climate of moral relativism, the concept of interest was born.

Interest as the organizing principle gained wherever allegiance to the feudal order weakened. *Interest* was the concept of the traders, the city-dwellers, the merchants, and that restless force in European history, the newly emergent middle class. It superseded *virtue,* which was the concept of theologians intent on controlling human vice. The attempt to constrain the vices through the elaboration of an order based on fealty and honor, the church and chivalry, gave way in time to a more energetic, mobile, and commercial culture organized around the nation-state.

What followed Machiavelli's formulation of the concept of interest was a series of modifications, first from national interest to the notion of group inter-

---

15. For a thoughtful study of these developments, see Albert Hirschman, *The Passions and the Interests: Political Arguments for Capitalism before Its Triumph* (Princeton, N.J.: Princeton University Press, 1977).

est, then to individual interest, and finally to economic self-interest. These transformations were largely the work of seventeenth-century English liberals.

From Group Interest to Self-Interest: The Rise of English Liberalism

Thomas Hobbes (1588–1679), who stands at the beginning of the English liberal line of thought, ridicules the tender notions of medieval feudalism, with its stations and classes, religious piety, network of obligations and duties, and overarching imagery of harmony and natural order. He speaks instead of the authority of the state in the imagery of a "Leviathan," who "hath the use of so much Power and Strength conferred on him, that by terror thereof, he is enabled to forme the wills of them all, to Peace at home, and mutuall ayd against their enemies abroad." In this Leviathan, declares Hobbes, "consisteth the Essence of the Commonwealth," and in the absence of such power, "men have no pleasure (but on the contrary a great deale of griefe) in keeping company."[16] So much for community life in any but the most artificial sense.

The basis for this extreme position was a new view of the meaning of life based solely and completely on the radical notion of individualism. It was this question of raw survival in the jungle of individual competition that melded personal appetites into a united and powerful group interest sufficient to justify extreme forms of government power.

Hobbes specified the mainspring of human behavior as the fear of death. John Locke (1632–1704), agreeing with his major premise, emphasized the crucial observation that people are rational. Their rationality provides the possibility of a community based on something a bit more ambitious than mere survival: an active interest in "the regulating and preserving of property."[17]

Locke saw us as having the capacity to understand our interests and the ability to regulate our interactions with others, whereas Hobbes allowed only the abandonment of all power over a crucial part of our lives in the hope of obtaining thereby the "preservation" of life and property. It is this notion of *regulation* that transformed Locke's system into a true theory of political community. Locke frequently referred, as Hobbes did not, to "community" as a synonym for "government."

Locke recommends a two-phase political construction. The society is based on a *contract;* the government is based on a *trust.* The *contract* brings individuals together for the purpose of settling disputes: "the community comes to be umpire, by settled standing rules; indifferent and the same to all parties."[18] So

16. Thomas Hobbes, *Leviathan,* ed. C. B. Macpherson (Baltimore: Penguin Books, 1968), pp. 185, 227–228.
17. Sir Ernest Barker, ed., *Social Contract: Essays by Locke, Hume, and Rousseau* (London: Oxford University Press, 1960), p. 25.
18. Barker, *Social Contract,* p. 50.

long as the society serves the purpose of regulating and preserving property, the contract cannot be revoked.

For the purpose of making this contract a reality, the members of the society create a government and *entrust* it with appropriate powers. The government exists to establish clear and specific laws, set up judges to settle conflicts, and supply the force necessary to penalize those who violate the law. The government stays in power according to the terms established for it and with the understanding that it will not exceed the purposes of its formation. Thus, regulation occurs within the polity.

Locke modified Hobbes's simple ideas of fear and instinct by centering his theory on people's rational interest in the protection of property. This interest becomes the basis for a political order. Locke declares:

> Political power, then, I take to be a right of making laws, with penalties of death, and consequently all less penalties for the regulating and preserving of property, and of employing the force of the community in the execution of such laws, and in the defense of the commonwealth from foreign injury, and all this only for the public good.[19]

Note that here Locke, like Smith, identifies the crucial role of government in ensuring the proper ordering of economic activity.

John Locke also appreciated the need for a sphere of personal belief that was to be protected and set apart from the power of the state. It is this arrangement that gives to liberal communities their amoral aspect. English liberalism has to do with ensuring freedom of choice in the acquisition and disposition of property, not with settling disputes over religion.

THE IMPACT OF ENGLISH LIBERALISM ON POLITICS   Hobbes sees no particular rationality in the claims of one person as against another:

> To this warre of every man against every man this also is consequent: that nothing can be unjust. The notions of right and wrong, justice and injustice have there no place. Where there is no common power, there is no law, where no law, no injustice.[20]

Thus, Hobbes's solution was force exercised in the name of the people, where Locke's rationalist solution tended more toward regulation and adjudication. The institutionalized performance of these two functions, for Locke, separated a political society, or polity, from the state of nature.

---

19. Barker, *Social Contract,* p. 4.
20. Hobbes, *Leviathan,* p. 188.

In legitimizing the concept of individual interest, Locke gives it a broad definition: the interest that draws individuals together is "the mutual preservation of their lives, liberties, and estates which I call by the general name, property."[21] In this broad definition, there is room for a fairly wide range of community concerns. Following a Lockean design, the U.S. Constitution gives to Congress the generous mandate to make laws to "provide for the common defense and to promote the general welfare of the United States." The point is that, although Locke developed a theory of limited government responsive to the people, he conceived of the functions that the people might delegate to the government as substantial and wide-ranging.

Locke's broad-based rationalist conception of the nature of individual self-interest gave new hope to those who continued to look for a solution to the old problem of controlling human vice. If an interest in "our lives, our fortunes, and our sacred honor" could be made the central principle of social organization, there might be a recipe for order that would tie each of us together in a durable social contract.

There were those who thought self-interest might be another name for avarice. However, the apologists of property were ready with two arguments: that commerce based upon property would induce order in the society and that it would discipline individuals through their citizenship in the state. These results would compensate for whatever concessions were made to avarice and greed. David Hume (1711–1776), the Scottish philosopher, speaks for this whole movement: "It is an infallible consequence of all industrious professions to . . . make the love of gain prevail over the love of pleasure."[22] If self-discipline is the virtue that results from industriousness, goes the argument, then the means to that end must be virtuous by implication. In this case, the means to the end is the pursuit of individual interest through the institution of private property.

The outlines of a liberal utopia are now beginning to emerge. So influential has Locke been that Louis Hartz can argue in *The Liberal Tradition in America* that the popular doctrine of "the American way of life" is nothing more than a "nationalist articulation of Locke."[23] Although other scholars disagree and cite important elements of traditionalism and natural law in the Constitution, there is no question that Locke was a major influence on our notions of contract, con-

---

21. In Barker, *Social Contract,* p. 73.

22. Cited in Hirschman, *The Passions and the Interests,* p. 66.

23. Louis Hartz, *The Liberal Tradition in America: An Interpretation of American Political Thought since the Revolution* (New York: Harcourt, 1962 [1955]), p. 11; for a contrasting view, see Staughton Lynd, *The Intellectual Origins of American Radicalism* (Cambridge, Mass.: Harvard University Press, 1982 [1968]).

sent, and property.[24] With these ideas, Locke succeeded in legitimatizing the authority of government while giving it limited powers.

RESPECTABILITY AND THE MARKETPLACE   The theme of this section has been the attempt to bring *interest* into the battle against the disorderly tendencies of human nature, and so to establish a benign polity. Machiavelli, Hobbes, and Locke all rely upon variations of this approach in their theories of politics. We have come now to the point of confrontation with the latent conflict between interest and vice. As Albert Hirschman tells it in *The Passions and the Interests: Political Arguments for Capitalism Before Its Triumph,* it was Adam Smith who re-engineered the argument into its most compelling form. It was indeed arguable whether self-interest could control such vices as avarice, or whether self-interest was in fact avarice by another name. For Smith, the problem was resolved by a simple and powerful reduction of the terms of the controversy.

Smith argues that the passions of lust, ambition, and vainglory, those durable villains of medieval religious thought, are in fact reducible to a single passion: the desire to be respected. Smith sometimes refers to this passion as *vanity,* however the point is that people mainly want to be well-regarded. It is preferment in the eyes of others that draws together all of our activity. According to Smith, "We desire both to be respectable and to be respected. We dread both to be contemptible and to be contemned."[25]

Rather than falling victim to a contest among the passions, then, we have only to learn how to bring the one grand passion, namely the desire for respect, into the service of order and we shall have resolved the central problem of political thought. Smith removes the opposition between interest and vice. He says that the pursuit of respectability, in the properly organized society, can work to the advantage of all. It is the desire for respect, captured and directed by the marketplace into productive activity, that is, paradoxically, to save us from our passions. Commerce reduces passion to interest. The pursuit of a self-interest in respectability through the marketplace leads us to be productive and law-abiding citizens.

24. See, for example, J. G. A. Pocock, ed., *Three British Revolutions* (Princeton, N.J.: Princeton University Press, 1980), pp. 265–289. On the variety of influences on American thinking in this period, see Donald Lutz, "The Relative Influence of European Writers on Late Eighteenth Century American Thought," *American Political Science Review* 78 (1984): 189–197.

25. *The Theory of Moral Sentiments* (Indianapolis: Liberty Fund, 1984), reproduction of *The Glasgow Edition of the Works and Correspondence of Adam Smith* (Oxford Univerity Press, 1979), ed. by D. D. Raphael and A. L. Macfie, p. 62. Smith sometimes labels this desire for respect as "vanity" or as "self-love," which implies self-indulgence and self-centeredness. However, the drive he is referring to requires for its satisfaction that others respond to us in an admiring or deferential fashion, hence *respectability* is the term that focuses on the nature of the interaction.

Adam Smith in fact has a low opinion of people who try to acquire respect only by material means. In his *Theory of Moral Sentiments,* Smith remarks:

> But, upon coming in to the world, we soon find that wisdom and virtue are by no means the sole objects of respect; nor vice and folly, of contempt. We frequently see the respectful attentions of the world more strongly directed towards the rich and the great, than towards the wise and the virtuous. . . . Two different models, two different pictures, are held out to us, according to which we may fashion our own character and behaviour; the one more gaudy and glittering in its colouring; the other more correct and exquisitely beautiful in its outline: the one forcing itself upon the notice of every wandering eye; the other, attracting the attention of scarce any body but the most studious and careful observer. They are the wise and the virtuous chiefly, a select, though, I am afraid, but a small party, who are the real and steady admirers of wisdom and virtue.[26]

Smith defined the meaning of one's self-interest not as arising from a natural endowment of talents and abilities, as Jefferson thought, or as every human being's desire to obtain and secure the means of subsistence, as Locke proposed. Rather, Smith placed self-interest in the psychological realm of identity. We want to be respected for who we are.[27] The activities we undertake are means to the end of achieving respectability. We may go about this intelligently or stupidly, and the polity has to be ready for either kind of approach. As Smith comments:

> Men may live together in society with some tolerable degree of security, though there is no civil magistrate to protect them from the injustice of those passions. But avarice and ambition in the rich, in the poor the hatred of labour and the love of present ease and enjoyment, are the passions which prompt to invade property, passions much more steady in their operation, and much more universal in their influence.[28]

So we need magistrates to protect against wayward strategies for seeking respect, and a marketplace where we can engage in the orderly exchange of labor and capital. These institutions are there to respond to the stupid things we do, as well as to our more intelligent efforts. We also need, says Smith, a government that will encourage us to seek respect by better means—through education, science, and the arts so that we may be purged of the "poison" of "popular superstition and enthusiasm."[29]

---

26. Ident.

27. Cf. Kenneth Hoover, James Marcia, and Kristen Parris, *The Power of Identity: Politics in a New Key* (New York: Seven Bridges/Chatham House, 1997).

28. *An Inquiry into the Nature and Causes of the Wealth of Nations,* Vol. II (Indianapolis: Liberty Fund, 1984), reproduction of *The Glasgow Edition of the Works and Correspondence of Adam Smith* (Oxford: Oxford University Press, 1979), ed. by R. A. Campbell and A. S. Skinner, p. 709.

29. *Wealth of Nations,* Vol. II, p. 796.

Smith's view is less inspiring than Jefferson's, and less based in rationality that Locke's. Adam Smith gave to classical liberalism a *utilitarian* orientation. In his view, magistrates and the marketplace are institutional means to psychological ends, namely, the formation of an identity based on respect. The justification of these institutions is based on their *uses* (thus *utilitarianism*) in helping us gain respect. Our own view of what will gain respect may not be particularly rational, as Locke might have thought, nor is it clear that our uniqueness is divinely intended, as Jefferson suggested. Rather, we seek respect by whatever means occur to us, and the institutions of society exist to channel that behavior in constructive directions.

BACK TO POLITICS: UTILITARIAN LIBERALISM   We have seen how Smith summarized all passion as the pursuit of self-respect and linked it to economic self-interest through the institution of the marketplace. The conservative aspects of this doctrine's implications for politics will be explored in Chapter 4. The more explicitly liberal political dimension of utilitarianism was formulated by Smith's younger contemporary, Jeremy Bentham (1748–1832). It is Bentham's radical proposal that self-interest be defined in even less discriminating fashion:

> Nature has placed mankind under the governance of two sovereign masters, *pain* and *pleasure*. It is for them alone to point out what we ought to do, as well as to determine what we shall do. On the one hand the standard of right and wrong, on the other, the chain of causes and effects are fastened to their throne.[30]

From this observation, Bentham deduces the famous principle of utility, which is to guide the judgment of each action by the "tendency which it appears to have to augment or diminish the happiness of the party whose interest is in question."[31] He allows that pains and pleasures are simply "interesting perceptions."[32] What Smith began when he reduced motivation to the single notion of respectability, Bentham finished by casting individual self-interest in a form so general that it defied all but the most rudimentary classification.

Yet politics is about the making of decisions, so interest does have to be defined in particular cases. That process of judgment, Bentham implied, must be placed in the hands of the people. Because there can be no general definition of pleasure and pain that holds for all individuals, a representative government must play the crucial role of summarizing the utilitarian calculations of all individuals.

30. Jeremy Bentham, "An Introduction to the Principles of Morals and Legislation," in *The Utilitarians* (New York: Doubleday, 1961), p. 17.

31. Bentham, "An Introduction to the Principles of Morals and Legislation," p. 17.

32. Bentham, "An Introduction to the Principles of Morals and Legislation," p. 41.

The society will then be guided by the principle of "the greatest happiness of the greatest number."

In his time, Bentham was seen as a great reformer, and he spent much of his life working on proposals for modernizing Britain's antiquated penal system. He was the author of the notion that punishment for crime should be calculated to dissuade potential criminals, and to reform those who are caught, rather than to punish them for their "sins." The great project of his life was the reform of the English legal code so that it would administer pain in such a way as to "place every member of political society in such circumstances that his private interest might coincide with the general interest."[33] He worked to purge religious conceptions from their role in public law.

What Bentham initiated was the ultimate democratization of liberalism. No longer did power have to be linked to a defined sphere of activity for "the protection of life, liberty, and estate," as in Locke. Public power might be deployed however the population wished. Bentham intended to free society from the shackles of tradition, custom, and privilege. While he was at it, his critics feared, he freed politics of all boundaries, morality of all content, and community of all meaning, save the collective pursuit of pleasure by whatever definition its current residents might have.

The long battle to free individuals from the yoke of traditional power and privilege acquired, by virtue of the work of Bentham and Smith, a powerful new theory. The simplicity of the pleasure-pain calculation opened the way to the reform of English politics and made utilitarianism the favorite theory of many men and women of progressive views. The institutional inventions of Smith and Bentham have drawn careful attention here because conservative versions of the arguments they generated are still with us in the works of theorists such as Friedrich Hayek who have influenced contemporary politics.[34] (See Chapter 4, on libertarian conservatism.)

Liberalism and Developmental Freedom

As the implications of utilitarian liberalism began to reverberate through English society, critics were quick to see that all pleasures might come out equal on the public scales and that anarchism (or despotism) could be the result. Conservative traditionalists foresaw a tasteless mediocrity overtaking English society. In addition, the proposal for so radical a form of democratic representative government

---

33. Guido DeRuggiero, *The History of European Liberalism,* trans. R. C. Collingwood (London: Oxford University Press, 1927), p. 103.

34. Kenneth Hoover, "Ideologizing Institutions: Laski, Hayek, Keynes, and the Creation of Contemporary Politics," *Journal of Political Ideologies,* 4 (1999) 1, 87–115.

offered the prospect of the blind leading the blind on serious questions of public policy.

It was up to John Stuart Mill (1806–1873), a protégé of Bentham, to rescue liberalism from these difficulties. In doing so, he gave the movement a powerful impetus, but changed some of its most basic assumptions. Mill attempted to save utilitarianism from the accusation that it fostered mindless pleasure-seeking. He did this by developing two powerful arguments.

Mill's first argument was that society must not just pursue the sum of individual interests understood at any given moment but, rather, must form rules that would serve for all individuals in similar situations. Although a temporary majority might decide that it would take great pleasure in eliminating people with green eyes, for example, the act of doing so would open up all other subgroups to threats of extermination, and society would descend into chaos. So, by Mill's *rule utilitarianism* (as opposed to *act utilitarianism*), no minority should ever be targeted for predjudicial treatment. This principle, applied to all policy questions, was intended to restrain the power of the majority to do as it wished.

The principle of rule utilitarianism can be institutionalized through constitutional protections and the election of wise people to public office, a point that brings up Mill's second major contribution to the revision of liberalism. Early utilitarians had seemed to argue that any person was as good a judge of pleasure and pain as any other. That principle appears to follow from the radically individualist assumptions that Bentham proclaimed. But Mill pointed out that if all human beings learn through experience, some have more experience than others. We should entrust public policy decisions to those who are the most experienced. Thus, he introduced an element of elitism into liberalism.

Mill limited the power of the majority, and of the elite, in another way, however. In his famous defense of civil liberties, *On Liberty,* Mill argues that whereas some may have more experience than others, no one knows for certain the whole truth about anything. It follows that free expression should always be protected, even from majority censure, because we can never be sure that any person's ideas are entirely without merit. This classic argument has inspired the struggle for freedom of expression ever since.

What Mill did, as Michael Freeden points out in *Ideologies and Political Theory,* was to bring to the surface the notion of *self-development* as a rationale for classical liberalism.[35] The point of liberty is not so that we may do anything we desire purely for the sensual pleasure of it, but rather that we have the freedom to "better ourselves" as human beings capable of thought, expression, and pro-

---

35. Freeden, *Ideologies and Political Theory: A Conceptual Approach* (Oxford: Clarendon Press, 1996), p. 147.

ductive behavior. Mill recast utilitarianism, with its doctrine of the pursuit of pleasure and avoidance of pain, as a way of emphasizing the importance of education and intellectual advancement. With respect to "pleasures of the senses" as distinct from "pleasures of the intellect, of the feelings and imagination, and of the moral sentiments," Mill states:

> Now it is an unquestionable fact that those who are equally acquainted with, and equally capable of appreciating and enjoying, both, do give a most marked preference to the manner of existence which employs their higher faculties. Few human creatures would consent to be changed into any of the lower animals, for a promise of the fullest allowance of a beast's pleasures; no intelligent human being would consent to be a fool, no instructed person would be an ignoramus, no person of feeling and conscience would be selfish and base, even though they should be persuaded that the fool, the dunce, or the rascal is better satisfied with his lot than they are with theirs. They would not resign what they possess more than he for the most complete satisfaction of all the desires which they have in common with him.[36]

John Stuart Mill and Harriet Taylor Mill were evangelists for the improvement of people's ability to live intelligently. They reformulated classical liberalism into a progressive ideology committed to clearing out practices based on tradition, superstition, or materialism they saw as hindering people's chances of becoming all that they could be. They practiced this evangelism on causes such as women's rights and experimentation with worker-owned cooperatives.

While ultimately skeptical of full-fledged communism because it might reduce everyone to a mediocre state, John Stuart Mill believed, not unlike Jefferson, that developmental freedom required some kind of democratization of economic as well as political power.[37] However, he feared that socialists might violate basic rights in their pursuit of class-based justice, and was concerned that simple majoritarian democracy would have the same problem. While the Mills came to no tidy conclusions about these questions, they opened the door to further elaboration of the idea of self-development as a rationale for classical liberal conceptions of freedom.

The system of ideas that Mill assembled was translated into a practical political program that deeply influenced Britain's politics and, through its empire and its intellectual influence, much of the world. The tensions between elitism and democracy in Mill's utilitarian liberalism, as well as those between the scope of

36. John Stuart Mill, *Utilitarianism* (New York: New American Library, 1974), p. 279.

37. See the correspondence between the Mills in *John Stuart Mill and Harriet Taylor: Their Correspondence and Subsequent Marriage,* ed. by F. A. Hayek (Chicago: University of Chicago Press, 1951), especially pp. 136–137.

government action and individual freedom, remained troublesome. As we will see, there were to be serious challenges on these and other issues from socialists, traditional conservatives, and anarchists.

The move toward basing classical liberalism on a conception of developmental freedom takes a further step in the late nineteenth century. Under the influence of liberal interpreters of G. W. F. Hegel (1770–1831), liberalism took a new form based not on experience, appetite, and interest but on the nature of the mind. Utilitarianism was based on people's direct experience of pleasure and pain. Hegel, on the other hand, represented a philosophical tradition that placed the essential characteristic of human beings not in the senses but in the intellect.

Thomas Hill Green (1836–1882), an English interpreter of Hegel, proposed a theory called *liberal idealism*. Green believed that what was missing in utilitarianism was any argument that brought individuals of differing interests into a true community. His study of Hegel convinced him that all individuals shared a common structure of intellect through the power of reasoning.

We all are capable of perceiving, with appropriate thought and education, the same principles of justice, because they are embedded in the mind. On the basis of this common structure, people can build a polity that realizes the inherent principles of justice appropriate to a humane existence.

The search for these inherent principles of justice proved to be challenging. Liberal idealists, powerful politically at the turn of the twentieth century, had a hard time stating clearly the exact content of their ideas. Nevertheless, liberal idealism represented another advance for arguments of developmental freedom and rationality. What was new was the added significance assigned to political community as the arbiter not merely of interest but also of justice. In this respect, Green was a transitional thinker to modern reform liberalism.

CONCLUSION

For all the power of these ideas, it was the advent of the industrial revolution that speeded the implementation of classical liberalism. In an age of entrepreneurs, shopkeepers, and newly independent workers, the concept of individuals pursuing their own interests fit neatly into the experience of the times. As the full consequences of utilitarianism in an era of industrialization became apparent, however, the foundations of classical liberalism came under increasingly critical scrutiny.[38] The miserable condition of the working class in nineteenth-century

---

38. For an interesting anthropological approach to relations of property and contract, see Lewis Hyde, *The Gift: Imagination and the Erotic Life of Property* (New York: Random House, 1983 [1979]), especially Chaps. 2, 5, 6.

capitalism, together with episodes of boom and bust, financial scandals, and widespread corruption, called into question the institutional assumptions of classical liberalism.

The Mills' commitment to developmental freedom ennobled the cause of classical liberalism. The search by Green and others for principles of justice fueled a reform movement in England that found its echo in American *progressivism*. We will see later how the problems they tried to address entered into the formation of reform liberalism in the United States.

The formulation of classical liberalism as the combination of a marketplace and a representative government became the principal force in reshaping political thought and, with it, the design and operation of political systems in many parts of the world. This powerful idea system is not without its challengers then or now. The remainder of our study of political thought will focus on the ways in which classical liberalism has been confronted by alternative ideologies.

We have become accustomed to hearing that the defense of the marketplace is a conservative position. In Chapter 4, on libertarian conservatism, we will see how that association developed. In Chapter 5, the story of how liberals came to believe in governmental intervention in the economy will be told. But before that, it is important to understand the position of classical liberalism's historical rival, traditional conservatism.

CHAPTER THREE

TRADITIONAL CONSERVATISM

elitist

[Conservatism] denies the existence of any irreconcilable antagonisms in a healthy body politic. It holds, on the contrary, that the efficiency and prosperity of each class—upper, middle, lower, each with its countless internal gradations—is essential for the well-being of the community as a whole. It recognizes the distinction between the classes as natural, fundamental, and beneficial; the same sort of distinction as exists between the head, the body, and the limbs of a man or an animal. But it regards the distinction as one of function mainly, and not necessarily one of honour or emolument.

recognize the individual
   notice the difference
want institutions to

F. J. C. HEARNSHAW
(1933)

Conservatives disagree with liberals principally on the question of the political significance of differences in people's abilities and characteristics. Liberals—and, to a considerably greater extent, socialists—argue that the common elements of people's need for self-development are such that public policy should be based on conceptions of basic rights and equal treatment. As we have seen in the previous chapter, classical liberal theories of individual rights remain a powerful element of modern politics.

Although conservatives believe in certain basic rights, they argue that the purpose of political institutions is to ensure that differences and distinctions among individuals will be recognized. For the *traditional* conservatives of the eighteenth and nineteenth centuries, this position meant a defense of customary institutions and practices of authority in class-based societies. This traditionalist view, muted in contemporary conservative thought, has been largely overtaken in the last thirty years by *individualist* conservatism (see Chapter 4). Contemporary individualist conservatives see the market, rather than governments, as the institution that will reward ability and hard work while redirecting the efforts of less productive people in society.

Both kinds of conservatives share a fundamental concern with the political significance of individual differences, but they diverge on the institutional meaning of this assumption. As we will see in this chapter, custom and tradition lead to political practices and policies that are, in interesting ways, at odds with the temper of modern, market-based societies. In the context of an acceptance of the inequality of individuals, which individualists and traditionalists share, there are contrasting views on the uses and limits of authority and power.

As is the case with classical liberalism and reform liberalism, there are differences between historical conservatism and its contemporary version. The tensions within modern conservatism can't be understood fully without a knowledge of both the traditionalist and individualist variants. In Chapter 4 we will explore the arguments for the individualist conservative position; here we will concentrate on justifications for the traditional conservative approach to politics.

THE TRADITIONALIST IMAGE OF POLITICAL LIFE

The traditional conservative image of political life begins from a view of the human condition that is strikingly different from the liberal conception. Where liberals see rational individuals capable of contracting with others for the mutual improvement of their lives and fortunes, conservatives see spiritual, fallible, limited, semirational personalities whose behavior cannot be perfected. Rather than using the state to move such creatures toward procedural equality and abstract justice, conservatives concentrate on establishing social and political institutions that will bring out the strengths and minimize the weaknesses in each distinctive personality.[1]

---

1. Clinton Rossiter suggests that conservatism is more skepticism about change than an analysis of human nature: *Conservatism in America,* 2nd ed. rev. (New York: Random House, 1955), pp. 6–18. Yet Burke endorsed the American Revolution, and conservatives today advocate drastic changes in economic and social policy. Cf. Samuel Huntington's threefold classification of attitudinal differences among conservatives in "Conservatism as an Ideology," *American Political Science Review* 52 (1958): 454–473. More serviceable for our purposes is the division between traditional and libertarian conservatives found in George Nash, *The Conservative Intellectual Movement in the U.S. since 1945* (New York: Basic Books, 1979), which is similar to the distinction between organic and individualist conservatism found in Kenneth and Patricia Dolbeare, *American Ideologies,* 3rd ed. (New York: Rand McNally, 1976).

a more social aspect

When traditional conservatives look at the mass of human activity that constitutes political life and ask what gives it order, they are most likely to answer that it is leaders and institutions, private and public. Conservatives see society as a web of particular arrangements, authorities, and beliefs arising out of habit, differences in abilities, and the limitations on human rationality. For the traditionalist conservative, the community is primary—it is not there merely to accommodate self-interested individuals. The community serves as the framework for the institutions, customs, ethics, and traditions by which personality is developed and order is maintained.

For each of life's functions, there are traditional institutions: the family, the church, government, corporations, schools and universities, craft unions, and private associations of all kinds. The conservative view of each of these institutions reveals something about the structure of the traditionalist view of political life.

Personal character is a key consideration. Rather than focusing on individuals as reasonable beings oriented to self-development, conservatives observe that people spend their lives struggling with great forces of temptation. The traditional vices, the pursuit of pleasure rather than duty, and the errors of egotism and self-indulgence confront us daily. They can be overcome only through discipline, faith, and institutional constraints. The basic line of defense against such weaknesses is *character*. The purpose of social, religious, and political institutions is to instill a sense of personal discipline, courage, and motivation. The other functions of these institutions involve dealing with the mistakes that people make.

The institution of the *family* has as its prime goal the nurturance of personality and the development of character. The differentiation of roles in the family follows from the need for physical, emotional, and intellectual growth as well as economic sustenance. For each person to play all these roles is to invite incompetence and disorganization. Many conservatives see this differentiation of roles as biologically determined, with the husband as provider and the wife as nurturer. Each has distinctive responsibilities that are essential to the well-being of the whole family.

In some traditionalist writing, the family becomes the metaphor for larger relations of authority. Familial imagery is often a part of conservative writing on government. Just as father, mother, and children have specific roles to play in the family, so do workers, managers, and leaders play roles in the proper operation of the society. A disordered society is one in which people move out of their roles without adequate background and preparation.

The *church,* as another example, exists not so much to provide a forum for the expression of private notions of spirituality as to furnish a link between people's spiritual inclinations and a larger order through faith in God. Traditionalists are skeptical of tidy schemes for salvation or justice, and they carry that skepticism into their attitude toward any religion that is too worldly in its concerns. It is the function of religion to console us as we experience our limitations, to reinforce faith, and to encourage discipline. In the latter respect, the alliance of the church and moderate forms of nationalism has found favor in conservative thought.

Conservatives view *government* with a mixture of respect and suspicion. Which of those attitudes a particular government evokes depends on two factors: how it is constituted and the role it plays with respect to other private and public institutions.

Because conservatives have a rather low opinion of the average person's abilities, they are most suspicious of simple democracy. To unite a majority around a program, the worth of which is allegedly proved by reason, without due regard for custom and tradition, is, from the conservative point of view, to invite the "tyranny of the majority." Conservatives see as particularly dangerous the kind of utopian democracy associated with the French Revolution, the Russian Revolution, and the utilitarian radicalism of Jeremy Bentham. A good government is constituted by good people: by the natural aristocracy of talent, breeding, and, very likely, wealth. An elite of experienced, disciplined, and moderate citizens is always to be preferred over a majority of the general population. Traditional conservatism is openly elitist.

wow

If a government passes the test of proper construction, the traditional conservative insists on a second test: that it be limited in what it does and, within its sphere of action, that it be strong and resolute. The purpose of government is to maintain the framework of order within which other private institutions can operate effectively. Where the government oversteps its bounds is where it usurps the function of private institutions, such as the family, the church, and the university.

Charity toward the poor is an obligation in any well-ordered society. Care for the poor by the church, voluntary institutions, and personal philanthropy appeals to the traditional conservative as protection against the rise of collectivism and, ultimately, tyranny. The state should provide a minimal level of support to those who can't take care of themselves. However, if the government's social mission is too broadly defined, the conservative fears, a welfare mentality begins to degrade political relations. Democratic majorities will use governmental power to increase subsidies at the expense of the truly productive people in the society.

In the conservative image of political life, the *schools* and *universities* have a special role. Liberals favor mass education and the "free marketplace of ideas"; conservatives quite explicitly endorse the notion that the purpose of an education is to instill the traditional wisdom of the society. Religion, as part of that tradition, is part of education. The curriculum should be an exercise in discipline for its own sake, as well as a conveyor of the cultural heritage.

*

tie to paper!

Academic freedom is a relative concept for the conservative, and the basic truths of the culture must not be undermined by "false" teaching. Fundamental principles, rather than mere sensory experience, should be the subject of education. Otherwise, in the view of Richard Weaver, a traditionalist theorist, "With knowledge limited to sensory experience, man [is] eventually lost in 'endless induction' and 'multiplicities.'" He adds: "Man [has] been in retreat for centuries, from first principles, from definition, from true knowledge—that is, the knowledge of universals."[2] Religion and ethics should be taught in the schools; radical critiques of society should be played down or dispensed with.

The remainder of the institutions of the polity should be organized around voluntary interests. Traditionalists look with horror on labor unions that operate as internal democracies seeking the same treatment for all workers. *Craft unions* are regarded more favorably, because they foster apprenticeship and seniority in the image of medieval guilds.

There seems to be a contradiction in the traditionalist view of political life. Conservatives believe in the dignity of the individual, on the one hand, and in order and hierarchy, on the other. But isn't the exercise of authority the principal threat to the dignity of the individual?

Resolving this contradiction requires an understanding of the traditionalist view of human strengths and weaknesses. A noted conservative writer, Peter Viereck, has defined conservatism as "the political secularization of the doctrine of original sin."[3] He means that institutions must do what the individual cannot do: provide the structures that will compensate for the limitations of human nature, while preserving the human potential for constructive action. People cannot fully develop without proper structures. The individual needs to be protected from weaknesses, nurtured in development, and given the means to express strengths.

The polity in these respects plays both a restraining role in relation to human weakness and a liberating role in cultivating individual potential. Robert Nisbet asserts:

> Genuine freedom is not based upon the negative psychology of release. Its roots are in positive acts of dedication to ends and values. Freedom presupposes the autonomous existence of values that men wish to be free to follow and live up to. Such values are social in the precise sense that they arise out of, and are nurtured by, the voluntary associations which men form.[4]

Paradoxically, in this view, freedom depends crucially on the role of institutions.

---

2. Summarized in Nash, *The Conservative Intellectual Movement,* p. 40.

3. Nash, *Conservative Intellectual Movement,* p. 66.

4. Robert Nisbet, *The Quest for Community* (New York: Oxford University Press, 1962), p. 269.

An emphasis on order remains in conservative thought, but there is a key distinction between *authority* and *power* that separates legitimate from illegitimate order. Power, according to Nisbet, is simply the application of force without consent—as much a possibility in a majoritarian democracy as in a dictatorship. Like most other traditional conservatives, Nisbet is suspicious of egalitarian democracy and sees it as a potential threat to the proper kind of order.

Authority, on the other hand, arises out of the "objectives and functions which command the response and talents" of people.[5] In Nisbet's view, authority is based on consent and commitment; power overrides consent and escapes limits. Conservatives attribute the rise of the powerful centralized state to the breakdown of legitimate authority. The key to the good society is that there should be a multiplicity of authorities serving many aspects of life. If the functions of these authoritative institutions overlap, that will serve the purpose of limiting and controlling the exercise of power.

ORIGINS OF TRADITIONAL CONSERVATISM

An irony of the history of conservatism is that the use of the term *conservatism* to describe an ideology is actually rather recent. The term appeared in Europe about 1830. Many strands constitute the roots of traditional conservatism. To assemble this history is to pick out the leading themes, to reconstruct where they came from, and to see how they changed over time. It is in these origins and changes that the conservative image of political life begins to take on various shades of meaning.

The history of conservatism is characterized by a series of unresolved arguments. These arguments reflect three basic tensions in conservative thought: the *relative strength of vice and virtue in human nature,* the *proper role of human action in politics,* and the *appropriate boundary between order and individual freedom.* As the preceding section suggests, the most important of these tensions involves estimating the weaknesses of human nature. It is the traditionalists' view of human limitations that we have seen to be the hallmark of the conservative position.

The arguments over these tensions have changed because the modes of justification in Western culture have shifted: from natural law to theology, to rationalism (or, in this case, anti-rationalism), and on to historicism and nationalism. Each of these larger frameworks of thought offered conservatives a way of restating their central arguments. The fundamental problems of human vice, the role of personal action, and the nature of order have all received attention in natural

---

5. Nisbet, *Quest for Community,* p. xii.

law philosophy, in theological defenses of monarchism, in conservative critiques of the revolutionary movements of the eighteenth and nineteenth centuries, and in conservative interpretations of the "meaning" of history and its implications for the destiny of nations. We will briefly explore the major developments arising from each of these modes of justification.

Conservatism and Natural Law

The oldest Western tradition of political theory comes from the natural law philosophy of the Greeks and Romans. As we have seen, arguments based on natural law were used as the basis for liberal individualism. However, another tendency in the natural law tradition helped form conservative ideology, and it deals directly with the consequences of human vice and virtue, with political action, and with order and freedom in society.[6]

Natural law philosophy places primary emphasis on the role of order in human life. Naturalism presupposes a meaning in life that lies behind appearances. For Plato, "reality" is not what we see around us; instead, reality is the inner principle that shapes these appearances. To understand these inner principles is to know the truth. Each human phenomenon thus contains the clues to some greater truth. So it is with political life. From the variety of political systems the Greeks observed, they attempted to distill the essential principles of politics. The Greeks were not constrained by cultural assumptions of individualism: for them human beings were social creatures, or, in Aristotle's phrase, "Man is a political animal." Thus, ideas about the good political life were the main subject of educated thought, and political philosophy was "the master science."

From this perspective, the polity is but human nature writ large, and it has the potential to reflect virtue as well as vice, strength as well as weakness. Because political life can be both good and evil, the work of designing the *polis,* to use the Greek concept, is a matter of will and intention. Ernest Barker points out that "in saying that the state is natural, [Aristotle] does not mean that it 'grows' naturally, without human volition and action. . . . Human agents 'construct' the state in cooperation with a natural immanent impulse."[7] So the work of creating the right

6. There is disagreement over whether natural law is an important basis for conservatism. Cf. Huntington, "Conservatism as an Ideology," and Russell Kirk, *The Conservative Mind: From Burke to Eliot,* 7th ed. (Chicago: Regnery, 1986). Huntington associates conservatism with a defense of existing institutions rather than a commitment to the notion of an intrinsic order, an assumption central to natural law. Yet it is hard to see how a theory that depends on institutions and prescription could escape a belief in an underlying natural order to human affairs.

7. Aristotle, *The Politics,* trans. Ernest Barker (New York: Oxford University Press, 1962), p. 7.

form of polity is a matter for human action. It has to be conducted according to principles that can be discovered by the examination of human nature.

For traditional conservatives, political institutions have a dual role: they correct for human weakness, and they express a natural order. The great Greek philosophers, impelled by the urgency of liberating human virtue from the clutches of personal vice, invite us to use observation and reason to understand the order that lies behind appearances and to fit our actions to it.

Plato's own utopia, described in his *Republic,* is a blueprint for the assignment of individuals with particular qualities to appropriate positions in the polity. Whatever their other differences, Plato and Aristotle had a highly developed notion of the immanent order, and there was a large role for the most intelligent citizens to play. The culmination of this notion is Plato's philosopher-king, who is to apply the highest powers of the mind to the task of shaping the life of the polity.

Looking back on the Greek tradition, modern conservatives see too much rational design in Plato's *polis.* They do not associate themselves with the utopian style of the *Republic,* being too skeptical for so large an act of faith. Yet traditionalists have never given up on the idea of a natural order. Given this view, achieving the good polity involves selecting leaders who can shape institutions according to the proper conception of order. Conservatives prefer to trust soundly constructed institutions rather than schemes for achieving a perfect community.

Feudalism, Revolution, and the Rise of Conservatism

Conservatives have always wrestled with the problem of power. How can fallible human beings be entrusted with power sufficient to bring order to political life? Medieval theologians saw dangers in giving great power to the sovereign, but there was an infinitely greater danger in having no central power at all.

Through their belief in original sin, these theologians could justify both the need for order and a reliance on divinely inspired monarchy. Only through divine inspiration of the ruler could God's requirement that there be order in human affairs be fulfilled without risking the abuses of tyranny. As this doctrine developed, feudalism, with its many protected statuses, gave way to absolute monarchy. The abuse of royal power led to the development of an opposition, organized ultimately as a parliament.[8] The scene was set for the downfall of monarchical government.

What catalyzed the formation of conservative ideology was the century of the Enlightenment, the eighteenth century, culminating in the French Revolution of 1789. Prior to that time, the involvement of traditionalist ideas in the absolutist

---

8. For a fascinating study of feudal society, see Marc Bloch, *Feudal Society,* 2 vols. (Chicago: University of Chicago Press, 1961).

monarchies of Europe came under attack by both English liberals, with their radical notions of contractualism, and the French *philosophes*, whose rationalism and secularism undermined the basis of traditional politics.

With the French Revolution and all the excesses that followed, conservatives had their target and their opportunity. What conservatives such as Edmund Burke (1729–1797) saw in the revolution was a perfect illustration of the beast in human nature, disguised in modernist clothing and turned loose to destroy society. It was precisely the elevation of reason over tradition, custom, habit, and settled practice that constituted the great evil of the revolution. In Burke's eyes, secularism was the scaffold of the guillotine, and rationalism was the blade. By forsaking all the other institutions and customs through which human intelligence operates, society was made the victim of unbridled radicalism.

On the other hand, Burke approved of the American Revolution. He saw it as essentially an effort by the colonists to retrieve their traditional rights as Englishmen from the hands of a king who had abused customary rights. Here the villain was the monarch, and the heroes were the citizens. Burke was offering no blind endorsement of democracy, however, but rather an assertion that the people, at least the propertied class, could legitimately and forcefully protect their status from the threat of misguided authority. To locate the wisdom of the polity in its property holders rather than in the monarch, his or her ministers, or the aristocracy was an important initiative in conservative thought. It made conservatism a contender in the new age of republican politics.

Burke was, in fact, more concerned with the method of change than with the agent. The political method he prefers is gradual, responsible, and carefully considered:

> The true lawgiver ought to have a heart full of sensibility. He ought to love and respect his kind, and to fear himself. It may be allowed to his temperament to catch his ultimate object with an intuitive glance, but his movements toward it ought to be deliberate. Political arrangement, as it is a work for social ends, is to be only wrought by social means. . . . Time is required to produce that union of minds which alone can produce all the good we aim at.[9]

Burke thus attempts to liberate the traditionalist position from blind royalism, reduce its reliance on the mysteries of natural law, and make it a popular philosophy attractive to all thoughtful, propertied citizens.

Conservatism, as Noel O'Sullivan points out, is a "philosophy of imperfection, committed to the idea of limits, and directed towards the defense of a limited style of politics."[10] Conservatism as a political theory has survived, in part,

---

9. Edmund Burke, *Reflections on the Revolution in France* (New York: Liberal Arts Press, 1955 [1790]), p. 197.

10. Noel O'Sullivan, *Conservatism* (New York: St. Martin's Press, 1976), p. 12.

because it set this limited style of politics in opposition to the reformist, revolutionary, and totalitarian movements that have punctuated history since the time of the French Revolution. The subtitle of Peter Viereck's book, *Conservatism Revisited: The Revolt Against Revolt,* suggests the meaning of traditional conservatism for politics.

MODERN CONSERVATISM

We have seen how conservatism drew upon the natural law tradition, relying on an abstract theory of a unified social order to justify a class-based hierarchy in political life. This basis for order fit with theological conceptions of a world presided over by a single God and ministered to by an institutionalized church. Yet the association of religion with institutionalized power created, as Luther pointed out, the possibility of manipulation by a privileged class of priests who could use their power to dominate the polity.

It was the project principally of G. W. F. Hegel (1770–1831), along with such British thinkers as Samuel Taylor Coleridge (1772–1834) and Thomas Carlyle (1795–1881), to develop a framework that became a new rallying point for traditionalists seeking social unity. They argued that history had a meaning and that the nation-state was the carrier of that meaning. For these romantic conservatives, the national experience represented the release of a force that was propelling the achievement of ever-higher levels of cultural expression. The task of politics was to find the inner logic of this plan and to facilitate its unfolding.

Nationalism, Historicism, Chauvinism, and the Rise of the "Mass Man"

Nationalism made conservative thought dynamic. The nation-state became the active agent of conservative designs. It expressed the moral order that traditionalists desired. Nationalism in Western European cultures represents a combination of forces, one lofty and philosophical and the other mundane and potentially murderous. These two forces are historicism and cultural chauvinism, and they are the different faces of the modern search for unity in Western society.

The great difficulty of locating the meaning of history in the nation-state is that the nation is not simply a territory enclosed within boundaries; it is also racial and ethnic. The German conception of the Aryans as a master race destined to rule the world had its origins in the belief that the mystical collectivity of the German people, the *Volk,* had a meaning above and beyond individual life (see Chapter 8).

The fascist horrors that followed upon the elaboration of *volkisch* ideology have obscured the traditional conservative critique of fascism and of the more robust forms of nationalism. Isaiah Berlin, in summarizing the phenomenon of nationalism, identifies four characteristics of nationalism when it is in full flower: the national group is perceived as *distinct,* as expressive of an *organic unity in society,* as uniquely *ours as opposed to theirs,* and as *supreme* in the chauvinist sense.[11] Although various conservative writers and theorists have endorsed one or another of these attitudes toward the nation-state, traditionalist conservatism really only requires allegiance to one characteristic: the organicism of society—the conception that society is an interdependent whole with each person having an appropriate status and function. With respect to all other characteristics, the conservative commitment to a "limited style of politics," in Noel O'Sullivan's phrase, precludes believing in the nation-state in a chauvinist or xenophobic fashion.[12]

A second political theme in contemporary conservatism grows out of the fundamental concern for the requirements of an interdependent society. A favorite subject of conservative ideologues in the middle of the twentieth century was the rise of what José Ortega y Gasset (1883–1955) labeled "the mass man."[13] For Ortega, the mass man is a person without judgment and principles, having only appetites. The capacity for creativity and for intelligent social relations is replaced by the illusion of self-sufficiency—and the reality of abdication to the power of the state.

In traditional conservative thought, the mass man was the conceptual opposite of the individual living in a properly constituted society. The distinction is subtler than one based merely on class. As Michael Oakeshott suggests, "the mass man is not necessarily 'ignorant,' often he is a member of the so-called intelligentsia; he belongs to a class which corresponds exactly with no other class." It is a class of people who claimed "the right to live in a social protectorate which relieved [them] from the burden of self-determination."[14] The mass man has no character. A nation-state of mass men would fall prey to tyranny because they could not supply order in their own lives. Insensitive to authority, they would become slaves to power.

A key difference between conservatives and liberals lies in what each means by self-determination. For the traditional conservative, self-determination means achieving the appropriate fit between personal character and the society's institutional requirements. The "mass man" is one who ignores the intricate code of institutionalized society, as well as the burden of self-discipline, favoring instead

---

11. Isaiah Berlin, *Against the Current: Essays in the History of Ideas* (New York: Viking Press, 1980).

12. O'Sullivan, *Conservatism,* pp. 11–12.

13. José Ortega y Gasset, *The Revolt of the Masses* (New York: W. W. Norton, 1932).

14. Michael Oakeshott, "The Masses in Representative Democracy," in *American Conservative Thought in the 20th Century,* ed. William Buckley (New York: Bobbs-Merrill, 1970), pp. 118, 121.

the mindless assertion of appetite and a preference for publicly provided security. He is, in short, the conservative's caricature of the liberal individualist who follows a self-interested course of pursuing pleasure and avoiding pain.

Traditional conservatives think that, if all individuals are left to pursue their own interests with a minimum of restraint, the result will be self-indulgence, anarchy, and a turn toward totalitarianism as the solution to the chaos that is created. Too much freedom in this simple, classically liberal, sense will lead to the loss of freedom as defined in the subtler conception of the traditional conservative.

The Problem of the Marketplace

In the twentieth century, the traditional conservative's preference for hierarchy and institutionalism has occasionally been reflected in a critical attitude toward the role of the marketplace. The marketplace is sometimes seen as a democracy in the area of economics in which only dollars, not character or breeding, count.

The problem that traditional conservatives have with the market stems from a concern for principles of justice. Conservatives have difficulty agreeing upon precise principles of justice; however, there are images of the natural dignity of human beings and of a natural order arising out of the inherent differences among people. But what do these images mean for the marketplace? Edmund Burke endorsed the marketplace, though he "always assumed that Liberal capitalist economics could be kept subordinate to the Conservative social ethic."[15] Burke's preferred social ethic was based on the values of duty, honor, and chivalry. The conflict between money and principle was not resolved by Burke, nor was it by traditional conservatives generally.[16] In modern conservatism, there is a line of traditionalist thought that develops the position of "distributism."[17] The idea is that property should be widely distributed so as to maximize the number of people who have a stake in the preservation of an orderly society. Whereas radicals have favored this principle as a key to equality, some conservatives see it as a way of encouraging widespread affiliation with the organized institutional life of the community. Modern forms of this view include home-

---

15. M. Morton Auerbach, *The Conservative Illusion* (New York: Columbia University Press, 1959), p. 37.

16. William F. Buckley defends both the censorship of ideas in the university based on the values of Christianity and the freedom of the marketplace in economics: *God and Man at Yale* (Chicago: Regnery, 1951). One reviewer, aware of possible conflicts, comments, "Now it is surely quite obvious that Christ and Adam Smith have very little in common." Review by Christopher Fullman in *Catholic World*, cited in John Judis, *William F. Buckley, Jr.: Patron Saint of the Conservatives* (New York: Simon and Schuster, 1988), p. 96.

17. Garry Wills, *Confessions of a Conservative* (New York: Penguin, 1979), pp. 135–42; cf. Auerbach, *Conservative Illusion*, pp. 106–130.

steading schemes and profit-sharing plans. For conservatives, distributism is a means of extending the affiliation of citizens to the structures of elite power that compose the vital institutions of the society.

CONCLUSION

The central problem of traditionalist conservatism has been to capture key political concepts in a formulation that will provide a usable standard for judging political action. The attraction of Bentham's liberal utilitarian formulation, "the greatest happiness of the greatest number," was its simplicity. Here was a test that could seemingly be applied to any policy question with an answer provided by the simple mechanics of democracy. For their part, conservatives have never solved that problem.

Simplicity is not possible in traditional conservatism. The effort to ally traditionalism with nationalism has largely borne sour fruit. On the contemporary scene, distributism sounds too much like reform liberalism.[18] There remains no simple way to summarize what traditionalism means for contemporary life.

For all of these difficulties, ideas that are labeled as conservative seem to have found a new appeal among electorates in industrialized countries. This appeal is due partly to a reaction against the excesses of individual freedom that were perceived to have resulted from liberal policy initiatives. Social conservatism based on religious values is a historic theme in traditionalist thought. The difference now is that the pressure is coming from "fundamentalist" religions rather than from the more established institutions of the society. Issues such as abortion, pornography, and school prayer have revived traditionalist arguments for limitations on freedom. "Moralist conservatism" is the modern face of traditionalism.

More significant, however, is the creation of a conservative version of capitalism that relies on the marketplace as the paramount institution in society. The marketplace, the great creation of utilitarian individualism, has been appropriated by politicians calling themselves conservatives! How this new form of conservatism came into being, and what has become of the tension between justice and economic power in the marketplace, is the story of the next chapter, on libertarian conservatism.

---

18. See Daniel Patrick Moynihan's excellent study of what happened when a Republican administration tried to implement a form of guaranteed annual income as a replacement for welfare: *The Politics of a Guaranteed Income: The Nixon Administration and the Family Assistance Plan* (New York: Random House, 1973).

CHAPTER FOUR

LIBERTARIAN CONSERVATISM AND ANARCHISM

If one wishes to advocate a free society—that is, capitalism—one must realize that its indispensable foundation is the principle of individual rights. If one wishes to uphold individual rights, one must realize that capitalism is the only system that can uphold and protect them.

AYN RAND
The Virtue of Selfishness (1963)

Conservatives of all kinds are bound together by the assumption that individual differences are more important than similarities. Traditionalists proceed to argue that institutionalized authority is the best response to this fact of the human condition. Another kind of conservatism offers a quite different response.

Libertarian conservatives present themselves as true believers in individual freedom. Their argument is that individuals are so different and so unique as to preclude any basis for prescriptive order based on tradition or any other standard. There is no set of principles, such as superior experience or character, by which one individual can be given authority over another. Attempts to do so will usually result in fraud and corruption.

The minimization of government is the prime political objective of libertarian conservatives. In this image of political life, the emphasis is on voluntary action. Personal expression is supreme, and rarely is a rationale for coercion, power, or force to be found. The only function of government is the protection of people and property from physical harm inflicted by others.

The free market is the essential institution of society and the metaphor for all other activities. Private enterprise is the vehicle for all economic activity and the model for public policy as well. Personal freedom is the central value for libertarians. What conservatism adds to libertarianism is an acceptance of inequality as the natural result of free behavior and as the consequence of differences in ability and motivation.

Viewed from either side of the political spectrum, the libertarian conservative movement bears a resemblance to anarchism. Anarchists assume that once governmental institutions are no longer there to inhibit and repress our sense of humanity, a great profusion of community activity will ensue. People will engage in all kinds of selfless mutuality and cooperation. Thus, anarchists see the overthrow of state authority as opening the door to the good side of human nature.

Libertarian conservatives, on the other hand, are more likely to see the reduction of governmental power as a wise accommodation to self-interested human nature. What fundamentally separates libertarian conservatism from anarchism is that anarchists see the removal of authority as the key to cooperative mutuality, whereas conservatives value the differentiation that competition brings.

Although libertarian conservatives and anarchists share some basic ideas and both draw upon classical liberals and other writers who value freedom for its own sake, their views of human nature are quite distinctive. These contrasting versions of life in a society with a sharply limited government bring into focus the uses and abuses of governmental power in political ideologies. By looking at them side by side, it is possible to see more clearly the implicit assumptions each has about human nature and the meaning of politics. After exploring the libertarian image of political life, its sources, and its implications for the conservative movement, we will see how it contrasts with anarchism.

THE LIBERTARIAN CONSERVATIVE IMAGE OF POLITICAL LIFE

In the ideal community of the libertarian conservative, there is little taxation, minimal welfare, and no conscription. No creed of any kind, religious or otherwise, is enforced. Private property is virtually inviolate.

Nearly all restrictions on private enterprise should be eliminated, save a minimum of regulations designed to protect the environment. Regulation itself should operate through the marketplace. The manufacturer, and ultimately the consumer, should bear the full costs of a production process. Damage done by strip mining, for example, should be paid for by the producer and reclaimed through the cost of coal rather than by taxation for environmental cleanup.

Libertarian conservatives would severely restrict the ability of the government to use its political power. Public services would be paid for by their users. To the greatest extent possible, political organization would devolve to the neighborhood level.

Limited government avoids an evil identified in the conservative suspicion of human fallibility. The power of officials can't be as easily abused when it is so carefully circumscribed. Taxation and regulation are conceived of as a means for entrenching advantage and position. All activity that is structured around collective consent or majority rule contains the danger that the weak will, through numbers, overtake and victimize the strong and the creative. The market, on the other hand, rewards the entrepreneurs, and they are society's most useful people.

Thoroughgoing libertarian conservatives are as suspicious of big business as they are of big government. They see government as the *means* by which big business can gain a position that pure competition in the marketplace would never allow. They view almost all governmental undertakings as efforts to use coercion to obtain what should be had, with legitimacy, only through the free market, whether of goods or ideas.

The libertarian conservative would introduce competition into elementary and secondary school systems. Forcing competition between schools would result in higher quality. The effort to provide a common basic education for all citizens has, in the libertarian view, led to mediocrity and conformity. The use of legal force to keep unwilling students in school has undermined learning. Rather than having a single public school system, individualist conservatives would prefer that students be given "vouchers" that could be used to finance an education at the school of their choice.

Restrictions on personal behavior are also to be removed. Laws against drug abuse are to be repealed, with individuals held responsible for their own behavior. Sexual behavior is likewise to be regulated only by personal responsibility for the consequences. Society has little or no mission to perform in salvaging people from their mistakes. A full burden of responsibility is placed on every person.

For the libertarian conservative, as for the classical liberal, such political community as there may be depends on individual initiative. The estimate of the kind and quality of civic activity varies with different writers. Some have worked with neighborhood self-reliance movements to see if voluntary activity could become sufficiently well developed to take care of many community functions.

On the far right of the movement is the utopia of Ayn Rand (1905–1982), to be found in her highly influential novel, *Atlas Shrugged,* where every interindividual transaction is reduced to selfish calculations of utility and personal favors are repaid in cash. In her romantic view, all notions of community were to be sub-ordinated to the need of the heroic individual for complete freedom from gov-ernment control, as well as social customs and traditions.[1]

A more moderate version of libertarian conservatism, sometimes termed *neo-liberalism,* is typified by the work of Friedrich Hayek (1899–1992). Hayek sees the market as an institution that makes efficient use of differences in individual knowledge. The market elicits particular talents and insights and mobilizes them for the satisfaction of social needs. While great inequality results from the spon-taneous behavior of individuals, the overall prosperity of society justifies the result. Where markets fail, as with monopolies or environmental issues or even the provision of subsistence incomes, governmental intervention is acceptable. However government must be strictly limited to establishing the legal framework for the market, and should go beyond that only for those functions that markets cannot perform.[2]

The History of Libertarian Conservatism

The history of libertarian conservatism is simple to tell, apart from a certain con-fusion about the labels used to describe it. The problem with the labels is that members of the movement often call themselves conservatives while acknowl-edging that their roots are in a libertarian version of classical liberalism.[3]

There are two reasons for this anomaly. Libertarianism is an ultraindividual-ist theory. Individual freedom is placed above all other community and social val-ues. In that sense, it claims to represent something special about the Western tra-dition prior to the rapid growth of state power in the 1930s. Thus, libertarian conservatives see themselves as *conservators* of an earlier political and economic tradition, even if they have borrowed some elements from a tradition that is more properly labeled classical liberalism.

---

1. Cf. Jerome Tucille, *It Usually Begins with Ayn Rand: A Libertarian Odyssey* (New York: Stein and Day, 1972); Claudia Roth Pierpoint, "Twilight of the Goddess," *The New Yorker,* July 24, 1995, pp. 70–81.

2. F. A. Hayek, "The Mirage of Social Justice," Vol. 2, *Law, Legislation and Liberty* (London: Routledge, 1982 [1976]). Cf. Kenneth Hoover, "Ideologizing Institutions: Laski, Hayek, Keynes and the Creation of Contemporary Politics," *Journal of Political Ideologies,* 4 (1999) 1, 87–115.

3. For a review of the political significance of this controversy, see Kenneth Hoover, "The Rise of Conservative Capitalism: Ideological Tensions within the Reagan and Thatcher Governments," *Comparative Studies in Society and History* (Cambridge University Press) 29 (1987): 245–268; Desmond King, "New Right Ideology, Welfare State Form, and Citizenship: A Comment on Conservative Capitalism," *Comparative Studies in Society and History,* 30 (1988): 792–799; and Kenneth Hoover, "Response to King on 'New Right Ideology,'" *Comparative Studies in Society and History,* 30 (1988): 800–803.

Libertarians also identify with much of conservatism's traditional analysis of human nature. They believe that imperfect as people may be, the best hope for the humane life lies in individual freedom. They concede less to the power of rationality than classical liberals do, and they appreciate much more the idiosyncratic and unique character of individual life. They see the principled individualist as something of a heroic figure battling against mass mediocrity, a conservative's answer to the utility-calculating economic man of the Benthamites. It is in these overtones of struggle, best evidenced in the work of Ayn Rand, that one can see the romanticism of the conservative showing through.

The roots of libertarian conservatism are found in the writings of Adam Smith and the group of late-eighteenth- and early-nineteenth-century writers, largely businessmen, known as the Manchester School of English utilitarians. What Smith promoted as laissez-faire for reasons of economic efficiency and moral discipline, the Manchester School advertised as the key to individual freedom for its own sake.

In the hands of Herbert Spencer (1820–1903), the doctrine was restated as Social Darwinism. The market was the means of natural selection among human beings. The "fittest" would survive its rigorous tests and would succeed. The weak would fail—but that is nature's and, according to Spencer, society's way. Setting aside the phenomenon of cooperation in nature, and the differences that human intelligence and social sensitivity might make among human beings, Spencer proclaimed competition as the natural principle of human life.

Antistatism

It remained for two Austrian economists, Ludwig Von Mises and his student Friedrich Hayek, writing in the spirit of crisis of the 1930s and 1940s, to identify the original Manchester tradition and free enterprise capitalism as the mainsprings of Western culture.[4] Some scholars saw the advent of totalitarianism in Germany as the reaction to excessive individualism, competition, and the rise of industrial capitalism. Hayek and Von Mises saw it, rather, as the consequence of the advance of "statism" and of the notion that the state could provide security for the individual. In their view, it was the resulting breakdown of individual self-reliance that made the Germans ripe for tyranny.[5] Using this example, they made the state the target of a powerful conservative critique.

---

4. Kenneth Dolbeare and Patricia Dolbeare, *American Ideologies: The Competing Political Beliefs of the 1970's,* 3rd ed. (Chicago: Rand McNally, 1976), pp. 60–62.

5. This generalization provides the libertarian theme in William F. Buckley's blend of individualist and traditional conservatism: *Up from Liberalism* (New York: Honor Books, 1959). Cf. John Judis, *William F. Buckley: Patron Saint of Conservatives* (New York: Simon and Schuster, 1988), p. 147.

The state and even the concept of security itself were seen as the enemies. Only the uncompromising assertion of individual self-determination could protect us from the conniving of craven security-seekers who would undermine our liberties and deliver us up to totalitarianism.[6] This was the theme of early libertarian manifestos and has remained as the consistent refrain of libertarian conservatism ever since.

Libertarians shared the traditional conservatives' disdain for the "mass man." It is typical of the difference between them, however, that the libertarians prescribed a solution quite different from the reinstitution of appropriate forms of authority. For them the threat was not in the personal weaknesses of the masses, but in the statist institutions and policies that removed the need for self-reliance. Were people truly free, they would lose their "massness" and become genuinely responsible.[7]

This moral tone in libertarian thought derives from a basic commitment libertarians share, a commitment that separates them from traditional conservatives. Morality consists of the exercise of individual choice. Behavior that is not freely chosen has no moral standing in libertarian eyes. It is the making of personal judgments that "leads some people to moral excellence and others to moral failure."[8]

The state is deeply suspect in libertarian thought. Murray Rothbard formulates the attitude toward the state in stark and simple terms:

> If, then, the State is not "us," if it is not "the human family" getting together to decide mutual problems, if it is not a lodge meeting or country club, what is it? Briefly, the State is that organization in society which attempts to maintain a monopoly of the use of force and violence in a given territorial area; in particular, it is the only organization in society that obtains its revenue not by voluntary contribution or payment for services rendered, but by coercion.[9]

By a "monopoly of the use of force," Rothbard is referring to the policing functions that give law its means of enforcement.

Thus, the state is the enemy of choice and therefore of individuality. The case against the state acquires a moral dimension: the institution is evil precisely

---

6. Friedrich von Hayek, *The Road to Serfdom* (Chicago: University of Chicago Press, 1944). While Hayek's views are used by libertarian advocates, his complete theory stresses the need for laws that maintain market relations and compensate for market failures. See Hayek, *The Constitution of Liberty* (1960).

7. Ayn Rand, *Capitalism: The Unknown Ideal* (New York: Signet Books, 1966).

8. Tibor Machan, *The Libertarian Alternative* (Chicago: Nelson Hall, 1974), p. 499.

9. Machan, *Libertarian Alternative*, p. 70. Rothbard's antistatist arguments provide a text for both libertarians and anarchists. See Alan Ritter, *Anarchism: A Theoretical Analysis* (Cambridge: Cambridge University Press, 1981), p. 180.

because it denies choice to those who oppose its decisions. Because choice is the beginning point of all morality, government and the coercion that is its method of operation are morally suspect.

In terms of the development of libertarian thought, the events of the late 1960s and early 1970s turned out to be quite consequential. Many libertarians separated themselves from the conservative establishment over the issue of the Vietnam War, and especially the draft, and went on to build a substantially separate movement. The movement centered on resistance to the statism that libertarian conservatives saw as pervasive in the rest of American society.[10]

Karl Hess, a former speech writer for the conservative 1964 Republican presidential candidate, Barry Goldwater, became an exponent of libertarianism as an alternative to the "system" politics of the conventional conservative movement. Hess became involved in an ambitious effort to establish an alternative community oriented to "understandable work, friends, someplace to stand, a reason to stand up, and a certainty of being counted, of being heard, of being a recognizable and not an indistinguishable part of the whole."[11] Freed of statist coercion, personal uniqueness could flourish. The numbing conformity of an institutionalized society could be overthrown.

The effort toward decentralizing and simplifying technology in order to meet human needs at the neighborhood and community level is a vital part of this movement. Technology is explicitly addressed as a key to self-sufficiency. Although Hess's initial experiment, in the Adams-Morgan neighborhood of Washington, D.C., did not survive after five years of innovative experimentation in self-sufficiency, the rhetoric of the movement found its way into the Reagan administration's emphasis on neighborhood-based self-help strategies for fighting urban blight and central city deterioration.

Libertarian conservatism represents the fulfillment of the anticommunity bias of classical liberal thought, with an added motif of suspicion and even hostility regarding all things governmental. What remains is a contradiction within the contemporary conservative movement. The traditional conservative and the libertarian are thus sharply split over the meaning and uses of both power and authority.

The Traditionalist-Libertarian Split

In comparing the two tendencies of conservative thought, George Nash points out that "while libertarians stressed the freedom of the individual in opposition

---

10. Jerome Tucille, *Radical Libertarianism* (Indianapolis: Bobbs-Merrill, 1970). Cf. Irving Kristol, *On the Democratic Ideal in American Life* (New York: Harper and Row, 1972), and Kristol's critique of libertarianism in *Two Cheers for Capitalism* (New York: Basic Books, 1978).

11. Karl Hess, *Community Technology* (New York: Harper and Row, 1979), p. 4.

to the State, traditionalists saw in the 'masterless man' a threat. While libertarians asserted the right of the individual to be free, the right to be oneself, traditionalists were concerned with what an individual ought to be."[12] In this contrast lies the difference between the two conservatisms. Libertarian conservatives are, for nearly all purposes, hostile to the notion of political community; the traditionalists regard community institutions as the primary vehicles of their philosophy.

The implications for community are clear. For libertarian conservatives, it is the capacity for choice that separates human beings from lower animals, and it is therefore the mission of the community to provide the circumstances in which free choice can be exercised most fully. Morality consists of minimizing structure and maximizing individual freedom. Traditional conservatives see the matter quite differently. Judgment is also important to a traditional conservative, but continuity and custom are more significant than independence and choice. Morality consists of exercising judgment within the confines of these sobering influences. Again, for traditionalists, the role of the community is precisely to nourish those structures that will constrain choice within appropriate boundaries.

Just as traditional conservatives are reluctant to make unrestricted individual choice the centerpiece of their philosophy, they are unwilling to see the state as the enemy of morality. For example, the use of state power to prohibit abortions, to mandate the offering of prayer in public schools, to enforce capital punishment, and, above all, to strengthen police power (whether locally or internationally through the military) are issues that separate libertarian from traditional conservatives. Libertarians generally oppose these measures; traditional conservatives support them.

It is here that traditionalists, their banner taken up by religious fundamentalists, meet libertarian conservatives in open confrontation. It is the traditional conservative appreciation of legitimate authority that has become the wellspring of the revolt against "permissiveness" with its consequences for such issues as the family, censorship, prayer in the schools, and gender equality. The chosen instrument of this revolt is government action—whether to build up the military, enforce school prayer, forbid abortion, or censor library books.

The conflict within the conservative movement between traditionalists and libertarians is ultimately deeper than even these sharp programmatic differences suggest. The libertarian version offers a democratic form of conservatism. All individuals are given the same freedoms from restraint by the state and other institutions. Traditionalism, by contrast, is not classless. It is precisely differenti-

---

12. George Nash, *The Conservative Intellectual Movement in the U.S. since 1945* (New York: Basic Books, 1979), p. 82.

ations in authority, based on class differences, that provide the means of social control within the context of powerful institutions.

The split finally comes home at the community level. If all social and political functions are subsumed in the service of the marketplace, the results for community may be quite the opposite of the traditionalist design. The continuity of community institutions, the stability of the family, the authority of the church, the independence of universities, and the fabric of social mores may all be dissolved by the acid of self-interest. Ultimately, in such social aggregations as these, there may be little of the institutional pluralism that distinguishes traditional conservatism and little of the personal freedom that libertarians hope for. Power may drift into the hands of the best organized and the advantaged, with the rest left to shift for themselves.

As political power declines, economic power increases in significance. In the U.S. system, political power has seemingly become more democratic, whereas economic power arguably has become more concentrated. Libertarian conservatives may discover that freeing the market from relatively democratic political control results in an increase in the economic power and political preeminence of a traditionalist upper class, a class that has historically favored stronger limits on personal behavior and more substantial forms of institutional control.

What holds these two conservatisms together in the current political scene is, very probably, the fact that the libertarian program of reducing taxation benefits no one so much as the traditional upper class. Whether that class will remain content with the results for social order of the decline in the role and strength of governmental institutions is one of the key questions for the future of the movement.

AN ANARCHIST PERSPECTIVE

Much less visible on the nightly news than conservatism is an ideology that has had a powerful influence on Western political history as well as American radicalism: anarchism. The term derives from the Greek roots *an-archos,* meaning literally "without a leader." Anarchists, along with libertarians, believe that the legitimation of the use of force through the state is the problem in society, not the solution, as in most other ideologies. However, anarchists are sensitive to sources of coercion apart from the state. The concentration of economic power through the institution of unlimited private property concerns them greatly. They are also suspicious of technology. Anarchists see in technology a tendency toward increasing the amount of hierarchy and domination in society. We will explore each of these themes briefly.

"Property is theft!" Pierre Proudhon (1809–1865) made this the rallying cry of anarchists determined to undo the basis of capitalism. The slogan could be seen in signs at the protest against the World Trade Organization Conference in Seattle in 1999. Proudhon's argument in a famous pamphlet, *What Is Property?* (1840), is that nature belongs to all humankind and that the use of it should be shared by groups of people living and working together in voluntary cooperation.[13] The notion of appropriating a piece of nature, calling it "mine," and erecting a government to coerce people into respecting its ownership is the root of the class system and the wholesale abuse of power that goes with it. Some anarchists, though not all, take the "liberation" of private property to be an excuse for "squatting" and even vandalism.

Murray Bookchin, in *The Ecology of Freedom: The Emergence and Dissolution of Hierarchy,* argues that the principle of *usufruct* should replace that of private property. In capitalism, private property can be acquired and kept almost irrespective of what is done with it; Bookchin makes an anarchist argument for the principle of usufruct: "Resources should belong to the user as long as they are being used." In a truly free society, the use made of resources would express both a communal and an individual need. "A collective need subtly orchestrates work, not personal need alone. . . . Hence, even the work performed in one's own dwelling has an underlying collective dimension in the potential availability of its products to the entire community."[14] He foresees a kind of spontaneous socialism that would operate by consent based on mutual need.

At root, anarchists believe that common sense will make evident the shared nature of basic needs once all the distortions introduced by institutionalized power are removed. The specialized, class-ridden system of production and distribution we now have must be dismantled. When work is specialized and regimented, it becomes alienating. All traces of individual creativity are removed. Management is substituted for initiative, and private coercion for personal incentive. In capitalism the race for survival permits exploitation of workers by managers, managers by stockholders, and stockholders by financial speculators. Everyone is set against everyone else.

True liberty will allow human beings to develop fully as the social creatures they are capable of becoming. Society will become the positive expression of human nature rather than the oppressive instrument of dominant classes.[15] Anarchists rely heavily on accounts of primitive or isolated societies, such as that of the Eskimos, to make their point.[16] Whereas anarchists realize that absolute

---

13. Pierre Proudhon, *What Is Property?* trans. B. R. Tucker (London: William Reeves, n.d.), p. 1.

14. Murray Bookchin, *The Ecology of Freedom: The Emergence and Dissolution of Hierarchy* (Palo Alto, Calif.: Cheshire Books, 1982), p. 50.

15. For the early history of these sentiments in America, see Staughton Lynd, *The Intellectual Origins of American Radicalism* (Cambridge, Mass.: Harvard University Press, 1982 [1968]), p. 110.

16. Bookchin, *Ecology of Freedom,* p. 51.

equality would itself require the forceful suppression of differences, they argue that all human beings have similar basic needs. In a just society, those minimal needs could be met through common action. What goes beyond the minimum is for each individual to work out, either alone or with others.

The principal of voluntarism, which is at the heart of anarchism, shapes the conception of politics found in anarchist writings. Anarchists distrust representative democracy as an invitation to the tyranny of the majority. It is, in the words of one anarchist theoretician, a "grand lottery" with no guarantee that the result will be characterized by wisdom or virtue. Anarchists prefer direct, as opposed to representative, democracy. Society needs to be broken down into groups that are capable of face-to-face exchange and common decision making. Participatory democracy is contrasted with representative democracy operating through politicians. Democracy without direct personal participation becomes a means of avoiding responsibility and opens the door to manipulation and corruption.

Technology and Hierarchy

Anarchists extend their rebellion against domination to the realm of technology. Modern anarchists do not reject technology per se, but they do see it as a dangerous phenomenon that must be used carefully on a scale permitting individual control and the maintenance of humane values.[17] Most recently, anarchists have attempted to incorporate this concern with technology into an ecological framework, arguing that the unity of our natural existence must be restored if we are not to destroy the planet. Technology's capacity to separate us from the natural environment is its greatest danger. The renewal of constructive and nurturing modes of exchange with nature are advanced as the cure for this malady.[18]

As a political movement, anarchism has influenced terrorists as well as pacifists.[19] In the decades prior to the First World War, six heads of state were assassinated by anarchist terrorists, including an American president, William McKinley. The anarchists were a major force in the Spanish Civil War (1936–1939), and their retribution against those who held power, whether through politics, property, or the church, was direct and brutal.[20] More recently, anarchist thought deeply influenced the U.S. countercultural left in the antiwar

17. See E. F. Schumacher, *Small Is Beautiful: Economics As If People Mattered* (New York: Harper and Row, 1976).

18. See Bookchin, *Ecology of Freedom*, p. 315ff. Cf. Mulford Q. Sibley, *Nature and Civilization: Some Implications for Politics* (Notre Dame, Ind.: Notre Dame University Press, 1981).

19. On the latter, see William O. Reichert, *Partisans of Freedom: A Study of American Anarchism* (Bowling Green, Ohio: Bowling Green University Press, 1976).

20. Murray Bookchin, *Spanish Anarchists: Heroic Years 1868–1936* (New York: Harper and Row, 1978).

era of the 1960s and early 1970s as radicals attempted to broaden the movement into a generalized revolt against "the system" and all of the relations of domination found in politics, education, culture, and personal life. Today, anarchist themes are taken up by the populist right in their crusade against government power, as well as by protesters against globalization.

For all that can be said about anarchist conceptions of how society might work, it remains, as one commentator put it, "less a political philosophy than it is a temperament. . . . Anarchism means . . . a grand struggle against evil, a secular crusade against the debasement of self, a fight against social degradation that the idea and the reality of the state seem to represent."[21] It is this temperament that influences anarchist modes of artistic and cultural criticism, as well as political agitation.

CONCLUSION

By examining libertarianism and anarchism together, we can see how government is but one power relationship in our lives. There are many others. Anarchists try to account for the whole structure of domination. Contemporary libertarian conservatives are mainly concerned with only one source of domination: government. From an anarchist point of view, the reduction of governmental power without the commensurate reduction of economic (and religious and social) power would simply mean that those sources of coercion would grow in significance with no necessary gain in true liberty.

A quite different perspective on the uses of power is provided by the next chapter, on reform liberalism. Here, we will see power of one kind, political power, used to counterbalance and regulate power of other kinds, economic and social.

---

21. Terry Perlin, ed., *Contemporary Anarchism* (San Francisco: Transaction Books, 1979), p. 3.

CHAPTER FIVE

REFORM LIBERALISM, POPULISM, AND PROGRESSIVISM

The first duty of the government is to the weak.

LORENZO DOW LEWELLING, POPULIST GOVERNOR OF KANSAS

Reform liberalism brings together ideas taken from populism, progressivism, and even socialism. These ideas merged in the New Deal, President Franklin D. Roosevelt's response to the near collapse of the U.S. economy in the early 1930s. The movement has gone through many phases over the past seventy years and reached a peak in the Great Society programs of President Lyndon B. Johnson in the 1960s. Since then, the reform liberal agenda has declined in influence under a sustained assault by conservatives.

Reform liberalism might more properly be considered a movement than an ideology, yet there is a thread that ties it together and distinguishes it from other ideologies.[1] Reform liberalism was not conceived by one systematic thinker. What began as an amalgam of ideas from many sources was trimmed and shaped by the practicalities of politics, leaving in place only those parts of the New Deal that conformed to a limited vision of reform. That limited vision is simply the notion that government should act to assist disadvantaged individuals so that they can compete effectively in the marketplace.

Reform liberals do not set out to abolish the marketplace but, rather, to use governmental power to remedy the inequalities of opportunity that it produces. This ideology is still liberalism, because it conceives of equality in terms of *opportunity* rather than *end result*. In the utopia of reform liberalism, substantial differences in people's material wealth would remain, but neither this situation nor any other remediable obstacle would prevent individuals from improving their position. Reform liberalism maintains the liberal focus on individual self-interest as the heart of politics. But its central objective is to use government to see that all citizens have a reasonable chance of participating in a competitive society.

We can differentiate classical liberals and reform liberals by understanding the distinction between *negative* liberty and *positive* liberty. Having negative liberty means that one faces few, if any, barriers to free choice. Classical liberalism provided negative liberty by authorizing a system of private property and individual rights that protected the possessions of one person from invasion by another. The free choice of what to do with one's possessions was not to be limited by the barriers of theft and violence. Similarly, classical liberalism restricted the power of government to interfere with freedom of expression and other basic rights.

Reform liberals accept this program, but they wish to go further. Even with every obstacle removed, some people may not have the *positive* means of exercising free choice. The unavailability of jobs, educational deficiencies, illness, the effects of racism, and poverty itself can mean that individuals find their options severely limited. The lack of barriers such as the threat of violence or state interference doesn't necessarily bring with it the realistic possibility of having choices

---

1. As Theda Skocpol points out, the choice of "liberal" as the name for Roosevelt's programs was deliberate: it was meant to appeal to progressives while keeping a safe distance from socialists. Although Skocpol uses Samuel Beer's term, practical liberalism, for this program, she describes it as "reformist" in every respect. The direction of the reforms clearly changed the institutional thrust of liberalism toward more government and was seen to be practical only in comparison with socialism and progressivism, not previous versions of liberalism per se. See Theda Skocpol, "The Legacies of New Deal Liberalism," in *Liberalism Reconsidered,* ed. Douglas MacLean and Claudia Mills (Totowa, N.J.: Rowman and Allenheld, 1983), pp. 87–104. Though differently defined, the phrase fits generally with the usage by Kenneth Dolbeare and Patricia Dolbeare in *American Ideologies: The Competing Political Beliefs of the 1970s,* 3rd ed. (Chicago: Rand McNally, 1976), p. 72ff.

in life. People may find themselves perfectly safe and secure but without the resources needed to develop a new vocation, care for loved ones, or participate in the life of the community.

Reform liberals attempt to remedy this imbalance through positive liberty. A person with positive liberty has the means of overcoming deficiencies—for example, education, health care, and job training programs—so that genuine options are available. The instrument of reform liberalism is governmental assistance and regulation.

The mission of government, then, is to provide substantive means for the improvement of individual lives. Reform liberalism seeks to serve the similar desires of all people for a secure and prosperous existence by using government as a means of reducing inequalities of circumstance and situation. In this way, it takes the "developmental freedom" of such classical liberals as the Mills one large step further (see Chapter 2).

Because governmental action is essential to this vision, the processes of government are themselves the target of reformist politics. The movement assumed that politics could be made honest through democratic reforms that would allow the multiplicity of interests in the United States to be fairly represented. A reformed process of government was to be the key to a reformed society.

We will see how this ideological vision plays itself out in the reformist image of the good society. With this image in mind, we will turn our analysis to understanding the ideas that were borrowed from progressivism and populism to change the agenda of American politics and shape new policies through several American administrations beginning with the New Deal.

THE REFORMIST VISION OF THE GOOD SOCIETY

Classical liberalism has one great flaw: to celebrate individualism is to accept extremes of economic inequality that leave some people far ahead of others in even the most basic prerequisites for survival. Historically, liberalism was a radical doctrine aimed at freeing individuals from the stifling hand of a hierarchical feudal society to pursue their own interests freely. The old order of separate "estates" and obligations for different classes was overthrown. Through the institution of private property, the communitarian basis of feudalism was transformed. A society was created based on individual self-development and contract. The consequence was a dynamic and individualistic society, but one in which inequalities of class based on heredity and status were replaced with a more fluid class system based on income and wealth.

At the beginning of this chapter, reform liberalism was defined as a movement centered on using government to assist individuals so that they have the substantive means of competing in a market society. What would it take to provide everyone with a chance of competing on a reasonable basis? The most obvious answers have to do with health, education, and economic welfare. In each of these areas, personal problems and misfortunes can disable and handicap anyone.

In the reformist vision of society, no one would be without medical care for serious illnesses and injuries. Health care would be insured privately where possible and publicly when necessary. In addition, government would actively pursue disease control and preventive medicine, along with the regulation of industry to avoid health hazards, and the administration of fair standards and pricing in health care institutions.

Similarly, education would be a public responsibility. Reform liberals share classical liberals' commitment to rationality as the method of a civilized society. Education is the means of cultivating reason and applying it to the strategies individuals use in improving their lives and participating as citizens. Consequently, good public education is an objective that involves the very foundation of society. What reformers added to the program was the active encouragement of those previously excluded from the educational system either by lack of means, discrimination, or deficiency of background.

Beginning with preschool programs and continuing through graduate education, those whose performance was limited by family background, income, deficiencies in basic skills, racial or ethnic barriers, and malnutrition would receive help. They would be offered extra classes, special tutoring, and personal support in the form of guidance and even income and subsidized meals. Educational institutions would be required to give preference to the hiring of teachers from disadvantaged groups. Admissions quotas would be established to ensure that disadvantaged groups had access to scarce places in professional schools. The educational process is the central channel for improving the upward mobility of the disadvantaged.

No one is to be denied the chance of living at a minimal standard of decency. Minimum income maintenance would be the right of all citizens. For those who were temporarily unemployed, there would be government-guaranteed unemployment benefits. Government programs would supply unemployment counseling, retraining, and employment services. Publicly financed work would be available to those unable to find employment. Projects such as building and maintaining public facilities and staffing public services would provide jobs. Private employers would be subsidized by the government for hiring the unemployed.

The lack of motivation that afflicts some of the poor would be dealt with by professionals trained in counseling, guiding, motivating, and organizing the disadvantaged. Rather than simply redistributing income directly, most reform liberals have advocated the extensive use of social services. The services should be coordinated so that a person unemployed because of ill health would be provided with medical assistance, family counseling, food stamps, employment training, and job placement services. The linking of these services would afford a coordinated approach to individual assistance.

In the marketplace, access to competition is opened up by strict enforcement of antitrust and price-fixing laws. Regulations to encourage bidding by minority firms bring in those previously excluded from obtaining contracts. Reforms of employment examinations to remove unfair quotas, racial biases, and unnecessary requirements would be designed to open employment opportunities to all.

Racism, which handicaps minorities in the competitive struggle, is to be vigorously opposed by governmental action. Segregation of public accommodations such as hotels and restaurants is made illegal. Discrimination, whether in hiring, admissions to educational institutions, or public transportation is outlawed. Public policy is redirected to give first consideration to previously excluded minorities in all aspects of hiring and promotion.

The denial of political rights through restrictions on voter registration or access to the polls is corrected by action of the federal government against offending local officials. To ensure the integrity and openness of the political process, reform liberals would use laws to regulate the nomination of candidates for public office. Primary elections or nominating caucuses open to all those willing to declare a party preference increase the effectiveness of democracy at the grass-roots level. The old system of nomination by power brokers and party "bosses" is cast aside in favor of these new procedures.

Civil liberties are protected from violation by government, private organizations, and even private individuals. The original conception of the Bill of Rights of the U.S. Constitution was that individuals must be protected from governmental interference in their freedom of expression. But what about threats to free expression from private groups such as the Ku Klux Klan, a self-appointed censor, or an employer? Reform liberals would make the enforcement of civil-liberties protections an active responsibility of government through legislation, executive leadership, and challenges in the courts.

The fundamental assumption of reform liberalism is that governmental action can overcome inequalities in background, wealth, and, most especially, power. Making the political process fair and open to all is a primary objective. Because political campaigns depend on expensive media advertising, campaign finance regulation goes to the core of the political process. Reform liberals want to be sure that elections cannot be bought by special interests or wealthy contributors. Limitations on private contributions, public reporting requirements, and the availability of public funding are used to prevent the buying of elections by special interests and wealthy contributors. These measures are intended to compensate for the political disadvantages of the poor and unorganized and to assure open access to the political process.

In the workplace, as in politics, reform liberals want to make the distribution of power fairer. The right of people to organize unions for the purposes of bargaining with their employers over wages and working conditions is protected by law. This option provides a basic tool for those who do not own the means of production to develop the power to confront those who do. The process of collective bargaining is regulated to define unfair practices, establish grievance procedures, and ensure honest elections of union officers.

Reform liberals stop short of endorsing measures aimed at absolute equality, such as drastic income redistribution. They do, however, believe that government can be an active and effective agent on behalf of the disadvantaged.[2] What we have seen is a sketch of the reform liberal's ideal society. Other illustrations of the extension of reform liberalism to environmental policy, foreign policy, and the protection of minorities will appear as we examine the emergence of these ideas and the movement that carried them forward.

THE HISTORY OF REFORM LIBERALISM

The origins of American reform liberalism really go back to the beginnings of the country. There was from the earliest period of European settlement a tradition of thought that diverged from the notion of individual self-interest as a basis for the "social contract." Whatever John Locke may have said about the influence of appetites and interests in shaping behavior and necessitating a social contract to provide order (see Chapter 2), there is also in Locke a claim that people have a certain natural reasoning ability and, with that, certain rights. The authors of the U.S. Declaration of Independence incorporated Locke's notion of government by consent in the context of a claim for equality and natural rights based on God's will:

> We hold these truths to be self-evident, that all men are created equal, *that they are endowed by their Creator with certain unalienable Rights; that among these are Life, Liberty, and the pursuit of Happiness.* That to secure these rights, Governments are instituted among Men, deriving their just powers from the consent of the governed. That whenever any Form of Government becomes destructive of these ends, it is the Right of the People to alter or to abolish it, and to institute new Government, laying its foundation on such principles and organizing its powers in such form, as to them shall seem most likely to effect their Safety and Happiness.

If human beings are created equal and if government is to "effect" not only our "safety," but our "happiness," then government must be something more

---

2. The debate that rages on whether the reduction of inequality is possible is analyzed from a reform liberal point of view by Philip Green in *The Pursuit of Inequality* (New York: Random House, 1981).

than a police officer for the property owners.[3] The Declaration argues that rights come not from the ownership of property but from God or, in a more secular version, from an "equal creation." Benjamin Franklin, Thomas Jefferson, Thomas Paine, and numerous others struggled over the relationships among property, individual rights, and the rights of the community as a whole. All endorsed the notion of private property, but they saw it as the creation of the community and as beholden to it in some limited sense.[4] Jefferson and Paine, in particular, distinguished the ownership of property as a civil right, accorded by society, from permanent and inalienable natural rights attached to human existence. That distinction became the basis for efforts to regulate inheritance and for proposals, rarely successful, to allow for government redistribution of land.[5]

Throughout American history there have been profound struggles over the issue of property rights versus human rights. The notion that slaves are people with rights, rather than property, was a basic factor in the Civil War. Efforts by debtors to weaken the power of creditors through monetary reform and efforts to limit the powers of banks have been frequent in U.S. political history.[6] Environmental issues are the most recent manifestation of this basic tension in the nation's cultural heritage.

We will explore the contributions made by populists to the development of the reform liberal tradition, and to the resurgence of conservatism toward the end of this century.[7] These movements are part of the story that includes *socialism,*

---

3. Benjamin Franklin put it very clearly: "The Combinations of Civil Society are not like those of a Set of Merchants, who club their Property in different Proportions for Building and Freighting a Ship, and may therefore have some Right to vote in disposition of the Voyage in a greater or less Degree according to their respective Contributions; but the important ends of Civil Society, and the personal Securities of Life and Liberty, these remain the same in every Member of the society; and the poorest continues to have an equal Claim to them with the most opulent, whatever Difference Time, Chance, or Industry may occasion in their Circumstances." In Albert Smyth, ed., *Writings of Benjamin Franklin* (New York: Macmillan, 1907), Vol. 10, pp. 58–60. Cited in Staughton Lynd, *The Intellectual Origins of American Radicalism* (Cambridge, Mass.: Harvard University Press, 1982 [1968]), p. 71.

4. This analysis is pursued in detail by Lynd, *The Intellectual Origins of American Radicalism,* pp. 20, 67–90. Cf. Dumas Malone, *Jefferson the Virginian* (Boston: Little, Brown, 1948), pp. 227–228; Joseph Ellis, *American Sphinx* (New York: Knopf, 1996), pp. 65–66; and Carl Becker, *The Declaration of Independence* (New York: Vintage, 1958).

5. Lynd, *Op cit,* pp. 76–77, 83. Thomas Jefferson proposed a clause for the Virginia constitution that would distribute 50 acres of land to every nonslave, male resident.

6. In the first version of the Wisconsin Constitution, for example, the chartering of banks was expressly *forbidden* because of anger over currency swindles by frontier bankers. See Robert Nesbit, *Wisconsin: A History* (Madison: University of Wisconsin Press, 1973).

7. For a discussion of the repression of these movements, see Alan Wolfe, *The Seamy Side of Democracy* (New York: David McKay, 1973), especially pp. 120–121.

progressivism, and *populism.* Socialism will be dealt with in Chapters 6 and 7, but populism and progressivism are crucial to the background of the New Deal, as well as to the continuing struggle over the meaning of equality for the process and policies of American government.

Populism: Origins and Early History

"Populism" has the same Latin root as "people." Populist movements claim to speak for the "little people" against the big interests. Historically, populists were concerned with two related forms of inequality: disparities in wealth and in power. The revolt against concentrations of wealth are the reform liberal part of the populist program, though recently the term *populist* has been revived by libertarian conservatives who want to reduce the power exercised by government in the marketplace.

Thomas Jefferson is, in many respects, the originator of populism in America. As Joseph Ellis points out:

> "[Jefferson] regarded himself as the spokesman for a latent majority of Americans who, if they could ever be mobilized, would assume their rightful place as true heirs to 'the spirit of '76.' And instead of talking about them as 'the public,' he began, in the 1790's to speak in the democratic idiom of 'the people.' These were prophetic words."[8]

What began in 1776 as a move *against* monarchism, increasingly became, in the mind of Jefferson and many of his allies, a move *toward* rule by the people directly through local democracies operating without strong national government. Jefferson saw himself as a "republican," by which he meant a believer in both democracy and sharply limited government. Jefferson opposed the "federalists" who wanted a strong presidency, a national bank, and the supremacy of the national government over the states. As Ellis summarizes Jefferson's later views in his letters to friends:

> "[Jefferson] and his colleagues of the revolutionary generation had seen through this trickery, but their successors 'having nothing in them of the feelings or principles of '76' were now completely duped into supporting 'a single and splendid government of an aristocracy, founded on banking institutions, and moneyed corporations . . . riding and ruling over the plundered ploughman and beggared yeomanry.'"[9]

The problem that arose very quickly, however, brought the two elements of Jefferson's views into sharp conflict: his belief in equality and his view of limited

8. Ellis, *op. cit.,* p. 158.

9. Ellis, *op. cit.,* p. 326.

government. Southern secessionists borrowed Jefferson's arguments for local control to justify "states rights" on the question of slavery. The fact that Jefferson himself became increasingly reluctant to face the slavery question played into their hands.

The result was that populism became an enduring current in American politics. The American Civil War settled, for a while, the preeminence of federalist views of the role of the central government. However, a rising tide of discontent following upon the economic troubles of the late nineteenth century revived populism, and it became the basis for a new movement in electoral politics. As John Diggins notes in his history of the American Left, the populist People's Party in the 1890s "could control or influence a dozen state legislatures and claim four senators and over fifty congressmen."[10] The broad populist movement, consisting of various parties and factions, was responding to pressures placed on small farmers by debt, railroad monopolies, and land speculators. To confront these forces, populists advocated government credit, railroad regulation, antitrust laws, and election reforms. The idea was to counterbalance the power of the wealthy minority with the power of the activated majority.

For all that populists sought to achieve by governmental action, however, they were not socialists. The socialist's distaste for private property ran against the grain of a movement that was part of the American experience of small landholdings and personal advancement through hard work. Populists of the left believed in active government on behalf of the average citizen, not the replacement of capitalism by a planned economy.[11] Originating largely among farmers in the South and Midwest, populism carried with it certain prejudices, as well as a political program, though the two were tied together.[12] In the South, many populists were also racists who continued to see the repression of blacks as a key to maintaining the precarious position of poor white dirt farmers. Efforts to ally poor blacks and whites under the populist banner ended in failure. In other areas, populists were anti-Catholic and saw the big-city Catholic political machines as corrupt and powerful enemies.

Whether populists were any more nativist and chauvinist than the general population is open to dispute, but the populist feeling of being victimized by other groups politicized prejudices in a powerful fashion. Anti-Semitism,

10. John Diggins, *The American Left in the Twentieth Century* (New York: Harcourt Brace Jovanovich, 1973), p. 41.

11. In North Dakota, a populist governor in the early 1920s succeeded in establishing a state-run bank, which exists to this day.

12. For a comprehensive history of populism's origins and development, see Lawrence Goodwyn, *Democratic Promise: The Populist Movement in America* (New York: Oxford University Press, 1976).

expressed as resentment against Jewish financiers and media interests, is still a part of populist movements in parts of the South, Midwest, and West.

The People's Party, the most successful American populist party, declined rapidly after 1896, largely because much of its program was taken over by Democrats and progressive Republicans. As one historian remarks,

> [Populism's] demands anticipated many changes to come in the twentieth century. If the demands for the recovery of public lands were never met, they anticipated the rationale of the conservation movement, the land as a public heritage. If the railroads were never nationalized, they experienced more effective state and federal regulation. And if the populists never elaborated a program for controlling the trusts, their condemnation of abuses in business helped advance corporate regulation and antitrust measures. Their demands for changes in political and electoral practices read almost like a catalog of twentieth-century reforms in that field."[13]

Populism gave to reform liberalism a whole range of meanings for the concept of positive liberty. By identifying concentrations of private and public power as threats to the interests of the common person, populists put the spotlight on crucial areas for reform.[14] Yet populism and reform liberalism are not identical, for reform liberalism has elements of elitism in its approach to politics that are counter to the democratic radicalism found in the populist movement. Where those elitist tendencies came from is, in part, the story of what the progressive movement added to the development of reform liberalism.

From Progressivism to the New Deal

Populism reached its peak as a visible political movement in the 1890s, as noted earlier, and thereafter became part of the mainstream through the adoption of some of its programs by the major parties. The progressives rose to prominence just after the turn of the twentieth century. The presidential candidacies of Theodore Roosevelt in 1912 and Sen. Robert La Follette of Wisconsin in 1924 made the progressive movement a significant force in electoral politics. While parties identified with the progressive label rose and fell, the movement was carried along on a broad stream of support in many states and cities where progressive ideas and officeholders were responsible for ambitious programs of reform.

Progressivism is a curiously American phenomenon. In a society that lacked a feudal history, a new kind of class system evolved in which a middle class of

---

13. George B. Tindall, *Populist Reader: Selections from the Works of American Populist Leaders* (New York: Harper, 1966), p. xv.

14. A history of these struggles is provided by Howard Zinn, *A People's History of the United States* (New York: Harper and Row, 1980).

independent farmers, shopkeepers, craftspeople, intellectuals, and white-collar salaried employees became a decisive force in American politics. These people were interested in creating a rational, orderly, honest society in which hard work would be rewarded and misfortunes could be overcome with the proper assistance. They found their target in abuses of the economic system through fraud and monopolies, and in the corruption of government through graft and bossism. Progressives led the attack on both, while developing a theory that government could be used to make capitalism work in a more equitable fashion.

William Appleman Williams identifies two broad themes in the program of the progressives: "They wanted to hold the large corporation at its existing level of power while raising other groups to positions of relative balance. They also sought minimum standards of equity and moral behavior."[15] This program appealed to vast sections of American opinion. Rejecting socialist designs for governmental control of the economy, progressives instead supported regulation to eliminate economic abuses such as monopolies, price fixing, and the exploitation of child labor. Angered at the role of big-city bosses in controlling the nomination of state and national officeholders, Wisconsin Governor Robert La Follette led a crusade for the establishment of open primaries in which nominees could be selected by the voters. Progressive journalists, such as Lincoln Steffens, exposed bribery and graft in government and crooked and inhumane practices by business executives.

The progressives' passion for clean government led them away from the customary ward politics of city machines and even fostered an aversion to party politics in the usual sense. Progressives believed in the independent expert, accountable only indirectly to public opinion and not at all to the political party leaders. The city manager form of government, the independent regulatory commission, and the professionalized civil service were all favorite proposals of the progressives. The objective was an efficient government free of the tainted influences of wealth and political bossism.

Progressives differed from populists in that they were not believers in radical forms of democracy. The use of expertise borrowed from the universities and the professions in the service of "good government" set progressivism on a course that would lead to accusations of bureaucratic elitism. Whereas Wisconsin's La Follette campaigned vigorously to replace boss-dominated political conventions with primary elections, he opposed the populist idea of the initiative, a form of direct lawmaking by the electorate.[16] He, along with most other progressives,

---

15. William Appleman Williams, *The Contours of American History* (Chicago: Quadrangle Books, 1966), p. 396.

16. A proposed law is placed on the ballot by petition, and if it passes, it either is referred to the legislature for action or takes effect upon adoption, depending on the kind of initiative process used. Several states permit the initiative.

believed that enlightened leadership was vital and that too much democracy would lead to demagoguery and bad policy. In his election campaigns he stated that, "A vote for me is a vote for the full expression of your views." This assurance meant that he and his fellow progressives would act on behalf of everyone's best interest, which was assumed to lie in rational, well-planned, and honestly executed public policy.

Critics on the Right saw progressives as meddlesome do-gooders who would stifle free enterprise. Big-city liberal politicians saw progressives as moralists who did not understand urban life, with its need for the accommodation and tolerance of diverse lifestyles.[17]

Critics on the Left were wary of the middle-class bias of progressive policies, the limited scope of progressive goals, and the elitism of the movement's leaders. Yet temporary alliances between progressives, urban liberals, and socialists were responsible for major policy initiatives on behalf of the disadvantaged. William Appleman Williams points out that the progressives

> were largely interest-conscious leaders united in a loose, and often mutually suspicious, alliance to check the dominant interest. Their greatest weakness was their lack of any broad and dynamic conception of how the system was to be coordinated and sustained. They did not like the large corporation, but they did not have anything to put in its place.[18]

Progressivism led to a patchwork of reforms and a mixed record of accomplishment. Most important, however, progressives, along with urban liberals and labor leaders, established models of governmental intervention in the economy that provided patterns for the New Deal as Roosevelt struggled to get the country back on its feet during the Great Depression.[19] The other principal legacy of the progressives was the idea that political reform meant opening up the parties to public inspection and participation. Both sets of ideas provided the agenda for the Democratic Party as it advanced new approaches to positive liberty from the New Deal, through the Great Society, to the age of affirmative action and environmentalism.

Yet reform liberalism is distinct from progressivism. The New Deal adopted progressive notions of governmental agencies employing experts to address prob-

---

17. For an account of the relationship of progressivism to urban liberalism, see John Buenker, *Urban Liberalism and Progressive Reform* (New York: W. W. Norton, 1974).

18. Williams, *Contours of American History,* p. 396.

19. A case study in the relationship between progressivism and the New Deal in the area of economic reform is provided by Melvin Urofsky in *A Mind of One Piece: Brandeis and American Reform* (New York: Scribner's, 1971). For a survey of other sources, see John Buenker and Nicholas Burckel, eds., *Progressive Reform: A Guide to Information Sources* (Detroit: Gale Research Company, 1981).

lems of the economy, but these agencies were dismantled by Congress just before the Second World War. The bureaucratic costs did not seem to be justified by the agencies' poor performance in rescuing the U.S. economy from the effects of the Depression. It was the massive governmental expenditures of the war that brought the economy around. The relatively small-scale projects of well-motivated experts could not bring sufficient resources to bear on the problems.

Progressive notions concerning government intervention in the economy were revived after World War II, but more significant were initiatives to create large-scale public employment programs and to implement price controls. The progressive style of reform was more successful, as we will see, in areas of national policy that used expertise and bureaucracy to attack social ills than it was in addressing fundamental economic problems.

From the Fair Deal to the New Frontier

The Fair Deal was President Harry Truman's label for his program of domestic activism on behalf of workers and farmers disadvantaged by postwar economic changes (1945–1953). The New Frontier was President John F. Kennedy's phrase for a revival of reform liberalism in limited areas of public policy (1961–1963). As illustrations of reform liberal ideology, these programs are as instructive for their limitations and failures as for their successes.

The most dramatic breakthroughs of reform liberals during both administrations concerned civil liberties. Racial discrimination became a high-priority concern of the Democratic Party in 1948 when Mayor Hubert Humphrey of Minneapolis led a walkout from the Democratic National Convention to protest segregationist practices by Democratic parties in southern states. Although the Truman administration had integrated the armed forces, it otherwise proceeded slowly in confronting institutionalized racism in the United States. Reform liberals wanted the government to take an active role by using constitutional reform and federal law to undermine the legal framework of segregation.

In the eight-year period between the Truman and Kennedy administrations, the modern civil rights movement gained momentum under the leadership of the Rev. Martin Luther King, Jr. (see Chapter 11). This movement forced President Kennedy to raise civil rights to the top of his agenda and to declare that "race has no place in American life or law."[20] Implementing this policy ultimately required the use of federal lawyers, voting registrars, and even troops. Southern governors, mayors, and sheriffs resisted federal efforts to enforce the rights of blacks to attend educational institutions and use other public facilities. Reform liberalism

---

20. Cited in Stephen Oates, *Let the Trumpet Sound: The Life of Martin Luther King, Jr.* (New York: Mentor, 1982), p. 238.

was enormously strengthened by the successes of Thurgood Marshall, architect of the courtroom strategy that breached the barriers of legalized segregation.

In a second respect, the two administrations were similar in their approach to reform liberalism. The goals of foreign policy were shaped by both Truman and Kennedy out of a determination to confront Russian and Chinese threats to U.S. interests. Communism is opposed by reform liberals precisely because it violates individual freedoms that are at the heart of the liberal creed. Both administrations pursued direct confrontations with communist military overtures, in Korea and Cuba. However, both presidents tried to use constructive means of defusing the appeal of communism: the Marshall Plan under Truman offered generous assistance to war-damaged nations in Europe, and Kennedy's Alliance for Progress was aimed at appealing to progressive forces in Latin America.

Liberal capitalism could confront communism through appeals to reason, idealism, and economic self-interest backed up by force when necessary. The reliance on force ultimately led reform liberals into an uneasy alliance with the growing power of the military-industrial complex throughout the cold war of the 1950s and on into Vietnam in the 1960s and 1970s.

An unsuccessful proposal in the Truman and Kennedy administrations was that contained in the Full Employment Act of 1946 for a form of national economic planning to secure jobs for the unemployed, if necessary through government-directed work programs. Price controls were similarly unpopular. Blocked by conservatives from using job programs to secure opportunity for the disadvantaged, reform liberals relied on economic growth, some of it financed by escalating military budgets, to expand welfare programs.

The Great Society

With the assassination of Kennedy in 1963, Lyndon Johnson became president (1963–1969). Raised in rural Texas, where reform liberalism had meant roads, rural electrification, and water projects, he transformed a wave of sympathy for Kennedy into support for a broad agenda of reform liberal programs.

Prodded by the increasing militance of the civil rights movement, Johnson pushed legislation to outlaw discrimination in voting, public accommodations, education, and employment. He extended the concept of the Peace Corps to a domestic version, Vista, designed to deal with poverty at home. Community assistance programs were established to channel resources to urban reform groups independently of the political machines, which restricted the power and prospects of poor people. Education received huge new subsidies, health care was opened up to public insurance and regulation, social agencies were expanded to deal with the complex needs of the poor, and basic subsistence benefits were increased. The theme of all of these efforts was active assistance to those in need of counseling, education, health care, income maintenance, and, to a limited extent, employment.

The failure to expand the Great Society into an effective program for providing public employment to the disadvantaged was largely attributable to the Vietnam War. The reform liberal style of using carefully rationalized, incremental responses to the war in Indochina led to an ever-escalating commitment of money and troops. Yet the conflict was rooted in decades of struggle by the Vietnamese to throw foreigners out of their country. It was a confrontation betwen technical expertise and raw nationalism that the United States, like France before it, could not comprehend. The war siphoned off money and support that might have made the Great Society more effective.[21] The same problem of limited scale that prevented a full test of New Deal reforms during the Depression restricted the impact of the Great Society.

The Decline of Reform Liberalism

The swirling currents of politics in the 1970s saw the furthest advances of governmental activism and, finally, the beginning of a broad-scale retreat.[22] The increasing cost of military budgets, the economic impact of rapidly escalating energy prices, and the deep-seated nature of many social problems cast a shadow on Great Society programs. But the essential unsolved problem was how to move the reform liberal agenda into serious involvement in resolving the distributive inequities of the economy.

The peak of redistributive policies came, paradoxically, in the administration of Richard M. Nixon (1969–1974). Nixon, at the urging of Rep. Daniel Patrick Moynihan (D. N.Y.) and others, put forward the Family Assistance Plan. The plan represented the culmination of a campaign to get traditional conservatives to agree with liberals that welfare should be placed on a national footing along with Social Security as a part of the nation's basic "safety net." Moving the responsibility for welfare from the states to the federal government permitted the vast disparities in state levels of support and fairness of administration to be addressed. The Nixon administration, however, withdrew its support in the face of opposition led by Gov. Ronald Reagan of California.[23]

---

21. Whether the Great Society succeeded or failed is widely debated; however, poverty levels decreased markedly. See John Schwarz, *America's Hidden Success: A Reassessment of Twenty Years of Public Policy* (New York: W. W. Norton, 1983).

22. See Kenneth Hoover and Raymond Plant, *Conservative Capitalism in Britain and the United States: A Critical Appraisal* (New York and London: Routledge, 1989).

23. Daniel Patrick Moynihan, *The Politics of a Guaranteed Income* (New York: Vintage, 1973), pp. 374–375. Cf. Christopher Leman, *The Collapse of Welfare Reform* (Cambridge, Mass.: MIT Press, 1980), p. 92; Lou Cannon, *Reagan* (New York: G. P. Putnam's, 1982, pp. 178–179).

The relationship of reform liberalism to welfare programs is more complex than it may appear. Reform liberals have historically stopped short of equalizing income for its own sake, and they have generally preferred government programs that offer education and other indirect forms of assistance rather than a handout. However, basic income maintenance for those least able to take care of themselves is seen as essential. Traditional conservatives also believe in basic support for the indigent. The definition of basic need is the key question, and reform liberals have a different one from that given by traditional conservatives.

Publicly provided welfare originated as a replacement for private charity. From the beginning, it was linked to conservative notions of the management of the lifestyles of its recipients. All the dominant social institutions made their mark: the family through the regulations associated with Aid to Families with Dependent Children, business institutions through regulations on employment, and the church through regulations on personal behavior.

The conservative objective is generally to reserve welfare for fatherless families of unemployable women and their children. Historically, employable men were to be excluded, cohabitation was forbidden for women on welfare, and income from part-time jobs was sharply restricted. Reform liberals, beginning with Social Security for older citizens, have attempted to broaden the notion of welfare so that it becomes a matter of right for any person falling below a certain income level. Individualist conservatives have opposed government-sponsored welfare programs for all but the most extreme cases, preferring instead to force self-reliance. Where that fails, private charity is the answer.

Reform liberals see the maintenance of a basic income as a prerequisite for entrance into competition for a decent standard of living. They have resisted the use of welfare to regulate personal behavior and have loosened eligibility restrictions. Liberals and conservatives could agree on "categorical" aid programs for the disabled, however, reform liberals worked toward a concept of minimum income as a basic right. It was this movement that began to fade with the defeat of the Family Assistance Plan in 1970, and with it came the beginning of the end of reform liberal ascendancy. This defeat was the first major victory of contemporary conservatism over reform liberalism, and it opened the way for a broader assault in the presidential elections of 1976 and 1980 by Ronald Reagan, the leader of the resurgent right.

Bureaucracy and larger budgets for social expenditures were the handmaidens of the implementation of the reform liberal agenda. Both attracted increasing fire from conservatives and those who resented the redistribution of opportunity, income, and power to the disadvantaged and to the public and private agencies whose programs assisted them. Libertarian conservatives feared the concentration of power in government. Traditional conservatives were caught in a dilemma: if welfare was restricted to fatherless families, as they felt it should be to enforce male job seeking, it encouraged fatherless families, a moral and social danger.

Welfare programs were, in this sense, designed to fail politically while not really addressing the basic needs of the poor for jobs, upward mobility, and the possibility of competing successfully.

Modest reforms of the welfare system failed to attract congressional support during the administration of Jimmy Carter (1977–1981), as did efforts to establish large-scale, publicly funded job programs. During that same period, the reform liberal agenda did advance in the area of environmental protection and affirmative action. New initiatives were taken toward ensuring equal rights for women, minorities, gays, and the handicapped. In this respect, reform liberals were adding to their program ideas gained from the liberation ideologies (see Chapter 9).

With the election of Ronald Reagan to the Presidency in 1980, a broad tide of reaction moved against the reform liberals.[24] Social spending was targeted as the cause of deficits and disappointing economic performance. Although government spending and deficits continued to increase dramatically, due to military expenditures, the growth in the domestic budget was sharply curtailed, and many social programs were eliminated. During the Reagan era, the enforcement of environmental and civil rights legislation was slackened, and unions were forced to make concessions.

Tax cuts became the advertised method of advancing economic growth and stimulating employment, rather than direct governmental assistance. Cuts in domestic expenditures, increased military budgets, and foreign borrowing to finance historic levels of deficit spending contributed greatly to reduced inflation and improved economic indicators, some decrease in unemployment, and higher levels of poverty. Reform liberal initiatives for positive liberty began to be abandoned as the Democratic Party puzzled over how to renovate the ideology in this new political environment.

In the 1992 primary elections, many Democratic candidates who advocated reform liberal solutions lost out to those who put forward the more conservative program of the "new" Democrats. The winner of the presidency, Bill Clinton, was a founding member of the Democratic Leadership Council, a group formed to advance "centrist" policies for the Democratic Party.

End of the Century: Back to Populism

In the 1990s, the label *populist* was claimed by both left and right. In one form or the other, populism has returned to the American scene to challenge both the programs of reform liberals and the doctrines of contemporary conservatism.

---

24. See Albert Hirschman, *The Rhetoric of Reaction: Perversity, Futility, Jeopardy* (Cambridge, Mass.: Harvard University Press, 1991), for a summary of the arguments used over the last two centuries, and most particularly in the 1980s, against progressive reforms.

Populism has become the underlying theme of movements protesting declining moral standards, environmental degradation, political corruption, and inequalities of wealth and power.

Conservative populists, angry over the actions of the Supreme Court in outlawing school prayer and protecting the civil rights of suspected criminals, mounted a campaign to reverse these decisions through changes in the Constitution.[25] The leaders of this movement, which is part of a broader reaction against moral permissiveness in American culture, have termed it populist because they see themselves rebelling against policies made by governmental elites. These elites, they say, are out of touch with popular feeling.[26] The alliance of the populist right with fundamentalist Christians produced a powerful political coalition that has influenced Presidential races, inspired anti-government rhetoric on talk shows, and motivated activists to run for office at all levels of the political system.[27]

Populists of the left in contemporary politics still identify concentrated wealth as their principal target. The rise of huge, conglomerate corporations and the spread of giant multinationals around the globe have evoked classic populist fears of exploitation. This response has led to probing analyses of both domestic and military policy in an effort to expose webs of influence and the self-serving policies that result.[28] Left populists have more recently begun to work with environmentalists and progressive labor unions to challenge "globalization" on the belief that it displaces workers, harms the environment, and leads to ever greater inequalities of income and wealth. Currently, protests against the International Monetary Fund and the World Trade Organization draw on populist convictions.

Both the populism of the left and that of the right play into conspiracy theories of how the United States is "run." The left highlights links between corporations, bankers, international trade organizations, and the military. The right is more concerned with the collusion of powerful bureaucrats and their supporters among labor leaders, intellectuals, and other groups identified as having suspect values.

Sometimes, both ends of the spectrum share theories of conspiracy and betrayal. At the turn of this century, as was the case at the end of the nineteenth century, there is a broad-scale attack on "elitism." By grouping all efforts to exer-

---

25. See Irving Kristol, "The New Populism: Not to Worry," *Wall Street Journal,* July 25, 1985.

26. See Richard Viguerie, *The Establishment vs. the People: Is a New Populist Revolt on the Way?* (Chicago: Regnery, 1983).

27. See Sara Diamond, *Roads to Dominion: Right Wing Movements and Political Power in the United States* (New York: Guilford Press, 1995).

28. See, for example, Kenneth Dolbeare, *Democracy At Risk: The Politics of Economic Renewal* (Chatham, N.J.: Chatham House, 1984) and Richard Barnet, *The Roots of War* (New York: Atheneum, 1972).

cise leadership under the rubric of elitism, no distinction is made between the coercive power, on the one hand, and moral or intellectual authority, on the other. Thus coercion by government and corporations appears to be the same as the development of legitimate authority in social movements, churches, universities, and other forms of noncoercive activity.

This new broad-spectrum populism is exemplified in the 1998 election of an independent candidate, Jesse Ventura, as Governor of Minnesota, over two "establishment" candidates, one of the Democratic Party and the other of the Republican Party. Ventura ridiculed the elites of both parties, along with cultural icons, such as public radio, the arts community, and organized religion.

Whether this new flowering of populism is a lasting phenomenon, or another passing wave of a movement that has been part of America since its founding, remains to be seen. It also remains to be seen whether populism will once again become the rationale for marginalizing unpopular groups, whether seen as "elites" or as minorities by reason of race or sexual preference, who differ from the majority in their cultural views and ways of life.

CONCLUSION

Reform liberalism remains a synthesis of many strands in American politics. It presents the alternative to a straightforward reliance on the vicissitudes of the marketplace as the arbiter of national life. Yet the favorite means of addressing this problem, government action, has become increasingly controversial.

The direct expense of poverty programs is more visible than the social costs of deprivation. Subsidies to the disadvantaged are more obvious than subsidies to the middle class and the beneficiaries of government contracts. The liberalization of norms of personal behavior have become associated in the public mind with the social consequences of welfare programs. The creation of a class of dependent citizens runs counter both to individualist values and to the original desire of reform liberals to enable all people to participate effectively in a market society.

Yet reform liberalism is being revived as inequalities once again become a center of public concern. There is no other alternative as a political response to the tendency of capitalism to produce great inequality of result. The plight of the homeless, the cost of imprisoning ever-larger numbers of convicts, and the impact of poverty on children are all forcing the issue.

Contemporary efforts to make reform liberalism acceptable to electorates in the United States and Britain focus on using the law to enforce private compliance with social goals, rather than establishing government programs that administer benefits directly. Proposals include requirements that private employers provide health insurance, family leaves in times of crisis or medical emergency, and facilities for disabled employees and customers. All of these uses of governmental power work in the direction of greater equality without requiring additional taxes.

The costs are borne by businesses who, when they can, pass them along to consumers. Rather than advancing developmental freedom by taxation and government provision, the same measures are advanced by requiring the private sector to operate according to legally enforceable standards.

Reform liberalism will continue to be a vital force in American politics insofar as it offers sensible solutions to the problems of poverty, the environment, discrimination, health care, and economic opportunity. Reform liberalism is, broadly speaking, the tradition that carries forward the vision of "developmental freedom" that is the legacy of classical liberalism.

The difficulty is that reform liberalism depends on leadership, whether by elected officials or the spokespeople for voluntary organizations. As the new millenium opens, American democracy will be tested yet again by the old struggle between its ideals of equality and justice, and its inborn suspicion of leaders and government. James Morone, author of *The Democratic Wish: Popular Participation and the Limits of American Government* takes a skeptical view:

> In a polity that never lost its Whiggish suspicion of government and governors, here is an alternative ideal offering its elusive chimerical promise: somehow, power can be taken away from the state and restored directly to the people. That ideal rooted in the crucial instant of the Revolutionary conflict, may be the most important false hope in American history.[29]

If populist protests not only frustrate governmental action, but also undermine authority in voluntary organizations, then the field is left open to the forces of conservatism rather than liberalism.

If, on the other hand, the populist faith in "the people" is borne out, and protest movements generate effective solutions and institutional changes in American politics, then the tension between populism and reform liberalism will have been constructive for the cause of developmental freedom.

---

29. Morone, *The Democratic Wish,* rev. ed. (New Haven: Yale University Press, 1998), p. 30.

CHAPTER SIX

MARXISM-LENINISM

A spider conducts operations that resemble those of a weaver, and a bee puts to shame many an architect in the construction of her cells. But what distinguishes the worst architect from the best of bees is this, that the architect erects his structure in imagination before he erects it in "reality."

KARL MARX
(1867)

Karl Marx (1818–1883) did not invent communism. The idea of people living and working cooperatively has a long history. Significant communal utopias can be found in the literature of the Greeks, the early Christians, the monastics, and the seventeenth-century English rebels against the institutionalization of private property.[1] Though his vision of communism may not have been original, Marx's distinctive achievement was a theory of how communism could come about, a development he advocated with intellectual skill and enormous energy. In the hands of Vladimir Ilyich Lenin (1870–1924) and his successors in the former USSR, Marxism became a justification for the centralization of state power in

---

1. For a history of these notions, see Frank E. Manuel and Fritzie P. Manuel, *Utopian Thought in the Western World* (Cambridge, Mass.: Belknap Press, 1982). Cf. Christopher Hill, *The World Turned Upside Down: Radical Ideas during the English Revolution* (London: Penguin, 1972).

the hands of the Communist Party. Mao Tse-tung led a revolutionary communist movement that had similar results in China.

Marx was a critic of classical liberalism. The targets of his impassioned writings were those who saw individual self-interest as the fundamental principle of society. He thought that human beings had a purpose quite different from the simple fulfillment of appetites or the pursuit of pleasure as described in the theory of Jeremy Bentham. He thought of people as creatures whose creativity required a particular form of social organization for its full expression. Marx forecast that a market-centered society based on the laissez-faire principle of separating politics from economics would be class-ridden and subject to ultimate collapse.

Like all other ideologies, Marxism proceeds from a view of the human condition to an analysis of politics. Marx's conception of the human condition began with a fundamental question: what is the difference between human beings and lower animals? From his answer to the question, Marx constructed an entire theory of the purpose of human life and the meaning of history. He also sketched a scenario for explaining how this purpose might guide the development of new forms of politics and community life. His imagery is compelling because it touches on basic human aspirations.

In the first section, we will look at the image Marx had of what life could be like in a society where true humanity had been achieved and people lived together as he thought they were meant to. In the next section, we will explore the framework of his analysis of capitalism and outline the steps that were to lead to communism. Finally, we will see how this vision was transformed into a system of politics that led to tyranny and tragedy.

MARX'S VISION OF COMMUNISM

Like other powerful philosophies, Marxism is based on an analysis of human nature. To the question of the difference between human beings and lower animals, Marx answered that it was not just the human capacity for thought or for communication that set human beings apart—as we know, animals have similar skills. Beyond that, he said, *human beings, unlike animals, are capable of conscious production*. People can transform one thing into another by choice. They can combine coal and iron to make steel. With steel they can create a sword or a plowshare. Animals, by contrast, produce only in response to instinct or by accidental variations of previously learned patterns. Bees and spiders can build structures, but not consciously as an architect does in choosing from alternative designs and fitting materials to a plan.

The force that drives human history is the urge each person has to express a potential for conscious production, whether physical or mental. Yet people are held down by class domination, which channels some to boring, repetitive jobs and others to lives of ease and leisure. Human potential is stifled by the inequality and injustice of a world that is not yet organized to maximize conscious production. Instead, people spend their working lives, for the most part, in forms of production, whether physical or mental, that offer them little choice about what they do or how it is done. The requirements of survival force people to work merely to serve basic needs. Work of this kind is a far cry from the expression of an inner urge to develop individual talents and creative possibilities.

Marx traced the historical evolution of the human species through various forms of society. He wanted to see how the species had struggled to realize its true nature. Marx was a contemporary of Charles Darwin and admired how he had separated the study of nature from theological conceptions of creation.[2] Marx's theory was constructed in a manner similar to Darwin's, but he replaced Darwin's notions of competition and natural selection with a dynamic view of human action as the agency of change. He wanted to show how history changed as a result of the creation of new forms of production and community life. He used this analysis to support his claim that there was a pattern to history that could be used to predict the future of the species.[3]

Marx viewed a communist society as having everything in place for a life of maximum conscious productivity. First of all, basic needs for food, shelter, and clothing would be provided by the community. Goods and services would be produced in a way that did not consume all of people's productive energy or destroy their motivation to be creative.

Marx also spelled out why attitudes would change so that people would willingly participate in such a system: everyone would work together for part of the present workday—say, three or four hours—at some socially necessary task. How could basic needs be supplied in such a short workday? Using a cooperative approach to the production of necessities, people would learn to work together for the common good. If production were organized so as to match individual abilities to the type of work, foster democratic techniques of planning, and remove the profit motive, the work done for necessity would be humanized. Eliminating the waste associated with competition, the frustrations of boring jobs, and the anger arising from relations of domination would make communal

---

2. Friedrich Engels remarked at Marx's funeral, "Just as Darwin discovered the law of development of organic nature, so Marx discovered the law of development of human history": "Speech at the Graveside of Karl Marx," in *The Marx-Engels Reader,* 2nd ed., ed. Robert Tucker (New York: W. W. Norton, 1978), p. 681. This overstates the relationship—one that has an interesting history: see Terence Ball, "Marx and Darwin: A Reconsideration," *Political Theory* 7 (1979): 469–483.

3. Here, Marx differed from Darwin, who thought that evolution had no particular purpose other than facilitating survival. Marx believed that humanity had a destiny. Cf. Ball, "Marx and Darwin," p. 473.

production more efficient. The creation of new technology would further reduce the need for drudgery.

Through work organized in this way, individuals would be entitled to receive the necessities of life. They would simultaneously be learning the attitudes appropriate to cooperative living. As Marx saw it, capitalism drives people apart through competition, manipulation, and domination. He believed that the rational organization of production in a communist system would overcome personal alienation and depression and permit the fulfillment of people's true social potential.

The maxim that would guide production and distribution in this "realm of necessity" would be "From each according to his ability, to each according to his need."[4] Individuals would receive from the community whatever was needed to support their particular contribution to the society. The work devoted to producing necessities would be the ticket to a life in which one would not have to worry about basic needs. Marx appears to have argued that without participation in such work, an individual would not be entitled to the benefits of communism.

To satisfy basic needs is not to fulfill entirely the purpose of life. It is only a preliminary condition to a life in which true humanity might emerge. In organizing production in the realm of necessity by these principles, Marx said, people will be freed of the dog-eat-dog struggle for survival, the boredom of specialization, and the pressures of competition that detract from their humanity. Theoretically, the efficiencies gained by this system would enable production to keep up with expanding social needs as new techniques and products for the improvement of life were invented. The enhanced quality of human interaction would make possible a more considerate approach to personal growth, social life, and the environment.

How does this happen? The answer, again, has to do with the proper human relationship to production. The fulfillment of the vision of communism is in what happens not in the *realm of necessity* but in the *realm of freedom*. The realm of freedom is where the promise of conscious production is fulfilled. It is that part of the day when people can produce whatever their abilities and interests allow without concern for supplying necessities.

Those who are used to the kind of work that Marx described as alienating might think that this "free time" would be spent in idle pursuits, sleep, and general time-wasting. Marx did not think so. Here is where true conscious productivity would manifest itself. Individuals would find the chance to express previously suppressed interests: to perfect various skills, make more refined products,

---

4. Pierre Proudhon, the French utopian socialist theorist, is credited with the authorship of this formula.

and challenge the boundaries of knowledge or achievement in a field of endeavor. Free rein would be given to intellectual curiosity and creative impulses. A librarian might learn to become a doctor. A doctor might learn to make furniture. Manual skills would no longer be divided from intellectual skills; people would have the freedom and the encouragement to develop both.

Why wouldn't people do the minimum and simply idle away the rest of the time? Marx's fundamental assumption about human creativity comes into play here. When people do crossword puzzles, they become bored with simple versions and move on to greater challenges. Hobbyists try to refine their techniques. Athletes aim for ever-higher levels of performance even when the competition is entirely voluntary. The human desire for expression and accomplishment will lead people to produce in an ever-more-interesting and creative fashion.

With the advance of communism, production would flourish. Rather than the gray, routinized social prison described by its detractors, Marx suggested, communism offers dazzling possibilities. Creativity would be liberated from exploitation. "Free" productivity might well become the dominant source of goods and services as individuals advanced old skills and crafts and invented new ones. A plenitude of ideas would stimulate fresh waves of productive energy, new technologies, and innovations of all kinds. Work would be valued for its human qualities rather than as simply a means to survival.

This vision of an egalitarian society of freely producing individuals is among the great utopias of Western political thought.[5] It has had enormous power as a political symbol for movements the world over. What went wrong? The answers are found partly in the complicated story of how this vision of utopia was translated into revolutionary politics and one-party rule. Understanding Marx's view, and the ways in which others used his legacy in actual political situations, requires a study of his framework for the analysis of history.

UNDERSTANDING MARX'S THEORY

Understanding Marx's ideas is a special challenge for people raised in capitalist societies. Much education and socialization have been directed toward discrediting Marxism. With the fall of communism in the USSR, Marxism has been consigned to a fate similar to that of fascism. Few students will ever have heard a discussion of Marx in his own terms.

Marx must be held at least partly responsible for the atrocities committed in the name of his theories by Stalin, Mao Tse-tung, and other "Marxist" leaders.

---

5. For a selection of excerpts from Marx on life under communism, see David McLellan, *The Thought of Karl Marx* (New York: Harper and Row, 1971), pp. 212–224.

As we will see, however, there is some reason to believe that he would not accept much of what these leaders have done as an expression of Marxism. Marx's influence extends far beyond the former USSR, with dozens of variations on his ideas to be found in the politics of Europe, Africa, Asia, and Latin America. There is, as well, a historically independent tradition of democratic socialism with which Marxism is sometimes confused. For all of these reasons, it is hard to arrive at a clear view of Marx.

A subtler problem in understanding Marx is that we are used to the specialization of knowledge. Universities are usually organized into departments of political science, economics, history, philosophy, and so forth. Each specialization separates one body of knowledge from another. Marx was a comprehensive thinker. His system of ideas reaches into all of these fields plus many more, such as sociology, anthropology, and even art, religion, and literature.[6] Marx tried to approach the human experience in the same way that we live it: as an integrated whole.

The key to solving some of these problems of understanding is to try to suspend one's preconceptions about his ideas and simply approach them afresh. It is important to understand the ideas in their own terms and then to apply critical judgment to the key assumptions, concepts, and evidence. A critique, or a belief, based on faulty understanding accomplishes little except the reinforcement of bias.

Marx explained most of what he had to say in the form of a scenario about the way human history had unfolded and was likely to develop in the future. Following the main elements of this story makes it fairly easy to grasp Marx's basic concepts. Once these concepts have been made clear, the work of analysis and criticism can begin.

To understand something about Marxism is not necessarily to understand the variety of ideas that are bound up in communist parties and movements around the world. Like Christianity, liberalism, or any other living tradition, communism contains new and old streams of interpretation, analysis, and innovation. For introductory purposes, however, Marxism provides the ideological core of communism.

THE HISTORY OF THE SPECIES ACCORDING TO MARX

Marx started from the assumption that the process of production shapes people's lives. Production is both a means to survival and the key to human nature. Our physical being and our very humanity are tied to the processes of work and cre-

---

6. See Terry Eagleton, *Marxism and Literary Criticism* (Berkeley: University of California Press, 1976), pp. vii, 15–17.

ativity. Whereas history is usually presented as an account of explorations, wars, and the rise and fall of rulers, Marx's version of history centered on developments in how people go about producing to fulfill needs and wants.

Were the history of human production simply the story of new inventions to make work more efficient, Marx's history would recount one technical development after another. But that version of history wouldn't explain the conflicts, the rebellions, and the wars that make history so dramatic. Marx pointed out that production is not just a matter of tools and raw materials but also involves the way people are organized to do the work.

From the organization of production come class structures. As capitalism develops, for example, two classes emerge: the bourgeoisie and the proletariat. One class, the bourgeoisie, owns and controls the *means* by which the other class, the proletariat, makes its living. By owning the factories, businesses, stocks, and other forms of property, the bourgeoisie exercises control over the lives of workers.

These two classes have quite different interests: the bourgeoisie is interested in profiting from the labor of others, and the proletariat is interested in survival. The difference between what workers are paid and the value they produce is the principal means by which capitalists gain their profits. Yet for the workers, wages are the means of their survival.

In capitalism, Marx pointed out, the owners of the means of production are the dominant class in the government as well as the economy. Where they do not rule directly through officials appointed or elected from their ranks, they rule indirectly by shaping the views, beliefs, opportunities, and career paths of those who do rule. Even if a working-class person ascends to a position of power, following the interests of the bourgeoisie is a condition of maintaining influence.

It is this relation of domination between classes that accounts for the major conflicts in history. As new technologies change the possibilities for organizing production, the old ruling class fights off new challengers.

An example of a Marxist explanation of historical events through class analysis would be the U.S. Civil War. In the middle of the eighteenth century, the Yankee mill owners who mechanized textile production were no longer interested in being subjected to the political power of the southern aristocracy. The plantation owners battled the northern mill owners. Southern plantation owners tried to preserve a class system based on slavery against the rise of a new order built on an alliance between Yankee industrialists and small midwestern farmers who did not enjoy competing with inexpensive slave labor. These real conflicts of economic interest were at the root of the Civil War, rather than lofty principles of human freedom.

Although one doesn't have to be a Marxist to engage in this sort of economic analysis, Marx's framework provides a larger historical perspective from which to view exploitation, class struggle, and revolutionary change. In Marx's terminology, the reason for conflict is that the relations of production (the class system by which production is organized) change more slowly than the means of production (technology and raw materials). The factory system spread rapidly in England because of the invention of steam-driven machines. Yet the old class system based on agriculture and craft production took many decades to wither in the face of a newly emergent commercial class of traders, bankers, and businesspeople.

Demands for new goods and services, as well as human inventiveness, mean that technologies are constantly being refined and the uses of raw materials improved. As these changes occur, they bring with them implications for the way in which production is organized. The groups losing power under the new arrangements resist change. History is a series of battles on many levels between rising and declining classes.

What makes history so complicated is that class structures pervade all the techniques of social control. Among these techniques Marx included religion, popular political ideas, and even the self-conceptions that people are taught to have of themselves. Socialization to cultural norms and habits is a powerful means of preserving class advantages. It is cheaper to use ideas to rule people than it is to hire police officers. Ideas are the velvet glove on the iron fist of power. Class-based control permeates our social and personal environment.[7]

Marx's scenario had many of the characteristics of a religious text. Contemporary struggles were explained, heroes were identified, victimization was clarified, and salvation was promised if a certain path was followed. In the confusion of a century filled with wars, economic cycles, and rapid technological change, Marx's theory provided an interpretation that could be made to fit a great variety of cultural circumstances. To analyze this scenario, one needs to escape the magnetic quality of the story line and examine the elements it is made of.

Just as Darwin used the concepts of variation and natural selection to explain evolution, so Marx had a set of basic concepts that were the keys to the dynamics of human history. Marx's scenario will begin to fit together as we examine the meaning of those basic concepts. Then we will see how he used his fundamental categories to explain history. Finally, we can follow the application of these concepts to the task of explaining how history moves from capitalism through socialism to communism.

---

7. Antonio Gramsci, the creator of the Italian Communist Party, develops the significance of political and cultural domination, or "hegemony," as the central aspect of class warfare. See Roger Simon, *Gramsci's Political Thought: An Introduction* (London: Lawrence and Wishart, 1982), specifically pp. 22–32, for a useful guide to Gramsci's often confusing writings.

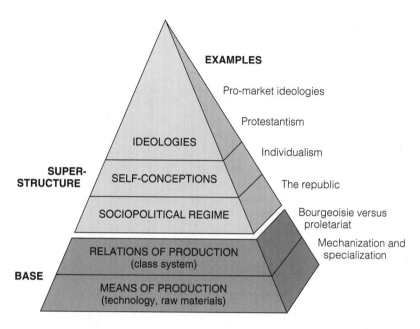

FIGURE 6.1   MARX'S CATEGORIES OF ANALYSIS

The Fundamental Categories of Marx's Theory

In order to see these relationships more clearly, it is helpful to simplify Marx's analytical framework. A Russian interpreter of Marx, G. V. Plekhanov (1857–1918), presents Marx's categories for the analysis of a society as shown in Figure 6.1.[8] The two elements of the base, the means of production and the relations of production, together shape the superstructure: the government, religion, and the beliefs that people are taught to have about themselves. When the introduction of new means of production generates changed relations of production, the conflict of new and old class structures is fought out through all levels of the superstructure. Rival classes battle over who is to control the government. Religions change. New ideas challenge prevailing self-conceptions.

As an example of how ideas become a method of shaping behavior, consider Marx's view of the "science" of economics as capitalists present it. In U.S. culture, economics is thought of as a matter of matching supply and demand. Goods and services for which there is a strong demand will bring a high price; unwanted

8. G. V. Plekhanov, *Materialist Conception of History* (London: Lawrence and Wishart, 1976).

goods or plentiful supplies will result in low prices. Economists concern themselves with market prices and do not distinguish between needs and wants or the conditions under which value is created by laborers under the control of capitalists.[9] This view places investment and the ownership of the means of production in a central role. Workers become "raw material" as suppliers of labor, rather than human beings with basic needs and a capacity for conscious production.

Idea systems such as modern economics serve the dominant class, according to Marx. That is why they are reinforced in the schools, churches, and workplaces.[10] Another example of the political use of ideas is Marx's view that the very concept of individualism works against the interests of true personal freedom. Free speech in a capitalist society becomes the right of the newspaper owner to drown out the voice of the lonely dissenter. Individual ownership of property becomes the justification for huge inequalities in the distribution of wealth. None of these circumstances really allows the individual to be the architect of his or her own destiny. According to Marx, true freedom is based on real changes in the means and relations of production, not on airy concepts of individual rights.

Changes in these configurations of power take decades and even centuries. Marx divides human history into periods differentiated by large-scale changes in which the power of a declining class at all levels of society gives way, over time, to the dominance of a new class. The decisive transitions are, for example, from the feudal reign of princes and popes to the rise of industrial capitalism and then to revolutionary socialism.

An illustration of the uses of Marx's categories for explaining change can be seen in the shift between historical epochs such as that which took place in Britain in the seventeenth century. The class that controlled the new means of production having to do with trade and commerce came to power through the strengthening of the parliament. The new bourgeoisie developed a republic centering on the power of property owners that confronted the authority of the hierarchy based on feudal relations of obligation and entitlement. The new parliament reduced the king to the role of an executive who shared power with representatives of property owners.

As the demands of trade and commerce required greater individual mobility, liberal ideas of individual freedom and economic competition replaced philoso-

---

9. See Bertell Ollman, *Alienation: Marx's Conception of Man in Capitalist Society,* 2nd ed. (New York: Cambridge University Press, 1976), pp. 193–194.

10. Marx comments, "The aim [of the economists] is to present production ... as encased in eternal natural laws independent of history, at which opportunity *bourgeois* relations [of production] are then quietly smuggled in as the inviolable natural laws on which society in the abstract is founded." Karl Marx, *Grundrisse,* trans. Martin Nicolaus (New York: Vintage, 1973), p. 87.

phies that emphasized each person's place in the larger order of things. Protestantism, with its theology of the individual's relationship to God, confronted the Catholicism of the rural aristocracy, with their ties to feudal structures of political and religious power.

All these changes, the conflicts included, are part of the enduring struggle by humanity to realize an inner desire to engage in conscious production. Major historical developments can be traced to the influence of economic changes upon various levels of society. Yet Marx did not mean to say that all of human behavior was determined by narrowly conceived economic factors, as if people had no part in creating their own destiny. His point was that the struggle for free productivity was worked out at many levels, the most powerful of which were the means and relations of production. Individuals play a role in creating new means of production and in responding to the pressures created by the relations of production, both in their working lives and in the many levels of the superstructure. History is dynamic. People supply the energy, and their need to produce creates patterns in how that dynamism is played out.

The Transition from Capitalism to Socialism

Marx's most famous prediction was that capitalism would crumble and be overthrown, to be replaced by a new socialist order that would prepare the way for true communism. Why did he think this would happen? His answer can be understood by applying the logic of his basic concepts. This done, we will explore his conception of socialism and, finally, return to the beginning point of this chapter: his vision of communism.

The fundamental tension in any historical period is in the poor fit between the relations of production (the way work is organized) and changes in the means of production (technology and raw materials). That is where we should look to understand Marx's analysis of capitalism. Marx adapted from the philosophy of Hegel the notion of a "contradiction" to explain how a society could be at odds with itself. Capitalism, according to Marx, is a mass of contradictions between what the species *wants* by way of conscious productivity and what it *gets* from the capitalist system of organizing production.

As Marx put it, the fundamental contradiction of capitalism is that it "presses to reduce labor time to a minimum, while it posits labor time, on the other side, as sole measurement and source of wealth."[11] The whole objective of management in a capitalist society is to break down complicated jobs into simpler, more

---

11. Karl Marx, "Grundrisse," in *The Marx-Engels Reader,* 2nd ed., ed. Robert Tucker (New York: W. W. Norton, 1978), p. 285.

specialized tasks. This approach allows management to minimize wages, cut down on labor time, and ultimately dismiss workers whenever machines can do the work more cheaply. Yet the proletariat, the largest class, exists by selling its labor and using the wages to buy the products of its own labor. How can a system survive that ultimately tries to abolish its own basis for creating wealth?

Add to this contradiction another one: capitalism creates in its factories the potential for huge enterprises where production *could* take place on a planned and cooperative basis, yet it does so in a way that pits one worker against another in competition. Or yet another: capitalism creates great wealth but distributes it to very few, while many remain in abject poverty.

All these contradictions present both an advance toward the goal of free productivity and an obstacle to further progress. Minimizing labor time is a good thing. Properly used, it could free everyone for conscious production. The abundance of goods and services brought into being by entrepreneurship is useful in making life easier and more secure. Yet the system forces people into ever-more-constraining and competitive roles. Cooperative production is a key to the provision of basic needs for all. Yet all of capitalism's achievements come at the price of a class system that benefits the rich and consigns many to spend their lives in a struggle merely to subsist.

So far, little has been said about capitalism that hadn't already been pointed out by non-Marxist socialists (see Chapter 7). Marx differed in his analysis in that he saw the change from capitalism to socialism as inevitable. Non-Marxist socialists, sometimes referred to as democratic socialists, generally believe that the change could come about through persuasion and electoral change.[12] Marx believed that it would happen for objective reasons of history and that it would involve revolution.

Marx's objective reasons for thinking that capitalism would fall had to do with the crises created by the contradictions. Two sets of crises will occur: for economic reasons, the rate of profit will decline; for sociological reasons, the proletariat will become a militant, revolutionary force bent on overthrowing capitalism. These two sets of crises bear closer examination.

THE ECONOMICS OF CAPITALISM'S COLLAPSE: CHANGES IN THE MEANS OF PRODUCTION

Profit is the key to capitalism. From it comes investment and the capacity of the system for renewal and expansion. Marx argued that there was an inner logic to capitalism that would ultimately lead to a collapse in the rate of profit. As managers try to minimize labor costs, they will introduce machines. There is a crucial difference between people and machines when it comes to generating profit.

12. Cf. Friedrich Engels, "Socialism: Utopian and Scientific" (1892), in Tucker, *Marx-Engels Reader*, pp. 683–724.

A machine is very simple in economic terms: either one can pay the fixed cost of operating the machine, or one can't. Workers are different. There is no fixed cost for labor except the price of human subsistence. A worker may produce a great deal of value but be paid very little as a result of competitive wage rates. The "surplus value," to use Marx's term, comes to the capitalist as profit. Separating the question of *value produced* from *wages paid* creates the potential for the profitable use of labor. The key to profiting from someone else's labor is to persuade or force the worker to accept wages that are lower, perhaps much lower, than the value the worker creates. Machines can't be persuaded or forced; it is either economical to operate the machine, or it isn't. A surplus is possible from a machine, but manipulation is not.

Under conditions of competition, the difference between laborers and machines becomes critical. If two manufacturers make the same product on the same machine, competition would force the price of the product down to the cost of operating the machine. The result would be little or no profit. If workers rather than machines make the product, however, there is a chance that profitability can be sustained by separating wages from the value created.

Even for labor-based production, under pure competition, wage rates could be forced down to the subsistence level. In the absence of unions or price fixing, the rate of profit might fall with labor-based production as it does with machines. However, machines do not consume their own products, nor can they be misled about the relation between wages and value. So the depressing effect on the rate of profit is speeded up when production becomes mechanized.

Even so, as long as the demand for goods holds up and there is imperfect competition, capitalists can continue to make profits. Profits fall and capitalism gets into trouble due to the cumulative effect of genuine competition in saturated markets, the reduction in the amount of surplus available to workers as purchasing power, and the displacement of workers by machines.

Some observers take the periodic recessions and depressions in capitalist economies as evidence that Marx wasn't completely wrong. In addition, it is often pointed out that governments have stepped in to prevent pure competition from occurring. At various times, governments have permitted large industries to operate noncompetitively, legitimated labor unions, established minimum wages, used tax revenues to prop up failing industries, and subsidized large sectors of the economy through the military-industrial complex. All of these policies have prevented the erosion of profits and wages that comes with pure competition.

Meanwhile, entrepreneurs have come up with new products and ways of increasing consumer demand through advertising and the planned obsolescence of cars and other products. Military force has been used to ensure markets and the supply of raw materials. These measures are seen by Marxists to have saved the capitalist system from its ultimate crisis. If Marx was right, however, governmental intervention and the expansion of markets would reach their limits. If markets for basic goods ever become satiated under pure competition, the contradiction between profit and the minimization of labor time should finally bring the economic collapse of the system.

We have been examining changes in the means of production that are to lead to capitalism's collapse. Yet revolutions do not happen without human action. What will make workers turn toward revolutionary socialism? To answer this question, it is necessary to understand the corresponding changes in the relations of production.

CAPITALISM AND CLASS CONFLICT   Marx argued that capitalism would lead to the increasing exploitation of workers by capitalists who were themselves driven by competition in the face of declining profit margins. Exploitation has many facets. In addition to extracting surplus value, capitalists try to dominate the cultural environment and even the personal life of workers. Intentionally or not, they make work ever more alienating, they repress dissent through manipulation and force, and they use political means to reinforce their power. Each of these aspects of exploitation comes back as revolutionary energy as the final crisis of capitalism approaches.

When capitalism matures, Marx argued, the distinction between bourgeoisie and proletariat will become ever clearer. Class differences will intensify. Classes left over from feudalism, such as professionals and artisans of various kinds, will be forced into the twofold class structure of bourgeoisie and proletariat. Class position will increasingly be determined by the ownership and control of the means of production. The owners will be a small class with sharply different interests from the workers'. As the rate of profit declines along with wages, the conflicting nature of these interests will become crystal clear.

Meanwhile, due to the increasingly specialized and routinized character of work under capitalism, workers will become alienated. Marx focused on the human consequences of the factory system that was just taking hold in England. The concept of alienation is one of Marx's most potent ideas. Alienation arouses feelings of self-hatred, attitudes of distrust toward fellow workers, and generalized anger and escapist behavior. Alienation means a sense of separation—in this case, a separation arising from the difference between what the worker has to do to make a living and the worker's innate desire to engage in conscious production.

Marx thought that wage labor under capitalism was a perversion of conscious production. Workers have no say in what is produced, the design of the product, how the work is performed, or what is done with the results. In the process of wage labor, people are forced to compete with fellow workers rather than cooperating. Personal relationships degenerate into calculations based on self-interest. Alienation at first distracts workers from organizing to solve their problems. Private forms of rebellion and escape substitute for satisfaction at work. Finally, alienation becomes so severe that workers are led to common action to redress their situation. Class consciousness begins to develop.

All these processes come to life politically when they are translated into action on behalf of the working class. Marx's vision of communism is one of alienation overcome by the creation of the best possible environment for conscious production. The formation of class consciousness is the key to action. Marx meant by class consciousness an awareness of one's true class position. Prior to the period of revolution, many people assume that their individuality is more important than their class position in determining their lives. Or people may have "false consciousness": they may think that they are part of the bourgeoisie because they are salaried, earn a middle-range income, or do white-collar work. In fact, they neither own nor control the means by which they make a living.

Perhaps the subtlest barrier to class consciousness is the cultural self-concept of individualism that is so prominent in capitalist societies. When people think of themselves primarily as unique individuals, they become politically confused. They become susceptible to appeals based on emotion, strong leaders, and vague theories of self-improvement. The ideology of classical liberalism, by stressing individualism, plays into the hands of the capitalists, according to Marx. As individuals, the people are a shapeless mass who can be manipulated. As a class conscious of its political mission, the proletariat becomes powerful.

Still, the rise of class consciousness comes only after other factors such as religious divisions, ethnic and racial differences, and regional separation are overcome. Workers must come to realize that nothing shapes their lives so much as their class position. The families of the working poor face a far different set of life chances than those of the inheritors of great wealth, regardless of religious belief, ethnic identity, or region. Capitalists manipulate these differences as a way of keeping the proletariat divided by playing off one race, ethnic group, or regional economic situation against another. Workers slowly learn to overcome these differences through common action.

When class consciousness takes root and begins to grow through political action, workers will see ever more clearly the true nature of their interests. They will begin to understand that they can get back the full value of their labor only if they are in control of the system. They will come out of their alienation into a movement that can seize upon the collapse of capitalism and overthrow the rule of the bourgeoisie.

The objective of the revolution will be the replacement of the capitalist ownership of the means of production by worker ownership through the state. By means of this revolution, the enormous productive power of capitalist industry can be harnessed to the socialist objective of providing everyone with the necessities of life. As the socialist system takes root and replaces capitalism, these tasks can be accomplished by cooperative, rather than competitive, relations of production.

The creation of a revolutionary situation along the lines of Marx's scenario depends upon the interaction between worsening economic conditions and intensifying political and sociological factors. It is not enough for the economy to fall apart; class consciousness must also have taken hold. The workers have to see clearly the position they hold in capitalism and the reasons why they are being exploited. As the rate of profit falls, workers get squeezed out, and their jobs become more routinized and specialized. Class consciousness must then be developed through political action.

Marx sees the revolution approaching through escalating crises:

> Hence the highest development of productive power together with the greatest expansion of existing wealth will coincide with depreciation of capital, degradation of the labourer, and a most straitened exhaustion of his vital powers. . . . These contradictions, of course, lead to explosions, crises, in which momentary suspension of all labour and annihilation of a great part of the capital violently lead [capitalism] back to the point where it is enabled [to go on] fully employing its productive powers without committing suicide. Yet, these regularly recurring catastrophes lead to their repetition on a higher scale, and finally its violent overthrow.[13]

If there is an economic crisis but little class consciousness, remedies such as the dictatorial centralization of all power in the state may be the result, rather than genuine socialist revolution. Some Marxists see the fascist repression of socialist movements in Germany in the 1930s as an example of this kind of failed revolution. On the other hand, if class consciousness is highly developed and yet capitalism is still healthy, the proletariat may not be strong enough to overcome the forces commanded by capitalists and bring off the revolution. The scenario for revolution can go wrong, but the factors that produce a revolutionary situation will recur so long as capitalism remains.

Building Socialism

The purpose of the revolution is to open the door to the development of a classless society—or, more descriptively, a society in which all people share the common tasks of providing necessities. The purpose is to "build socialism" and create the conditions for the transition to communism. The stage of building

---

13. Marx, "Grundrisse," in Tucker, *Marx-Engels Reader,* pp. 291–292.

socialism is quite different from the stage of communism itself. Because this is the stage that the former USSR claimed to be in prior to its collapse, it is particularly important to see how it was supposed to proceed.

The task of building socialism has three major thrusts: the reorientation of economic relations to the socialist mode, the defeat of bourgeois institutions and attitudes, and the construction of a new socialist superstructure affecting all aspects of the society. The factories and offices need to be reorganized along socialist lines so that workers have a controlling voice in how the work is carried out. The production goals must be coordinated to meet the needs of society. This is a huge task, similar to what was done in mobilizing the U.S. economy for participation in World War II.

While the economic base is being reoriented to socialist production, the revolution will have to be defended against attempts by the bourgeoisie to reclaim their power. Marx envisioned a revolutionary period followed by subsequent skirmishes and smaller conflicts. The subtler part of the struggle to secure the victory of the proletariat will lie in the battle for people's "hearts and minds." Bourgeois ideas must be attacked and replaced with socialist conceptions. Workers have to see themselves as "comrades" rather than competitors. Religious ideas must not be used to distract people from rebuilding society by the promise of rewards in the afterlife. Art and culture should make people see the real relations of power and struggle that underlie society. The mission of education is to explain the rationale of the new order.

The directing force for all these changes is to be, in Marx's phrase, the "vanguard of the proletariat." The vanguard comprises those who most thoroughly understand the class struggle, the requirements of revolution, and the necessity for personal discipline in building socialism. Marx referred to the vanguard's role in building socialism as "the dictatorship of the proletariat." He did not describe this vanguard or its method of operation very carefully. Some socialists read Marx as having argued that the vanguard might be a majority of the society ruling in the name of the proletariat through the devices of democratic government.[14] However, the prevailing interpretation of who is in the vanguard is shaped by the work of Lenin, the creator of the Communist Party.

For Lenin, only a highly centralized party could plan the economy and defend the revolution in the service of building socialism.[15] He viewed Communist parties as a completely different kind of organization from the voluntary parties

---

14. This was the view of Rosa Luxemburg (1870–1919), the Polish Marxist revolutionary and critic of Lenin, Trotsky, and others. See Martin Carnoy, *The State and Political Theory* (Princeton, N.J.: Princeton University Press, 1984), pp. 61–65.

15. See Alfred Meyer, *Leninism* (Cambridge, Mass.: Harvard University Press, 1957), especially pp. 97ff.

familiar to Western democracies. The role of the Communist Party is to implement the revolution at all levels of society, from the factory floor to the highest offices of government. Thus, party membership is open only to the truly dedicated and qualified. The party is to include citizens who are leaders in their workplaces and whose lives demonstrate uncompromising commitment to the revolutionary goals of Marxism-Leninism.

Building on the notion of the dictatorship of the proletariat, the party under Lenin and, especially, under his successor, Joseph Stalin (1879–1953), became an all-pervasive force controlling the lives of Soviet citizens.[16] In the end, the party became an end in itself and corrupted every aspect of the revolutionary vision that Marx had created. The Communist parties of the former USSR and its satellite states became a law unto themselves, using ideological rhetoric to justify personal privileges for members, repression of dissent, manipulation of all of the institutions of society, violence, and murder. To "purify" the party and the revolution, Stalin instigated purges in which millions of people perished.

The state, acting at the direction of the Communist Party, assumed the major role in building socialism. State ownership of the means of production did not turn out to be the same as worker ownership. The centralization in the state of the power to transform not just production, but all aspects of culture and society, led to results that bore little resemblance to Marx's ideals. If Marx thought that individual rights in capitalism were largely illusory, he would have a hard time justifying the complete denial of workers' rights in communist systems.

Not all Marxists agreed with the turn toward the party as the essential vehicle of the revolution. Leon Trotsky (1879–1940), Lenin's ally and the rival of Stalin, argued that the revolution must be an active and ongoing process among the working class itself as it directly created the forms of socialist life and work. Though Trotsky had been a principal figure in establishing the power of the Communist Party, he came to oppose the Stalinist position that the revolution must be primarily the work of the state and the party elite. He was assassinated by a Stalinist agent in 1940. His legacy of an antistatist version of Marxism lived on, particularly in the Third World, where Marx's nineteenth-century image of industrial capitalism never did have much relevance.[17]

---

16. See Leonard Schapiro, *The Origins of the Communist Autocracy* (Cambridge, Mass.: Harvard University Press, 1977). On Stalin, see Robert Tucker, "The Rise of Stalin's Personality Cult," *American Historical Review 84* (1977): 347–366.

17. See Terence Ball and James Farr, eds., *After Marx* (Cambridge University Press, 1984), and Carnoy, *The State and Political Theory,* for a discussion of the varieties of Marxist thought.

The Transition to Communism

Before reviewing the reasons why history did not proceed as Marx had predicted, let us complete the account of his scenario for the arrival of communism. Once socialism is firmly established, the gradual transition to communism can begin. When the socialized factories and offices are producing efficiently, the proportion of the day devoted to producing necessities can be reduced. Wasteful production of nonessentials will be eliminated through planning. As workers become accustomed to cooperative production, they will be increasingly receptive to socialist ideas about the purpose of society and the need for reforms in education, religion, and culture generally. As a new generation is raised with these ideals in mind, the momentum of the socializing process will increase. A new kind of socialist citizenship will replace the old capitalist individualism.

These changes will lessen the amount of conflict and crime in the society. Inequalities will be dramatically reduced, removing a major motive for theft and other criminal acts. Because the government will no longer have to devote its energies to maintaining capitalist control over the means of production and the policing of crime will take fewer and fewer resources, the government itself will "wither away." What will remain are planning functions organized so as to respond to the people's priorities. Democracy based on true equality will operate from the ground up in communities, factories, and offices. Planners and managers will be held accountable through elections.

By degrees the phase of building socialism will end, and communism will arrive. In the *realm of necessity,* production will be organized by socialist principles, and distribution will take place on the basis of need. In the USSR, this took the form of highly subsidized housing, transportation, education, and health care. The true cost of these services was not borne by the individuals who used them but, rather, by the revenues generated from a planned economy.

In the *realm of freedom,* a plenitude of individual creativity will assure a world full of interest and stimulation. People will approach the attainment of human "species-being" as masters of necessity, conscious producers, and free human beings in the genuine sense. The vision described at the beginning of this chapter will come into focus as human society arrives at its highest level. The basic structure of society needs no further development because human beings have realized their inner natures.

Marx reviews the whole story in a single famous paragraph in Volume 3 of *Capital,* his masterwork:

> Just as the savage must wrestle with Nature to satisfy his wants, to maintain and reproduce life, so must civilized man, and he must do so in all social formations and under all possible modes of production. With his development this realm of physical necessity expands as a result of his wants, but, at the same time, the

forces of production which satisfy these wants also increase. Freedom in this field can only consist in socialized man, the associated producers, rationally regulating their interchange with Nature, bringing it under their common control, instead of being ruled by it as by the blind forces of Nature; and achieving this with the least expenditure of energy and under conditions most favorable to, and worthy of, their human nature. But it nonetheless still remains a realm of necessity. Beyond it begins that development of human energy which is an end in itself, the true realm of freedom, which, however, can blossom forth only with the realm of necessity as its basis. The shortening of the working day is its basic prerequisite.[18]

This scenario for the development of communism Marx sometimes presented as inevitable, although he also foresaw that there could be false starts when the key elements were not all in place and that a revolution could fail. Many of his historical writings analyze the relationship of key factors in struggles such as the French Revolution, the American Civil War, and nineteenth-century English society.

Lenin took Marx's ideas and fashioned them into a rationale for revolution in the USSR. Some Marxists point out that Russia was neither capitalist, nor industrialized, nor even a nation in some respects in 1917. It was, in this view, a vast collection of more than a hundred nationalities and ethnic groups governed by a feudal czarist regime that collapsed under the pressures of the First World War. In the confusion, a small, disciplined, brilliantly led communist minority was able to take over and implement a revolutionary regime.

The problem was that capitalism hadn't completed its work of building up the productive base. So the new government had to do that by force while, at the same time, finishing with the First World War and repelling invaders from the capitalist nations (the Americans and the British in 1921, during the Russian Civil War, and the Germans again in 1940). The result was a totalitarian dictatorship that left its people stultified and its economy woefully inefficient. The Soviets have tacitly acknowledged the difficulty of following Marx's scenario. In 1961, the Communist Party put forward a plan that was to deliver the Soviet Union to communism beginning in 1980. In 1985, with that goal unattained, the new planning document set no date but called for "advances" on all fronts. In 1992, the system collapsed, and a perilous transition to a democratic, market-based economy commenced.

China is seen as another example of a peasant economy vaulted into socialism without industrialization through the wartime collapse of a corrupted capitalist structure. Today, China flirts with competitive relationships of production in order to stimulate the kind of economic development that is so hard to

18. In Tucker, *Marx-Engels Reader,* p. 441.

achieve through force. Marx's scenario depends upon an abundance of production to provide for social needs. Neither the Soviet nor the Chinese economy achieved it.

Although the former USSR and China can be seen as deviants from the Marxist scenario, it is also true that there is no clear example of a nation that has followed the script. Variations on Marxism have been tried in many developing countries. The results in some countries led to increases in literacy, land redistribution, health-care reform, and other services. Yet in the end the concentration of power led to waste, corruption, and often tragedy. Virtually all European countries have adapted socialist ideas to their politics, although those ideas have come out of the democratic socialist tradition more often than out of Marxism.

The United States seems to represent the clearest refutation of the scenario. Capitalism has suffered its economic crises, and it is revealing to use Marx's categories to analyze them, but it has survived and spread prosperity to millions. There is a largely submerged U.S. history of Marxist thought and political action, but Marxism never succeeded in achieving a mass basis. Class consciousness is a factor in Republican and Democratic politics, but it has been overshadowed by a general consensus on free enterprise as the best way to organize the economy.

Marxists, on the other hand, point to the unique character of the United States as essentially a new nation possessed of abundant resources, with a working class divided by region, race, ethnicity, and gender, so that class consciousness has developed only slowly. Moreover, serious economic crises have been met by governmental action to prop up the economy. Government intervention, and the development of unions that have saved workers from the worst aspects of capitalist competition, have retarded the movement toward revolution, in the Marxist view.

In the century after Marx's death, there developed a vast body of interpretation that sponsored many variations on Marxist politics. The analysis of these works is beyond the scope of this book, but all the important variations accept his view of the human condition. They differ primarily over his analysis of how contradictions are worked out within capitalism, the role of the state, and the relationships among economic, political, and social power.

Modern Marxist thinkers moved away from the lockstep interpretation of his scenario for the arrival of communism. They concentrated on interpreting the subtleties and dynamics of class conflict and the functioning of the state in highly complex Western societies.[19] Marx is used as a guide to understanding the strategies of competing interests rather than as the authority on the timetable for revolution.

---

19. Carnoy, *The State and Political Theory*.

Prior to their dissolution, the Communist parties of Western Europe generally arrived at the position that the revolutionary overthrow of capitalism was not the appropriate method for achieving communism. Rather, they adopted the path of participating in elections and working within parliaments and governments in the same fashion as other parties.

THE DOWNFALL OF MARXISM-LENINISM

We have now completed a sketch of the Marxist scenario for the transition to communism, and we have seen what became of it in practice. What was it that allowed Marxist ideas to be used to justify gross violations of people's lives, liberties, and personal dignity? There are several answers, some unique to Marxism and others similar to the explanations offered for the sins of fascism, of monarchism, or of ideologies and religions generally.

Fascism, as an example, permitted inhumane actions of every variety because it offered a kind of salvation, at least for a certain race of people. When the higher good becomes collective in character, as with a race, faith, nation, or class, as in the case of Marxism, then the potential for abuse of fundamental human values appears. Nazis carried out genocide against Jews; Christians burned heretics and witches; Serbs have massacred Muslims. All believed they had moral reasons for their actions.

These atrocities become particularly likely when the question of the collective good is decided by other than democratic means. With Fascists, it was the *Führer* who defined the needs of the race and the nation. In Leninism, it was the Communist Party through its leadership that set the terms of individual sacrifice. It is one thing to concede these decisions to leaders voluntarily, as believers in a religion may wish to do, but it is quite another to live in a system where "the forces of history," or some other abstraction from people's daily experience, dictate who shall make the decisions wholly apart from individual consent or any kind of accountability.

Marxism-Leninism allowed a privileged group to claim for itself the power to decide nearly every issue affecting the lives and prospects of people in communist societies. This was done in the name of a scenario for the liberation of all workers, but in practice it permitted the flagrant abuse of power. The Communist Party had a system for the internal evaluation of its members and functionaries, but there was no process for holding the party itself accountable to the people. Lacking the credibility that comes with popular support, the internal party apparatus became ripe for favoritism, sycophancy, and corruption.

Democratic accountability depends upon intelligible standards of evaluation. People have to be able to judge what is being accomplished and whether the sacrifices made in the name of the common good are yielding worthwhile results. From a democratic point of view, the defect of Marxism as a political theory is that the key concepts rest upon abstractions about a potential transformation of the human condition.

Although Soviet leaders were fond of citing data on kilowatts of power generated or bushels of wheat grown, their fundamental claim to legitimacy lay in Marx's ideas about how human creativity could be satisfied through the reorganization of production and the development of a classless society. The meaning of these benchmarks was to be found in Marx's theory. The fault lay in the failure to establish a politically accountable relationship between theory and practice.

Just what is a classless society? Does it mean that there are no variations in the respect accorded to different individuals, the amount of work expected, or the attention that should be paid to advice given by people regardless of qualifications? How is production to be reorganized, exactly? Jobs differ in difficulty, tedium, danger, skill, and many other aspects. There may never be a match between people's interests and abilities and the work that needs to be done.

Marx's answers to these questions moved to ever higher levels of abstraction about solidarity, classlessness, the end of alienation, and the ultimate goal of free creative production. Because of the structure of his theory, there was no real way to agree on how to assess progress toward the ultimate revolution.

The important point is that Marx and millions of his followers did not think of themselves as cynics or opportunists. He was engaging in a form of theoretical analysis that uses abstraction to illuminate new possibilities in the human condition. The vision he created spoke powerfully to people's aspirations. It is worth a bit of exploration to see exactly how this form of analysis separates his values from the exigencies of political practice.

The problem centers on his use of language. To put it in academic terms, Marx defined concepts by their relationship to one another, rather than by some specific, consistent, and even measurable properties. For example, the concept of class can be defined by an income test: lower class could mean those making less than $20,000 a year.[20] Marx, by contrast, defined class in relation to other concepts, such as alienation, exploitation, bourgeois-proletariat relations, or, indeed, its opposite, the classless society.

---

20. For a discussion of this method of definition and the uses and limitations of the social scientific form of explanation that builds upon it, see Kenneth Hoover and Todd Donovan, *The Elements of Social Scientific Thinking*, 7th ed. (New York: Bedford, St. Martin's 2001). For a summary of the conventional critique of Marx's definition of class, see Peter Calvert, *The Concept of Class: An Historical Introduction* (London: Hutchinson Publishing Group, 1982).

Marx did this because he saw that class meant one thing in nineteenth-century French society amid the remnants of a struggle among the feudal nobility, the rising bourgeoisie, and the developing urban proletariat but something quite different in a modern industrial society. The difference lies, according to Marx, in the way in which inequalities among people are generated by relationships based on various ways of producing goods and services. Because class is, in part, "defined" by its relation to changing modes of production, Marx's method allowed him to capture this difference in a way that more conventional definitional techniques might miss.

The problem for the reader, or the citizen in a communist society, is that definitions in this framework are inherently abstract and changeable over time. The key concepts that justify the regime are not used consistently in a way that permits measurement and accountability. It may be easy to tell if one is lower class or upper class when the measurement is income, but the concept of class becomes quite vague when it is defined through attitudes, relationships to historical circumstances, or even the changing circumstances of power in a workplace, family, or social situation. If classist behavior is a crime and the definition is vague, the people who control the meaning—namely, the party—have great power.

There is a danger in the other direction as well. Terence Ball argues that Marx's collaborator, Friedrich Engels, defined Marx's ideas in a (falsely) static way so that they could be understood in the familiar methodological style of a science. The danger was realized when Lenin and Stalin used this mechanical interpretation of Marx to create the Communist Party as an instrument for the uncompromising and insensitive administration of a theory of class conflict and revolution. Ball suggests that the dynamism of Marx's thought was lost, only to be replaced by a "scientific" form of socialism that was coercive and ultimately totalitarian.[21]

Yet the final justification for Marxism, and for the communist regimes he inspired, lies in the notion of a superior form of individual and social life. The content of that image is a philosophic abstraction that has been controlled in practice by the arbiters of power and authority. Tyranny can be exercised in the name of science, though the procedures of verification and proof offer some protection against it. But tyranny can also be exercised in the name of philosophical abstractions, and most especially so when the meaning of them cannot easily be challenged.

Marx's method of definition does offer considerable possibilities for exploring relationships in society. This is the method that allowed him to see capitalism as a whole system of interrelated phenomena embracing everything from art to

---

21. Terence Ball, "Marxist Science and Positivist Politics," in Ball and Farr, *After Marx*, pp. 235–260.

religion. The method also has the advantage of capturing the dynamism of history, but in practice, it invites arbitrariness and self-serving behavior rationalized as philosophy.

CONCLUSION

Although Marx's recipe for class warfare and revolution has been discredited, his critique of capitalism retains some appeal for people who are concerned about the inequalities, crime, and materialism that seem to accompany capitalist development. For most of the twentieth century, serious political discussions resolved into a comparison of Marxist, democratic socialist, and capitalist approaches to problems and possibilities. With the collapse of the Soviet Union and the changes apparently under way in China, this discussion will change form.

Concerns about inequality, crime, and materialism will continue to find expression, but few will see the state-centered socialism advocated by Marx and Lenin as the solution. In fact, the fall of communism in the Soviet Union may unbind the discussion of these problems from the cold war rhetoric of capitalism versus Marxism. Critics of capitalist political economies will be led to look for solutions other than state control of the means of production, and defenders of capitalism will no longer be able to dismiss critics as agents of Marxist revolutionary ideology.

A critical judgment of Marx depends upon analyzing his fundamental assumptions about the human condition and the connections to his theory of revolution. Is it true that human beings are destined to struggle toward achieving a world in which conscious production can be maximized for all and necessity is reduced to a minimum? In this prophecy lies the almost mystical appeal of his doctrine, and from it flow the analytical ideas that make him such a potent critic of capitalism. Or is his model of human nature either inaccurate or too simple? Do other aspects of human nature besides the relationship to production have to be taken into account?

If Marx was correct about human nature, does his scenario for the downfall of capitalism and the rise of revolutionary communism necessarily follow? Can a revolutionary regime redirect the state toward the implementation of socialism and organize the transition to communism without becoming corrupt and repressive? Is there another path to utopia? Democratic socialists believe that there is, as we will see in the next chapter.

As the Marxist scholar Bertell Ollman makes clear, all of Marx's key concepts are derived from his fundamental assumption about the human drive toward conscious production. A class-based society inhibits the fulfillment of people's humanity; exploitation derives its evil character from the way in which that conscious productivity is denied to some for the profit of others, and so on. Marx's whole theory can be evaluated critically through the analysis of the validity of this fundamental assumption as it is worked out through his conceptual system. Upon this base stands his entire analysis of the meaning of alienation, the purpose of history, and the nature of politics.[22]

The question raised by Marx is the classic issue of the meaning of life. In the chapter on liberation ideologies, we will see that subsequent theories have given us different and more sophisticated models of what is involved in the full development of human potential. Although "conscious production" is an element in contemporary models of human development, other dimensions have to be taken into account as well.

22. For further exploration of Marx's methodology, see Ollman, *Alienation,* and Paul Thomas, "Marx and Science," *Political Studies* 24 (1978): 1–23.

CHAPTER SEVEN

DEMOCRATIC SOCIALISM

*Despite its failure everywhere to
measure up to its original ideals,
[socialism] has been one of the most successful political movements of all time.*

ALBERT FRIED
Socialism in America (1970)[1]

Socialist ideas influence the public policy of every country in the world. Public schools, public transportation and utilities, and social security are all examples of institutions and policies advocated by socialists, often in alliance with other movements. In this sense, socialist ideas are present in all but the most libertarian party programs.

For most of the twentieth century, democratic socialist parties provided the principal alternative to conservative rule in European countries. Variations on socialist parties and regimes have held power throughout Africa and in parts of

---

1. Albert Fried, ed., *Socialism in America: From the Shakers to the Third International—A Documentary History* (Garden City, N.Y.: Doubleday [Anchor], 1970), p. 1

the Middle East and Central and South America. Canadian and U.S. politicians have adopted many ideas from the socialist tradition. Parties of socialist origin are in power in France and England presently.

All this has come about in the last century and a half, and much of it since the 1930s. What powerful vision lies behind this movement? What ideas is socialism made of, and where did they come from? What are its strengths and weaknesses? Has socialism run its course, to be replaced by a worldwide capitalist political economy?

For many Americans, socialism appears as an idea that is vaguely understood and routinely dismissed as impractical. To many, socialism means governmental control of the economy, the loss of personal freedom, and economic inefficiency. There is some truth in all these generalizations, but they are parts of a stereotype that conceals more than it reveals about the socialist tradition—both its theoretical development and its impact on everyday life in the United States and throughout the world.

Our purpose will be to look for common themes in the variety of socialist visions rather than to examine the entire spectrum. Although we will see some general distinctions among broad streams of socialist thought, the description of the ideology has been synthesized from many sources. The history of socialist ideas presented here will include only the essential concepts.

Throughout this chapter, we will be exploring democratic and *evolutionary* approaches to socialism that contrast with Marx's conception of *revolutionary* socialism as a stage on the path to communism. The imagery of these two conceptions of socialism occasionally overlaps, but fundamental differences of both ends and means distinguish them.

THE SOCIALIST VISION

Socialists start from the belief that human beings are inescapably social creatures. A life dedicated only to the satisfaction of individual appetites is no life at all. To see ourselves as completely independent creatures having no essential bond with the rest of humanity is to engage in a fantasy having no basis either in the facts of biology or in the realities of daily life. The experience of communicating in a common language, of working with others, and of making society responsive to the developmental needs of all its members is what makes for the fulfillment of human potential.

Socialists do not deny the significance of individual freedom. However, their conception of what freedom means, and how it is attained, differs greatly from that of conservatives. For socialists, individuality and sociality (to adapt a word) are not opposites; they are *complementary*. To be fully human is to be engaged with others in the manifold tasks of life. Only in a properly constituted society can people develop their personal talents and abilities.

Freedom seen as autonomy from society is an illusion. In a socialist society the individual would achieve freedom by participating as a mature citizen in a community of equals. Individual differences would be expressed as a matter of choice rather than of necessity.

The quest for essential kinds of cooperative relations is itself part of human maturation. The great question of socialism is how to secure this kind of cooperation. Should cooperation be strictly voluntary? Can institutions such as cooperatives provide a framework for relationships of mutuality? Should the democratic state become the means of enabling cooperation? Do we have a *right* to expect minimum levels of sustenance from others in society? If so, should the state have the power to enforce that right through taxation and redistribution?

Socialists argue that the pressures of competition in capitalist society keep individuals divided on the basis of class, ethnicity, race, gender, and the struggle for survival. In capitalism, individuals can consume only what they are able to pay for, and the means of earning money are distributed very unequally. Through luck, class position, inheritance, or corruption, as well as hard work, some individuals gain an advantage over others. To combat the structures of power that keep capitalist property relations in place, socialists of various kinds have embraced varieties of resistance tactics, cooperatives, communal experiments, and forms of state intervention.

In the socialist ideal, goods and services would be distributed according to *need*. Need is defined generally as basic necessities plus whatever is required to support the individual's ability to function in society.[2] In return, people would be asked to contribute to society on the basis of *ability*. "*From* each according to ability, *to* each according to need" is the rallying cry for socialists of all kinds. In capitalism, they argue, the reverse happens: we work out of necessity, and only those with rare abilities are rewarded adequately for their level of effort.

In a secure environment with basic needs provided, individual talents could be cultivated without being held back by a class system or undermined by ruthless competition. The result would be undreamt of levels of creativity and productivity. All the waste that goes with competition, advertising, the policing of property relations, and the damaging effects of violence would be diminished or dispensed with.

---

2. For a thorough analysis of the concept of human need, see Patricia Springborn, *The Problem of Human Needs and the Critique of Civilization* (New York: Allen and Unwin, 1981). Nancy Fraser extends the concept of need to include participative parity. See Fraser, *Justice Interruptus: Critical Reflections on the "Postsocialist" Condition* (New York: Routledge, 1997).

Socialism would not abolish disagreements among people or resolve all differences. However, its advocates think that democratic methods offer the best chance of settling disputes and making publicly beneficial decisions. Instead of a few powerful figures ruling by virtue of wealth, socialists foresee those most affected by these decisions holding power. By allowing people to share both participation and accountability, socialists expect that work would be performed more efficiently, productivity would be maximized, and the humane life would be possible.[3]

The main emphasis of socialism is on mutual relationships of common work and shared expression "in which productive wealth is *owned* and *controlled* by the community and *used* for communal ends *(italics mine)*."[4] This classic definition of socialism sets the framework for the remainder of this chapter. Struggles over how best to deal with the three issues of *ownership, control,* and *use* of productive resources constitute the history of socialism. An additional defining issue is the *scope* of cooperative relations.

As we will see, there are both statist and nonstatist answers as to how such resources might be owned collectively, how they might be controlled democratically, and how they might be used to benefit all members of the community. There are also important differences over how far cooperative and communal relations should extend into the realm of personal life.

Evolutionary vs. Revolutionary Socialism

In Chapter 6, we examined Marx's communist utopia. He adapted the socialist ideal for his own purposes and emphasized its communal aspect by calling the final stage of history *communism.* It is important at this point both to see the differences between communist and democratic socialist ideas and to explore the contemporary issues raised in socialist thought.

Marxism is frequently distinguished from socialism on at least two grounds. Many socialists do not believe that revolution is the proper means for transforming society, relying instead on the possibility of peaceful transition through democratic political institutions. Marx, on the other hand, thought that socialism required a revolution and had to be enforced by the state as a means of achieving communism.

Secondly, some socialists think Marx's vision of communism goes overboard in sharing too much of what must remain private if individual freedom is not to be lost to conformism and the terrors of the police state. For democratic social-

---

3. For a modern essay on socialist utopianism, see Michael Walzer, *Radical Principles: Reflections of an Unreconstructed Democrat* (New York: Basic Books, 1980), pp. 273–290.

4. Robert Kilroy-Silk, *Socialism since Marx* (New York: Taplinger, 1972), p. xv.

ists, preserving civil liberties is as important as sharing wealth and power. Christian democratic socialists see religion as a spiritual counterpart to socialism, rather than as the "opium of the masses" to be suppressed by the state.

The differences between democratic socialists and revolutionary communists over how to bring about change are profound. Contrast the following statements. The first is from the post-World War II "Rules of the Fabian Society," an influential British democratic socialist organization.

> The [Fabian] Society consists of socialists. It therefore aims at the establishment of a society in which equality of opportunity will be secured and the economic power and privileges of individuals and classes abolished through the collective ownership and democratic control of the economic resources of the community. It seeks to secure these ends by the methods of political democracy.
>
> The Society, believing in equal citizenship in the fullest sense, is open to persons irrespective of sex, race or creed, who commit themselves to its aims and purposes and undertake to promote its work.[5]

The second statement is from Marx's *Communist Manifesto:*

> Our epoch . . . has simplified the class antagonisms. Society as a whole is more and more splitting up into two great hostile camps; into two great classes directly facing each other: Bourgeoisie and Proletariat. . . .
>
> The Communists . . . openly declare that their ends can be attained only by the forcible overthrow of all existing social conditions. Let the ruling classes tremble at a Communistic revolution. The proletarians have nothing to lose but their chains. They have a world to win. WORKING MEN OF ALL COUNTRIES UNITE![6]

Notice that the Fabians appeal to all; Marx addresses the working class. The Fabians endorse equal opportunity; Marx advocates class rule. The Fabians propose to use the "methods of political democracy"; Marx incites revolution.

Although there are common elements to their visions of the good society, the means of getting there are sharply different. This difference in method led Friedrich Engels (1820–1895), Marx's collaborator, to label non-Marxist socialism as "utopian" socialism, whereas Marxism was to be seen as "scientific" socialism.[7] For Engels, the term *utopian* was one of mild contempt. Engels admired the

---

5. From the rules as amended in 1949. In Anne Freemantle, *This Little Band of Prophets: The British Fabians* (New York: New American Books, 1959), p. 265–266.

6. In Robert Tucker, ed., *The Marx-Engels Reader,* 2nd ed. (New York: W. W. Norton, 1978), pp. 473–474, 500.

7. "Socialism: Utopian and Scientific," in Tucker, *Marx-Engels Reader,* pp. 683–717.

early socialists, but he scorned their simple faith that reason and idealism would somehow lead people to adopt these new forms.

History may judge differently which version of socialism was utopian. The ideas of modern democratic socialists owe much to the visionaries whom Engels dismissed. Contemporary democratic socialist politicians added to these visions a healthy respect for parliamentary democracy and the limits of the uses of power in achieving change. The record of democratic socialist governments is far less bloody than that of revolutionary communist regimes. The reforms they have achieved in education, health care, and worker participation in management, while not always successful, have by and large withstood the test of time and free elections.

Socialism and Personal Life

Socialists have classically argued for the extension of democracy from politics to economics—and also to social relations, including the family. What this means for parent-child relations and for sexual behavior has always been a source of controversy among socialists and a principal area of confrontation with traditional conservatives.

Socialist criticism of the family begins from what is clearly a stereotype, though one that has much historical validity: the family unit as consisting of a father who holds a job and dominates the power relations of the family; a mother whose work is confined to the home, who receives no wages, and who has minimal civil and political rights; and children who are subservient in every respect to their parents. Few families fit this description today, and for many families the stereotype always did overstate the reality of male domination.[8] However, the laws of Western societies have historically reinforced that pattern. It is these laws and the conditioning to hierarchical authority in the family that socialists and other reformers have tried to change.

Socialists favor various kinds of emancipation from this version of the family with its male-supremacist, authoritarian characteristics. From the beginning of this century, socialists in the United States struggled for voting rights for women, equal access to jobs, and day care for children. Legal reforms were to allow women to own property in the same way as men and to have an equal stake in the property acquired after marriage. The rights of children were advanced through child labor laws and legal protection from parental abuse. Socialists are in the forefront of struggles for an expanded role for the community and the state in the education and socialization of children.

---

8. Less than 20% of the U.S. population lives in families that fit the pattern of an employed father, an unemployed mother, and children.

Apart from these reformist measures, the principal improvement of family relations comes from the socialist principle of substituting cooperation for competition in work life. In a socialist society, men would be released from the pressures of playing the dominant role. Because people would be treated humanely in the workplace, the connection would be broken that makes "macho" behavior a compensation for powerlessness and exploitation on the job. The humiliation that socialists see as the result of class domination, competition, and alienation would be missing in socialist society, and the result would be healthier family relationships.

Some of the great socialist visionaries, including Marx at times, advocated communal sexual and familial relations, an idea that still remains controversial among socialists.[9] Marx thought that the family was merely a disguised form of bourgeois rule over the emotions, supported by property relations and surrounded with hypocrisy. In the family under capitalism, he saw adultery and the reduction of romantic feelings to property relations.[10]

Many socialists would agree with this critique and would add that the family under capitalism is where children are socialized to a world of inequality and domination. There is less agreement on what the family should be and how politics is related to its development. Although Marx advocated communalizing personal relations, the simple model of common kitchens, communal nurseries, and free sexual relations has declined in popularity among socialists.

Socialists today generally attempt to introduce elements of democracy into personal life as a critique of relationships based on traditional parental authority or economic dominance. Most socialists favor community day-care centers, for example, not as a way of destroying the family but as a means of breaking the monopoly of male power over the household. By this reform and others, a socialist society attempts to supply the supports that increase the level of voluntary cooperation within the family. All socialists agree that the family will ultimately be a much healthier institution in a society that removes economic desperation, provides basic necessities, and encourages cooperation.

Contemporary American socialists are likely to view the family with more ambivalence than distaste. It is seen as the place where a caring environment of mutual commitment can make life under capitalism bearable. At the same time, under the pressures that capitalism creates, it can become a source of mental and physical oppression and of conditioning to a materialistic and competitive system. Given these polarities, some contemporary socialists favor the legitimation

---

9. Lenin quickly disavowed this movement in Russia. To one socialist who claimed that sexual relations should be as free as drinking water, he responded that no one likes to drink from a dirty glass!

10. The fact that Karl Marx fathered an unacknowledged child by the Marx family maid suggests that his way of dealing with family responsibilities may have its problems as well.

of many different living arrangements, including traditional heterosexual relationships, with or without legal sanction, collectives for single people, and gay and
lesbian marriages. The determinant should be the needs of the individuals
involved for personal growth and development, rather than legal restrictions or
economic and social pressure.

Socialists recommend these alternatives as both a release from the exploitative relations of capitalism and a way to realize the freedom that a society should
allow in personal life.[11] Their advocacy of diversity is part of an effort to build a
coalition of groups that feel oppressed in modern capitalist society.

The controversies over how socialism is to be achieved and what it means for
personal life are important in the history of this ideology because they have often
defined the limits of its appeal in democratic countries. At times, the liberalization of social mores has been a popular cause in the West, and socialism's support
has helped make it so. Women's suffrage was accomplished by building a coalition of socialists and many other reformist groups. In more conservative periods,
socialism has been hampered by the reaction of moral traditionalists. The "New
Right" in the United States has used traditional moral concerns as powerful
issues against socialists, liberals, and the Left generally.

Similarly, the association of socialism with radical change, if not revolution,
has tied the fortunes of the movement to changing tides of public satisfaction and
discontent with the prevailing system. Socialism gained respectability in the
United States in the 1920s and 1930s. A number of cities had socialist mayors;
there were many socialist legislators. The Second World War and the reaction to
the atrocities of the Stalin era, however, discredited much of the Marxist and
non-Marxist Left.

Socialism became marginally respectable again only in the 1970s following
the development of the civil rights, feminist, and antiwar movements. But with
the development of a full-blown conservative critique of socialist programs in the
1980s and 1990s and the fall of the Berlin Wall, socialism entered another period
of decline.

Although popular issues have affected the appeal of socialism, the heart of
the ideology is a vision of a more democratic relationship among the individual,
work life, the state, and society generally. There are many recipes for achieving the
socialist ideal, from small communes where everything is shared to planned societies where the principal industries are publicly owned and managed by the state.
Socialism has taken many forms, and I will summarize the development of the
key ideas and experiments in the next section.

---

11. See Lois Rita Helmbold and Amber Hollibaugh, "The Family in Socialist America," in *Socialist
Visions,* ed. Steve Rosskamm Shalom (Boston: South End Press, 1983), pp. 194–196, 216–222.

FIGURE 7.1   SYSTEMS OF POLITICAL ECONOMY

RESOURCE	STATIST SOCIALISM	COOPERATIVE SOCIALISM	CAPITALISM
OWNERSHIP	Government	Workers	Stockholders
CONTROL	Voters/bureaucracy	Managers/councils selected by workers	Managers selected by stockholders/boards
USE/ DISTRIBUTION	According to need/ government plan	According to work/ value added	According to supply/ demand as reflected in market price

THE HISTORY OF SOCIALIST EXPERIMENTATION

Socialists share a commitment to a distinctive mix of equality, democracy, and freedom, but the ideas that have shaped socialist thinking have emerged as much through practice as theory. This brief history will include an account of major socialist experiments as a frame of reference for the development of socialist ideology.

Socialists extend the struggle for democracy and egalitarianism from the sphere of politics to the domain of economic relationships and personal life. The struggle for greater democracy in economic relations is really about the three parallel issues of the *ownership, control, and use or distribution* of productive resources (see Figure 7.1).

As we will see, capitalism has been challenged throughout its history by many experiments and political movements organized around the two versions of socialism. Cooperative socialism preceded the rise of state socialism, so we begin with early efforts at communal living and the alternatives that were generated out of the experience of industrialization.

Socialist Prehistory: From Christian Communalism to the Rise of Cooperatives

Early Christian socialists believed that a simple life based on common work offered the best prospects for living the spiritual life. These believers took literally the biblical teaching concerning the equality of God's children and the pre-eminence of virtue over material gain.[12] Monastic communities arose as an

---

12. Cf. Alexander Gray, *The Socialist Tradition: Moses to Lenin* (New York: Harper and Row, 1968 [1946]), pp. 40–42ff.

expression of this ideal. Monks and nuns take the classic vow of poverty, chastity, and obedience designed to discipline the vices of greed, lust, and vanity. Communal living in a self-sufficient environment provides a separation from the sinfulness of the world and a means of reinforcing religious commitments that make the vow meaningful.[13]

These visions of combining spirituality with egalitarian forms of work and social life inspired seventeenth-century English rebels against the institution of private property. On the basis of religious inspiration, the Levellers, led by Gerard Winstanley, aimed to "assemble a community, dig up and plant the commons, and live on their produce."[14] These movements were poorly conceived and badly led, but they gave fresh life to the ideal of spiritual reform through the organization of production on a cooperative basis.

The civil wars and revolutions of the seventeenth century led to the foundation of classical liberalism in the work of John Locke. However, his version of the social contract was too limited for radicals and romantics. Jean Jacques Rousseau (1712–1778) took the notion of the social contract to a more profound level and had a major influence on the style and development of socialist thought. He focused on the fundamental question of how to get people to look beyond their immediate self-interest to the larger interest of the whole community. He termed this larger interest the *general will*. People would be guided by the general will if certain conditions were met. There would have to be a measure of equality so that "no citizen is rich enough to be able to buy another; and none so poor as to be forced to sell himself."[15]

Without such arrangements, Rousseau observed, the result is tyranny: the rich supply the financing for despotism, and the poor supply the tyrants themselves, a chilling prophecy of what happened in Germany in the 1930s. There needs to be liberty of expression, active and effective participation of all citizens, agreement that all laws will be made democratically, and a consensus that the rule of law will be supreme. Under these conditions, individuals might become true citizens participating in the general will.[16] Inspired by the American War of

---

13. See Albert Hirschman, *The Passions and the Interests: Political Arguments for Capitalism before Its Triumph* (Princeton, N.J.: Princeton University Press, 1977).

14. Frank E. Manuel and Fritzie P. Manuel, *Utopian Thought in the Western World* (Cambridge, Mass.: Belknap Press, 1982), p. 349. Cf. Christopher Hill, *The World Turned Upside Down: Radical Ideas during the English Revolution* (London: Penguin, 1972).

15. In "The Social Contract or Principles of Political Right," *Jean Jacques Rousseau: Political Writings*, trans. and ed. Frederick Watkins (Madison: University of Wisconsin Press, 1986), p. 55.

16. See Sheldon Wolin, *Politics and Vision: Continuity and Innovation in Western Political Thought* (Boston: Little, Brown, 1960), pp. 370–371. Cf. Jacob Bronowski and Bruce Mazlish, *The Western Intellectual Tradition* (New York: Harper and Row, 1960), pp. 283–304.

Independence, the French Revolution was filled with Rousseauist rhetoric about equality, liberty, and fraternity, but was lacking in orderly process and common sense. The result was a counterreaction that led to the dictatorship of Napoleon Bonaparte from 1799–1815.

In the wake of the disappointments of the French Revolution, visionaries such as Henri de Saint-Simon (1760–1825) and Charles Fourier (1772–1837) constructed recipes for the establishment of ideal communities outside the realm of state power. These experimental communities involved the shared ownership and control of textile mills, among other forms of production. They also experimented with varying degrees of communal living.[17]

As industrialization took hold of Western civilization, socialists focused on cooperative forms of factory production. Robert Owen, a Scottish industrialist, operated a large cotton mill in New Lanark from 1800 to 1829. He looked after the educational and social needs of workers and their families, and this became the basis for his belief in cooperative communities with shared ownership of the means of production. Owen had many imitators. Though these utopian communities ultimately failed for various reasons, they set a style for socialist thought. Variations have been tried many times since; the notion of participative management has even found its way into the literature of contemporary business administration.

Owen also reinforced in socialist thought the Rousseauist idea that a person's character is the product of environment rather than personal choice. If the environment could be changed to reinforce habits of cooperation and sharing, people would be less greedy and selfish. The vices attributed to capitalist competition and inequality would fade away. There would be no more vulgar displays of personal wealth and no poverty, theft, or prostitution. Owen's successful tenure at New Lanark demonstrated that these results were possible, at least in a paternalistic community that provided adequate services for its workers.[18]

The thesis that character is shaped by the economic environment separated many socialists from Christian theology, with its emphasis on personal responsibility for sinful behavior. In another sense, however, it allied socialists with various crusaders for moral reform. The essence of the argument was whether human nature is capable of improvement by other means than personal self-discipline.

---

17. Not all of these experiments were socialist. A fascinating example of a capitalist effort at devising an ideal community is provided by Saltaire, a woolen mill in northern England. Titus Salt, the owner created a village with many amenities designed to instill virtue in the lives of the workers. See http://members.tripod.co.uk/saltaire/index.html.

18. The title of Owen's book illustrates the point: *The Revolution in the Mind and Practice of the Human Race: or the Coming Change from Irrationality to Rationality.*

Socialists contend that changing the system of production, providing education, and breaking up concentrations of wealth will improve people's lives *and characters*. Socialism offers a path to the virtuous life in addition to the path of religious commitment.

The impetus to form utopian communities spawned numerous efforts in the United States and other countries.[19] However, in England, the movement for cooperative socialism ran into serious problems with the economic failure of several notable efforts. These were attributed by Sidney (1859–1947) and Beatrice Webb (1858–1943), leaders of the socialist Fabian Society, to the worker's lack of education and their inability to bring together the capital resources to finance industrial modernization. To address the education problem, they founded The London School of Economics and Political Science in 1895, which remains today as an internationally respected institution of higher learning. The Webbs assumed that an institution devoted to academic freedom and social scientific inquiry would lead its students toward socialist views. Today, the faculty represents diverse points of view, and generations of students have benefitted from lively disputations about the practical and philosophical merits and difficulties of all manner of ideas.[20]

To remedy the need for a much more powerful way of wresting ownership and control of production from capitalists, the Webbs worked with trade union leaders to found the British Labour Party in 1900.[21] In half a century, the Labour Party would rise to power and attempt to transform the relationship between government and the economy.[22] The turn away from cooperative forms of socialism to statist approaches would have immense consequences for twentieth century politics.

Socialism, Economic Planning, and the State

The cooperative movement is but one strand of socialist ideology. The growing power of the nation-state in the early part of the twentieth century placed the role

---

19. See, for example, Charles Pierce LeWarne, *Utopias on Puget Sound, 1885–1915* (Seattle, University of Washington Press, 1975).

20. Ralf Dahrendorf's *A History of the School of Economics and Political Science, 1895–1995* (New York: Oxford University Press, 1995) offers a fascinating perspective on the history of relations between intellectuals and movements for reform in Britain. Cf. Jose Harris, *William Beveridge: A Biography* (Oxford: Oxford University Press, 2nd ed., 1997).

21. The Webbs ultimately concluded that moderate reforms would not work, and became advocates of the Soviet form of communism in the 1930s. This course was rejected by the leadership of the British Labour Party, and the Labour Party came to power in 1945 by democratic means.

22. For a brief account of these struggles, see Kenneth Hoover, "Ideologizing Institutions: Laski, Hayek, Keynes, and the Creation of Contemporary Politics," *Journal of Political Ideologies*, 4 (1999) 1, 87–115.

of government at the center of socialist interest. Socialists advocated the democratization of political participation. They battled to extend the vote to women and minorities and to establish presidential primary elections in the United States, among numerous other measures.

Along with improving access to political power for millions of citizens came efforts to extend the reach of that power to more and more areas of community life. Socialist reformers favored publicly financed educational systems, the provision of basic utilities such as parks, electric power and public transportation, and the regulation and, in some cases, public operation of basic economic institutions such as banks and communication systems.

The most characteristic expressions of the statist approach to democratic socialism were the efforts in Britain and other European countries to combine parliamentary democracy with socialist economic institutions.[23] The widespread animus against the upper classes for their role in the disasters of World War I and the depression of the 1930s contributed to the spread of socialist sentiment. World War I brought democratic socialists to power in Austria. The movement grew in other parts of Europe, and it soon became an occasionally successful contender for power in Sweden and Britain.

The early democratic socialist governments concentrated on improving services and laying the foundation of the modern welfare state. World War II brought new life to socialist ranks. In 1945, Britain's Labour Party won a surprising victory over Winston Churchill's Conservative Party. The Labour government nationalized the Bank of England, the railroads, and large elements of the coal and steel industries. The British Labour government also established a publicly financed health system, with medical services and prescriptions available to all without charge.

In France, the government developed variations on planning that involved private owners in cooperative arrangements with the government, the establishment of governmental planning agencies with considerable powers, and the extension of government responsibilities to a wide range of policy areas.[24] These innovations in Britain and France, among other countries, produced mixed systems in which the economics of the marketplace and the politics of democracy existed side by side in uneasy partnerships.

These arrangements were occasionally associated with reasonably successful strategies for economic modernization and growth, as in the Scandinavian coun-

---

23. A useful examination of these experiments is found in Bogdan Denitch, ed., *Democratic Socialism: The Mass Left in Advanced Industrial Societies* (Totowa, N.J.: Allanheld, Osmun, 1981).

24. For a survey of French socialism, see Stuart Hams, ed., *Socialism in France: From Jaures to Mitterand* (New York: St. Martin's Press, 1983).

tries, but also with big government and high taxes. The minimum socialist objective of providing for basic security was met through an extensive system for sustaining the disadvantaged. The larger goal of engaging people in a higher level of participation in the productive process remained more elusive. Nationalization of industries gave unions enormous power to strike against the government as a major employer, as in the coal mines or the railroads, and thus shut down the economy. This strength led to wage rates that improved the lot of workers considerably, though sometimes at the expense of the position of an industry in international competition.

The power of capital was now confronted with the power of organized labor acting through socialist political parties. These confrontations have generally been nonviolent, but they have been bitter nevertheless. In Britain the dream of a peaceful transition to a successful form of socialism was interrupted by the realities of economic decline as the British Empire was lost to independence movements in Africa and Asia. The rigors of increasing competition with low-wage Third World countries, and the burden on the social service system of increasing numbers of immigrants, older citizens, and children, are forcing West European electorates to reevaluate the cost of providing high levels of publicly financed services.

Perhaps of longer term significance than the cost problem is the decidedly mixed results of the cumbersome process of having politicians make economic decisions. Socialist enterprises have had a hard time competing in a world economy in which multinational corporations have the advantages of quick decision-making, sophisticated marketing, political leverage, and mobile financial arrangements. Experiments with increasing the participation of workers have usually taken second place to the necessities of meeting the competition by using the techniques of centralized management.

State socialism added another often remote and concentrated center of power, the bureaucracy, to the struggle for control. Critics on the left as well as the right began to point out that socialist political parties were losing their creativity and sense of vision. Governments became bogged down in deciding between competing groups aiming for a larger share of the pie.

The powerful critiques of socialism developed by the Austrian political economists Ludwig Von Mises and Friedrich Hayek slowly eroded the conceptual legitimacy of socialist ideas.[25]

Hayek's *The Road to Serfdom* (1944) characterized socialist central planning as inevitably inefficient. Hayek saw socialism as the twin of fascism in that it

---

25. See Kenneth Hoover and Raymond Plant, *Conservative Capitalism in Britain and the United States: A Critical Appraisal* (New York and London: Routledge, 1989), for an analysis of this critique.

overbuilt the role of government and thus constituted a threat to individual freedom that would eventuate in a modern form of "serfdom."[26] George Orwell, author of the satire of communist totalitarianism, *Animal Farm,* replied that: "(Hayek) does not see, or will not admit, that a return to 'free' competition means for the great mass of people a tyranny probably worse, because more irresponsible, than that of the state."[27] Orwell was more fearful of the arbitrary power of capitalists to determine the fate of their workers than he was concerned about the authority of a democratically elected government.

This struggle between privately exercised power operating in the marketplace, and publicly accountable power exercised through government, has become the defining feature of modern politics. Democratic socialists continued to try to find democratic ways of controlling the power of capitalists over the use and disposition of resources, both human and material.

Perhaps the potential evils of statism were illustrated most clearly in the socialist countries of the former Eastern bloc, such as Poland, Hungary, Czechoslovakia, Romania, and Yugoslavia. Here the introduction of state socialism came from a combination of internal movements and Soviet political and military manipulation. The goal of socializing these societies by increasing the level of democratic participation was clearly subservient to that of fitting the policies of each country to the requirements of Soviet control over foreign policy and economic development.

East European socialism remained under the shadow of Soviet domination and of the system of rule by the Communist Party originated after the Russian Revolution. In practice, this meant that the party had a tight grip on all the major institutional positions of power—the media, universities, the military, factories, and so on. Only the Catholic Church remained partially independent. In the Soviet orbit, state socialism was given a much more potent form due to the alliance between the governmental bureaucracy and the party that effectively undermined democracy.[28]

The former USSR put down post-World War II movements toward democratic reform in Hungary in 1956, in Czechoslovakia in 1968, and in other satellite states as well. These reform movements were mainly directed at escaping

---

26. See the fiftieth anniversary edition, introduction by Milton Friedman (Chicago: University of Chicago Press, 1994). Cf. John Gray "Postscript" in *Hayek on Liberty,* 3rd ed. (London: Routledge, 1998), pp. 147–161, for a critical assessment of Hayek's politics.

27. In Noel Annan, *Our Age: The Generation That Made Post-War Britain* (London: Fontana, 1990), p. 586. Cf. Hoover, "Ideologizing Institutions: Laski, Hayek, Keynes, and the Creation Contemporary Politics," *Journal of Political Ideologies,* 4 (1999) 1, 87–115.

28. See Donald Hodges, *The Bureaucratization of Socialism* (Amherst: University of Massachusetts Press, 1981).

Soviet domination, rather than overthrowing socialism and accepting capitalism. The Catholic Church, headed by Pope John Paul II, a native of Poland, became a center of resistance. The failure of the Communist bloc to adapt to democratic pressures and nationalist sentiments led to the final collapse of the whole system.

Socialism had become synonymous with rule by the Communist Party, and the party owed its allegiance to Moscow. The struggle is now under way all across Eastern Europe and throughout the former Soviet Union to implement a form of democratic capitalism that will take some account of socialist aspirations.

In Africa, experiments with socialism were undertaken amid the pressures of the decline of colonialism, the Cold War, black nationalism, and tribal rivalries (see Chapter 11). Many African leaders were deeply influenced by socialist ideas as they brought their countries to independence in the 1960s. In some cases, considerable gains were made in literacy, education, and public health. Yet it proved virtually impossible to translate European socialism into an African form of postcolonial political economy that could surmount the problems of underdevelopment in the midst of global economic competition. The centralization of economic power opened the way to favoritism and corruption. Many avowedly socialist countries turned toward attracting investments from multinational corporations as a matter of economic survival.

Socialist movements in Latin America were sharply influenced by the forcible overthrow of the democratically elected socialist government in Chile in 1973. Chileans angered by the redistributive policies of the socialist government rebelled with American help, and a military dictatorship resulted. Democratic socialism as an alternative to the revolutionary model provided by Cuba has seemed an impossibility because of the military strength of the forces of capitalism.

In the 1980s, the socialist Sandinista government in Nicaragua followed a less repressive version of the Cuban model and attempted to implement socialist educational and economic reforms in the midst of severe interruptions of its society from within and without by forces opposed to socialism. After prolonged intervention by the U.S., the effort ended in the election of an anti-Sandinista government.

The twentieth century has provided ample proof that the advancement of socialist ideals by the coercive power of the state is exceedingly risky. Yet the impulse to extend equality to wider spheres of life continues to take new forms through political movements and innovative experiments in the democratization of productive and communal life. Some of these experiments will be discussed in the final section. First, however, the distinctive history of socialism in the United States needs to be examined.

Socialism in the United States

American socialism is in many respects more complex than the European versions. Its sources are varied, from the Christian and secular communitarianism practiced by early settlers to the dissent against private property at the time of the adoption of the Constitution. Add to this mix successive waves of immigrants, among them all manner of socialists, reformers, and revolutionaries. The weaknesses of socialist movements in America say as much as the successes about the meaning and relevance of socialist ideology.

The high point of electoral success for a party carrying the name Socialist came in the first two decades of this century. The United States at the turn of the century was the scene of massive labor struggles to establish the right to organize in a few basic industries.[29] The Socialist Party had more than 100,000 members, and its candidate for president, Eugene Debs (1855–1926), twice received in the neighborhood of a million votes. There were fifty-six socialist mayors, including leaders of some of the largest cities in the country, and numerous socialist newspapers and local organizations.

The ideas in the platform of the Socialist Party were at times shared by populists and progressives and even elements of the Democratic and Republican parties. What was distinctive about socialists was their class-based approach to change. Progressives believed in strong government as an agent of reform, but they tried to appeal to all classes. Populists believed in the average citizen rather than elites, but not in the theory of the working class as the bearer of a special historical mission for the transformation of society. Socialism had its middle class and even wealthy advocates, but the appeal was always to the special virtues and historical significance of the working class.[30]

Socialism is an ideology that sees the potential for a different world from the one we know. Socialists believe that changes in social conditions will improve human behavior. For most socialists the working class is the agent of such change, both because it is most directly involved with the key condition, the system of production, and because it is the direct victim of capitalist exploitation. The working class knows intuitively the meaning of work, the possibilities for the

---

29. For an excellent review of this period, see John P. Diggins, *The American Left in the Twentieth Century* (New York: Harcourt Brace Jovanovich, 1973), pp. 57–63. Diggins reports that between 1881 and 1906, there were "some 30,000 strikes and lockouts, affecting almost 200,000 businesses and over 9.6 million workers" (p. 57). Cf. Diggins, *The Rise and Fall of the American Left* (New York: W. W. Norton, 1992).

30. Aileen Kraditor, *The Radical Persuasion 1890–1917: Aspects of the Intellectual History and Historiography of Three American Radical Organizations* (Baton Rouge: Louisiana State University Press, 1983).

democratization of the workplace, and the necessity for change. The powerful fig-ures of American socialism, Debs, Daniel DeLeon, and Big Bill Haywood (1869–1928), as well as intellectuals such as Max Eastman, understood and tried to work with this analysis.

Yet there were many obstacles to the development of class consciousness among American working people. Some derived from the special nature of American experience, others from the way in which issues advanced by socialists divided working-class loyalties. No more diverse "working class" could be found on the face of the earth. Unlike the homogeneous European nations, the United States is largely an aggregation of ethnically and racially diverse immigrants. There were even divisions within ethnic groups, such as that between the first wave of German immigrants, influenced by Marxist radicalism, and the second German wave, inspired by Ferdinand LaSalle's democratic socialism. These dif-ferences complicated what was already an unlikely prospect for the growth of militant class consciousness.

For class consciousness to develop, there needs to be a concentration of masses of people. Yet in the United States, until recently, the frontier attracted dissenters. The working class must also have movements to unite it around a clear, ideologically based program. Yet in the United States the labor movement was divided into many sectors. The most powerful unions had a much simpler program than socialist reform. In the famous words of Samuel Gompers, a form-ative leader of the American Federation of Labor, the program consisted of one word: "More!" The only major attempt at "one big union," the International Workers of the World, under the leadership of Haywood in the 1920s, fell prey to government repression, internal division, and a flirtation with violence that cost it its association with the Socialist Party.[31]

The notion of working-class solidarity had its internationalist dimension. On the American scene, internationalism undercut the socialists' ability to deal with the tides of popular opinion in two world wars. Debs opposed American entry into World War I; he went to prison for arguing that it was a capitalist war for which the proletariat provided the cannon fodder. The argument was popular among the believers, but the fight among the leadership and in the ranks over participation in the war sapped the Socialist Party and reversed its momentum. The "Red scares" of the twenties added official repression to internal weakness, and class consciousness was weakened and dissipated.

With the consolidation of the Russian Revolution in the early 1920s, many American socialists found new hope. However, Lenin's path to change through the Communist Party was not based on any conception of democracy recogniza-

---

31. Diggins, *The American Left,* p. 60. Cf. David Milton, *The Politics of U.S. Labor* (New York: Monthly Review Press, 1982), for a sympathetic view of Depression-era labor radicalism.

ble in the United States. As American leftists drifted toward the Communist Party, they became tied to Russia's foreign policy and to the Soviet model of centralized governmental planning directed by the party.

When the Depression seemed to fulfill Marx's prophecy of the collapse of capitalism, the Left became further entangled in the currents of Soviet politics. But when Stalin temporarily made a nonaggression agreement with Hitler, the notion of international working-class solidarity suffered a deadly blow. Although the Nazi invasion of Russia set the stage for a U.S.-Soviet alliance against Hitler, it did not restore the essential element of socialist politics: working-class solidarity. The American-Soviet alliance, which gave way soon after World War II to cold war politics, was clearly based on national political interests, not the common struggle of working people.

An additional reason for the failure of class consciousness was the success of reformers who borrowed ideas from socialist ideology but left aside the rhetoric and the larger analysis of class conflict. From Franklin Roosevelt's New Deal to the Great Society programs of Lyndon Johnson, American politicians proved to be adept at using socialist ideas to address grievances and rectify the most glaring effects of inequality. Their programs have often borrowed some of the ideas that socialists offer, but not the critique of capitalism.

The only version of socialism that succeeded at all in the United States was based on democratic politics and a reformist program. It was called "sewer" socialism. The program concentrated on the efficient operation of public utilities and the expansion of public control to include transportation systems and small public housing projects. Coming to power in a number of U.S. cities in the 1910s and 1920s against a background of corruption and favoritism, the socialists emphasized clean government and democratic participation rather than class warfare.[32]

Capitalism has not, on the whole, seemed exploitative to the U.S. working class. Rising prosperity has been attributed to capitalist efficiency and productivity, though it could be argued that it had something to do with massive government investments in the military and the regulation of resource use and business practices by the government. However, this ability of capitalist political and economic systems to generate great wealth has disarmed class-based analysis and thereby deprived socialists of their basic tenet.

Socialism, Democracy, and Capitalism in Contemporary Politics

While class warfare is a subdued theme of contemporary politics, socialist conceptions of democratization and greater equality continue to influence public

---

32. See Richard Judd, *Socialist Cities: Municipal Politics and the Grass Roots of American Socialism* (Albany, N.Y.: SUNY Press, 1989).

policy and even forms of corporate organization. Thus, the broad tendency toward greater democratization carries forward elements of the socialist agenda, even if socialism as an ideology falls out of favor. Whatever else the twentieth century brought, a tremendous increase in democratization is clearly in evidence. From 1900, when no nations offered universal suffrage to today, when 62% of the world's population live in states with democratic systems, there has been a great advance in human rights.[33]

When economic considerations are added to the analysis, it is apparent that the modern industrialized political economies of the west are mixed systems, neither entirely capitalist, nor socialist. While state socialism of the classic sort is in eclipse, there are aspects of state socialism that remain prominent in Western European political economies. Government health care systems remain in place, and German law requires that workers be represented on the boards of major corporations. Governments formed by historically socialist parties were in power all across Europe at the end of the twentieth century, though their commitment to state ownership of productive resources no longer holds.

The United States is predominantly capitalist though, as we shall see, there are surprisingly significant extensions of worker ownership, and even control, apparent in the private sector. The "safety net" of Social Security and welfare measures, though diminished in scope, remains a major feature of public policy. Furthermore, the spread of democratic egalitarianism has greatly influenced contemporary social attitudes and religious views.

Our purpose in this section is to illustrate the influence of socialist ideas, rather than provide a complete history. We will focus on the democratization of resource *ownership* and *control*. In Part Two, on contemporary ideologies, we will look at environmentalist ideologies as a reflection on struggles over the *use* of resources, and we will explore the influence of socialist egalitarianism on attitudes toward gender, race, and identity.

While statist socialism has gone into decline, there has been a revival of cooperative socialism. Of the cooperative experiments, perhaps the most striking is the one named after the community in which it began, Mondragón, in the Basque country of northern Spain. Mondragón is built around a network of producers' cooperatives that include some of the largest appliance manufacturers in Spain. Workers in the cooperatives contribute an initial share of money and participate in the direction of the enterprise through elected councils that hire managers. The cooperatives originated as a worker education movement in 1943, and a small manufacturing operation was established in 1956. From there, the Mondragón

---

33. Freedom House, "End of Century Survey Finds Dramatic Gains for Democracy," report available online at http://freedomhouse.org.

"experiment" has grown to include more than a hundred enterprises with 23,000 "cooperators."[34]

In Mondragón, cooperatively organized banking and educational institutions have flourished to the point where they provide for the credit and training needs of the larger system. The bank, now one of the largest in Spain, also lends money for initial shares to prospective workers. Mondragón has weathered rapid growth, as well as economic recessions, without laying off workers or losing its momentum. Workers no longer needed in one industry are retrained through the educational system for other jobs.

The Mondragón example is now being carefully studied by socialists and others interested in a progressive form of productive community that is built from the ground up, rather than implemented by the state. While these experiments suggest that cooperative socialist principles may be workable in a modern industrial economy, the cooperatives have moved away from more direct forms of control by worker's councils toward a centralized managerial system in order to meet the needs of a fast-paced global economy.[35] They continue, however, to generate for the cooperators a much higher standard of living than capitalist firms in the region.

If we broaden our conception of cooperatives to include partnerships, stock option plans, and other ways of spreading the wealth and power within organizations, there are many examples to consider. In the U.S., doctors and lawyers have long formed partnerships that approximate cooperatives in arrangements for distributing income and controlling the conditions of work. Universities, among the most durable of all organizations, have historically operated on the basis of faculty control of curriculum and personnel decisions, and tenured appointments to protect academic freedom. These forms of democratized *control* are being eroded by managerial techniques as medical practices move toward health maintenance organizations, and universities are pressured to respond to externally determined standards of accountability.[36]

The most interesting recent developments in the democratization of *ownership* are found in the burgeoning software and e-commerce industries. Extensive

---

34. See William Foote Whyte and Kathleen King Whyte, *Making Mondragón: The Growth and Dynamics of the Worker Cooperative Complex,* 2nd ed. rev. (Ithaca, N.Y.: Cornell University Press, Institute for Labor Research, 1991); and Kenneth Hoover, "Mondragón's Answers to Utopia's Problems," *Utopian Studies* 3 (Summer 1992): 1–20.

35. They have also begun to employ workers on a noncooperative basis—up to 40% of the workforce in some cases. See Tim Huet, "Can Coops Go Global? Mondragón Is Trying," *Dollars and Sense,* November/December, 1997, available on the web at http://www.igc.apc.org/dollars/issues/nov97/mon.html.

36. It is ironic that, as corporations become more like universities, with "campuses" instead of "head-quarters," universities are being pressed to imitate hierarchical corporations.

employee stock-options program are typical in these industries. Upper level employees have become independently wealthy. While control usually remains centralized, the informal style of teamwork, and the de-emphasis on titles and hierarchy, are part of the culture throughout the software industry.[37]

A similar phenomenon may be seen in e-commerce and mass retailing where firms such as Amazon.com and Home Depot build initiative through an employee stock-options program.[38] Even the airlines and defense industries are utilizing this principle. A majority share of United Airlines is employee-owned, and they have had a direct impact on decisions about the company leadership. Another example is Science Applications International Corporation, a major defense contractor, which is employee owned.[39] In fact, of the 58 publicly held corporations on the *Fortune Magazine* list of "100 Best Companies to Work For," 36 offer stock options to all employees.[40]

The spectrum of democratized economic and political organization runs from communes through to major corporations. Firms at either end of the spectrum operate very differently. Each has its strengths and weaknesses. Democratizing *ownership* through employee stock options contributes greatly to the incentives for productivity. The diffusion of wealth that results helps to create a more independent and self-sufficient workforce. On the other hand, democratizing *control* through elected councils appears to slow down decision-making so that competition in a global economy becomes difficult.[41] However, informal modes of cooperative production through task-oriented teamwork have increasingly become the norm in modern corporations.

Currently, socialists have come to acknowledge the efficiency of the marketplace in allocating scarce resources.[42] Centrally planned economies run by governments are clearly prone to inefficiency and corruption. The use of government

---

37. See James Fallows, "Inside the Leviathan: A Short and Stimulating Brush with Microsoft's Corporate Culture," *The Atlantic Monthly,* February 2000, pp. 34–38.

38. "Getting the Chance to Do It Himself: Out of the Shadows to Run Home Depot," Jennifer Steinhauer, *New York Times,* May 13, 1998, p. C1.

39. See Carolyn Geer, "The Book on Dr. B.," *Forbes Magazine,* December 1, 1998, available on the web at http://www.forbes.com/forbes/97/1201/6012157a.htm.

40. "The 100 Best Companies to Work For," *Fortune,* January 10, 1999, p. 83. The stock of these companies rose 50% faster over the past three years than the average for public companies generally. Nearly all of them offer such working conditions as "flextime," jobsharing, telecommuting, and family leave arrangements.

41. On the problems of collectives as experienced by a veteran participant, see "Unavaoidable Inequalities: Some Implications for Participatory Democratic Theory"; *Social Theory and Practice,* Karen Wendling; Summer 1997. Text available through the Proquest database.

42. See David Miller, *Market, State and Community: Theoretical Foundations of Market Socialism* (Oxford: Clarendon Press, 1989).

coercion to plan the economy threatens individual liberties. However, private ownership of resources is similarly plagued by waste and misappropriation of assets and human resources. A large percentage of business "start-ups" fail, and for every corporate success story, there are many examples of decline and collapse.

Historically, socialists have favored public accountability through the political process as a method of ensuring greater equality of treatment. However, the enhanced productivity that results from diffusion of corporate ownership and control suggests that the discipline of the marketplace in a framework of law can also structure private behavior in ways that favor broader participation in the rewards of labor.

In any case, for reasons as congenial to capitalism as to socialism, the voluntary sharing of ownership and control has become more pervasive. The recognition that these modes of participation are more productive than the rigidly hierarchical corporation has become more persuasive than any ideological program. The irony of socialism as the century ended was that the corporation rather than the state may have become the more promising arrangement for advancing at least some of the economic objectives that inspired the original socialist vision. From a socialist perspective, what remains for the democratized state is the role of providing what private corporations cannot: guarantees of basic rights, including the social and material requisites of life in a civilized society.

The search continues for modes of ownership and control that will return value to those who created it, make the best use of the workers' knowledge and initiative, and generalize fair treatment to all. Debates over how best to advance democratization are sometimes obscured by rhetoric about capitalism and socialism. However, engagement through participation in ownership, and even control, is spreading. The *means* of democratizing ownership and control are demonstrably available, however the major question remains how far those means can extend to the *ends* of securing greater equality for all citizens. Meanwhile, the battles over the distribution and use of resources continues to unfold as the safety net is redesigned and environmental issues become ever more prominent.

CONCLUSION

Socialists in the United States have been effective mainly by communicating ideas that enter the mainstream of party politics. The lack of a broadly based socialist movement makes the United States distinctive among industrialized countries. It suggests that where class is less recognized or relevant, the socialists must pursue strategies other than emphasizing class conflict if they hope to expand their base.[43]

---

43. For an analysis of a contemporary American experiment in middle-class socialist politics, see Mark Kann, *Middle Class Radicalism in Santa Monica* (Philadelphia: Temple University Press, 1986).

Meanwhile, reformist ideas have entered the mainstream of politics from other sources. Mass movements seeking advances in civil rights, women's rights, and environmental protection prompted large-scale changes in rhetoric and policy. The countercultural movements of the 1960s and 1970s spawned many interesting conceptions of politics. The expansion of social scientific research in the areas of psychology and sociology opened up new ideas about human nature and its political possibilities. These initiatives are, in many cases, tied together by the theme of *liberation,* the subject of Part Two. First, however, it is important to understand the reaction against Marxist and democratic socialist ideas that gave rise to fascism.

CHAPTER EIGHT

FASCISM

Before mass leaders seize the
power to fit reality to their lies, their
propaganda is marked by its extreme contempt for facts as such, or in their opinion
fact depends entirely on the power of [the person] who can fabricate it.

HANNAH ARENDT

(1958)

The term *fascism* calls up memories of Adolf Hitler and Benito Mussolini and images of totalitarian dictatorships in Germany, Italy, and Japan during the Great Depression and Second World War. Interesting as these topics are historically, fascism seems dated as an ideology. Fascism is important not so much because there are active movements by that name, though there are. It is important because through the study of fascism we realize the power of racist, nationalist, and authoritarian ideas in whatever form they take—and they take many potent forms in contemporary politics.

Fascism is a combination of racism, nationalism, and authoritarianism that centers on a mystical faith in the superiority of a specific group of people.[1] This definition is illustrated most clearly by German fascism, with its doctrines of Aryan superiority, the historic mission of the Third Reich, and the belief in the *Führer* principle of absolute dictatorship. However, every country influenced by Western civilization has probably had some form of fascist political movement, and the United States is no exception.

Because the perception of wars is mainly shaped by the winners, current generations have come to see fascism as a ridiculous and delusionary ideology. It is hard to see what could have captured the imagination of millions of Germans, Italians, and Japanese and the sympathy, however temporary, of many U.S. editorialists, political leaders, and ordinary citizens. The hardest task of all is to estimate the potential for a fascist revival in current political manifestations of racism, nationalism, and authoritarianism.

We begin, once again, by constructing a vision of a fascist society. Fascists, like socialists, attempted to form utopian communities.[2] From these experiments, and from the history of fascist thought, we can see what a fascist utopia would be like.

A Fascist Utopia

There is a scene in a famous German propaganda film, *The Triumph of the Will*, involving a huge encampment of Nazis at Nuremberg in 1934. Members of the National Socialist, or Nazi, Party are gathered to celebrate the consolidation of power in the hands of Hitler. Prior to the spectacle of massed formations of disciplined followers, there are scenes of activities in the camp: early morning exercises, the sharing of work in preparation for the serious ceremonies to follow, roughhouse fun, and hearty meals of sausages and potatoes. The film's director, Leni Riefenstahl, uses these scenes to convey a sense of the happy simplicity, the purity of motive, and the integration of play, work, and loyalty that the Nazis wished to project. The dream of drawing together feelings, beliefs, and everyday activity in one idyllic environment has a powerful fascination.

---

1. This descriptive definition follows from the work of George Mosse, *The Crisis of German Ideology: Intellectual Origins of the Third Reich* (New York: Grosset and Dunlap, 1964), and A. James Gregor, *The Ideology of Fascism* (New York: Free Press, 1969), pp. 10–15. For a review of the controversy over the definition of fascism, see Gilbert Allardyce, "What Fascism Is Not: Thoughts on the Definition of a Concept," and the responses by Stanley Payne and Ernst Nolte, in *American Historical Review* 84 (1979): 367–398.

2. See Mosse, *Crisis of German Ideology*, Chap. 6.

What is required to make this vision possible? In the German case, the Nazis thought that a united people, having a homogeneous racial background and the special character of the common *Volk* ("people"), was capable of such an existence. The ideology of the *Volk* developed in the revolt against industrialization and democratization that began to affect Germany in the late nineteenth century. Its myths identified in the German people a native wisdom, a virtuous character, and a feel for the spiritual meaning of life. In Japan, the superiority of the Japanese among Asian peoples was the center of a corresponding myth; among Italian fascists, the chauvinism was directed against Africans and, after Mussolini's alliance with Hitler, against Jews.[3]

In the early German fascist utopias, pure Aryans would live together in a kind of rural paradise where land would be provided by the state and all would play their assigned role in its cultivation. Women would bear children, keep the household, and assist their husbands in the work of the community.[4] Men would hold the positions of power. The community would be united in its belief in the leader and in common dedication to the protection of the *Volk* from dilution by other races, their customs, and their behavior.

The rules of the community would be the result not of bargaining and compromise in a political process but, rather, of the leader's interpretation of custom and tradition on behalf of his people. The mythical tradition of racial superiority supplied the symbols and rituals that sanctified the role of the leader as interpreter of the national will.

On a more directly political level, the leader would work through his most loyal followers, his "bold nucleus," in Mussolini's words, to instill the proper attitudes and virtues in the general populace and to help them emulate the model of racial perfection in their daily lives.[5] Membership in the National Socialist Party was, as in the case of the Communist Party, a distinction earned on the basis of loyalty, commitment to the ideal, and willingness to sacrifice everything for the cause.

The focus of politics would be on interpreting the meaning and mission of the *Volk* rather than on responding to individual desires and settling differences.[6] Character would count for more than reason and logic. Purity of character, the

---

3. See Bertram Gross's summary of the comparative development of the three "classic fascisms" in *Friendly Fascism: The New Face of Power in America* (Boston: South End Press, 1980), pp. 11–31.

4. On the role of women in Nazi Germany, see Jill Stephenson, *The Nazi Organization of Women* (Totowa, N.J.: Barnes and Noble, 1981).

5. Ernst Nolte, *Three Faces of Fascism* (New York: Holt, Rinehart and Winston, 1966), p. 158.

6. See Hannah Arendt's discussion of law in a totalitarian society in *The Origins of Totalitarianism*, 2nd ed. (Cleveland: World Press, 1958), p. 462.

Nazis believed, comes from purity of race. They believed the Germans were a special race whose history proved that they were capable of great feats of bravery, faith, and duty. The motto of the Nazi SS, or special police, was "My loyalty is my honor." There was no room for an independent code of honor or for personal judgment—only loyalty to the *Führer,* leader of the Fatherland.[7]

The *volkisch* community would be split neither by racial divisions nor by class divisions. Industrialization and democratization were seen paradoxically to have introduced division into society. The emergence of an organized working class, a proletariat, was deeply threatening to the German middle class as well as to the peasants. Such conflict would only divide in the presence of Germany's enemies what was meant to be united: the German people, history's most advanced race.

The antidemocratic character of fascism was presented as a remedy to the problems of division among the German people. The effort to introduce parliamentary government during the Weimar period after the First World War accentuated the divisions. The divisive partisan controversies seemed only to discredit the ideal of democracy and confirm the decline of a once unified society.

Yet the Marxist desire for a classless society was even more threatening. Fascists believe that each person has a different level of ability from every other. The point, however, is for each person to give full effort to whatever part the state requires him or her to play. During the revival of the German Army after World War I, privates saluted one another to show that the lower ranks were as worthy of respect as the officers. But to ally with others as a class, and to set that class interest above the interest of the whole community, was perceived as selfish and irresponsible.

The leftist challenge to the unity and organic harmony of German society was particularly unwelcome. The fact that many Communists and socialists, including Marx, were Jews confirmed the alien character of this development. The fact that class division was most pronounced in cities made the rural orientation of fascist imagery all the more significant.[8]

Fascism manages to combine an appeal to classlessness with extreme authoritarianism. In the fascist utopia there is solidarity but not equality. Solidarity is based on the common commitment to the ideals of the *Volk* rather than on a false leveling.[9] What differentiates people is not so much their individual preferences

---

7. On the role of the cult of the strong leader in rendering political participation meaningless, see Piero Melograni, "The Cult of the Duce in Mussolini's Italy," in *International Fascism: New Thoughts and New Approaches,* ed. George Mosse (Beverly Hills, Calif.: Sage Publications, 1979).

8. Mosse, *Crisis of German Ideology,* p. 22.

9. Arendt, *Origins of Totalitarianism,* pp. 360–361.

and styles as their function in the common enterprise. In the Nuremberg rally of 1934, a huge formation of workers performed a military-style rifle drill with their shovels. The ceremony dignified menial labor and identified workers with the patriotic heroism of the army. The uniforms defined the place of workers in the larger order of the society.

In this context, industrial work was viewed by the Nazis as a new form of craft, and industrial workers were to see themselves as members of a guild of artisans on the medieval model. The Marxist notion of a union of workers from different plants advancing their interests at the expense of management was abhorrent to the Nazis.

Genetic Purity, Physical Culture, and the Role of the State

Family life would be structured in the first place by genetic considerations. Only persons of the correct racial stock, excluding Jews, foreigners, and inferior physical specimens, would be encouraged to have children. The Nazis set up camps where proper Nordic types could breed more productively than the family structure would allow. Nazi regimes mounted campaigns to reward motherhood with medals, as in a military campaign—the more children, the higher the decoration.

Family relations would be conducted along the lines of fascist belief. The authoritarian position of the father would not be challenged. The mother would be honored for her carefully circumscribed role as keeper of the home. Children were to be inculcated with the Nazi spirit through home instruction as well as participation in youth clubs, festivals, and ceremonies.

In Nazi Germany, physical culture was considered to be an important part of personal development. Perfection of the body was celebrated above the cultivation of a free intellect. The mind was valued only as it enabled the spirit to be understood and translated into practical achievements. Intellectuals who evaluated and criticized were censored, their positions in universities destroyed, and their books burned.

In such a closed universe, the spirit of the race is the motivating force, and its indications, as interpreted by the leader and his loyal followers, are the guiding precepts of the community. Any person or practice that does not contribute to the unified effort is beneath contempt and subject to the wrath of the community.

Fascism has its religious characteristics as a system of faith. The faith centers on a myth of the innate superiority of a race and nation. Leaders play the role of priests rather than politicians by presiding at ceremonies, interpreting the myth, and condemning heresies. There are elements of myth in all ideologies, but fascism places myths of racial supremacy and authoritarianism at its very core.

THE ORIGINS OF FASCISM

Ernst Cassirer points out in *The Myth of the State* that "myth does not arise solely from intellectual processes; it sprouts forth from deep human emotions."[10] To understand the mythic basis of fascism, and of forms of racism and nationalism that lead to authoritarianism, it is important to explore some of the emotions that create the myths.

Scholars commonly explain the rise of fascism to a fever pitch in the 1930s as a response to the devastation of the First World War and the economic crises that followed. Fascist political organizations were founded in Germany, Italy, and Japan in the same year: 1919. In Germany, the loss of face and the destruction of people's savings and investments through the inflation in the 1920s and the Depression of the 1930s created a desperate population bereft of belief and ripe for the assurance that a powerful myth and a skillful leader could provide. In the National Socialist Party's appeal to the voters in the 1932 elections, for example, the connections are made directly:

> HITLER is the last hope of those who were deprived of everything: of farm and home, of savings, employment, survival; and who have but one possession left: their faith in a just Germany, which will once again grant to its citizens honor, freedom, and bread.[11]

Scholars who have taken the longer view emphasize the dislocation caused by the conversion from a traditional peasant society to a modern capitalist economy.[12] As George Mosse points out, the *Volk* movement "used and amplified romanticism to provide an alternative to modernity, to the developing industrial and urban civilization which seemed to rob man of his individual, creative self while cutting him loose from a social order that was seemingly exhausted and lacking in vitality."[13] Hitler presented himself as the personification of both the fall and the rise of the German people.

The elaboration of key elements of the myth preceded Hitler. The proposition that the German people had a historic destiny was rooted in a generation of German philosophy of which the leading figure was Hegel. Hegel argued that history was the unfolding of a divine plan by which superior forms of civilization

---

10. Ernst Cassirer, *The Myth of the State* (New Haven, Conn.: Yale University Press, 1946), pp. 46–47.

11. Joachim Remak, *The Nazi Years: A Documentary History* (New York: Prentice-Hall, 1969), p. 42.

12. For a statement of the "modernization" thesis concerning the rise of fascism, see Peter Stearns, *European Society in Upheaval* (New York: Macmillan, 1975), p. 2. Cf. David Schoenbaum, *Hitler's Social Revolution: Class and Status in Nazi Germany, 1933–1939* (New York: Doubleday, 1980), pp. 13–15.

13. Mosse, *Crisis of German Ideology*, p. 17.

would replace primitive forms. He associated European Christian civilization with this higher level of development.[14]

A crucial next step was taken by Houston Stewart Chamberlain (1855–1927), the son-in-law of the German composer Richard Wagner, who made the link between Darwinian theory and nationalism at the end of the nineteenth century. Chamberlain argued that a truly superior people proved itself by outdistancing others in production, culture, and military strength. He brought in this dubious interpretation of Darwin's scientific conclusions about animal evolution to bolster the credibility of the myth of Aryan supremacy.[15]

What was seen to have corrupted this special race of people was the influence of foreigners and those lacking in the historical rootedness of the German people. The vast changes that swept European society in the late nineteenth and early twentieth centuries had undermined the traditional basis of German culture. A rural, aristocratic, religious, and orderly nation was rapidly being overtaken by forces of industrialization, democracy, secularism, and liberality.

These changes, felt in every aspect of life, were accentuated by the calamity of the First World War, which had confirmed the downfall of the traditional order. In the economic and social crisis that followed, the search for a scapegoat was on. The Jews, who were seen to represent rootlessness, the commercial spirit, and the urban lifestyle, were accused of undermining the natural state of affairs. They were the enemies, along with the socialists and Communists, who added the dimensions of secularism and democracy to the disorder of German life.

The revolt against modernity, with its emphasis on mobility, reason, science, and secularism, has preoccupied many analysts of ideology. Research on the personality types most susceptible to the appeal of totalitarianism has indicated a correlation between personal insecurity and a willingness to believe in authoritarian solutions.[16] The pressures on personal life created by rapid change lead to the quest for certainty beyond reason and doubt.

Everyone struggles with the need for belief and commitment. How far into politics this struggle is carried has a great impact on the practice of politics. The similarity of fascist political behavior to gang behavior in the cities of the United

---

14. Marx was also a student of Hegel, but he thought that history revealed itself not through the spirit as expressed in culture and the actions of leaders but through the process of production. Revolutions in the relationship between the productive process and the class system would bring about a higher level of development, not the leadership of a *Führer*.

15. In the ideology of the *Volk*, the Aryans were portrayed as a people originating in India who had found their way westward to Europe, developing in the process traits of strength and self-reliance, and who had served as the racial stock for the Nordic races and the Anglo-Saxons. Mosse, *Crisis of German Ideology*, pp. 88–90.

16. T. W. Adorno et al., *The Authoritarian Personality* (New York: Harper, 1950), pp. 753–783.

States, and indeed the adoption of fascist symbolism by certain gangs, illustrates the link between insecurity as experienced by displaced young people, and by citizens who have lost their livelihood and social dignity.

The combination of modernization and economic collapse that afflicted Italy and Germany after the First World War created a crisis mentality. Socialists offered a critical analysis of Germany's faults. Hitler provided an impression of certainty and a practical program of reemployment through a military buildup. Although circumstances as extreme as this do not arise in everyone's life, the experience of Nazism makes clear how far such a myth can go in shaping people's political behavior.

There were similar movements in most European countries. The French nationalist ideologist Charles Maurras (1868–1952) proposed that the state and the soul were parallel concepts and that the nation was the soul writ large. By this analogy, the state is beyond reason; it is the expression of the enduring meanings of life, and its rituals have a religious quality. Participation in the rituals of the state confers a positive identity on people for whom an identity based on work or personal accomplishment is beyond reach. Nationalism, and through it racism, becomes a recourse against the stresses of modern life.[17]

The Volk and the State: National Socialism in Germany

Myths about the nation-state help people respond to feelings of personal ineffectiveness and alienation. Socialists point toward a revolution in the way that production is organized as the key to solving this alienation. Fascists offer a different solution: the submission of individual desires to the will of the state as expressed by its leader—hence the title of the film mentioned earlier, *The Triumph of the Will*. The justification of this "ideology of the will" is that it fulfills the historic mission of Germany, just as the principle of natural selection in Darwinian thought ensures the survival of the fittest. All other aspects of society are to be subordinate to this exercise of, literally, *will* power.[18]

With obedience to the will of the *Führer* as the primary principle, the Nazis in Germany worked toward a theory of commercial organization that would imitate socialism by placing control of key economic decisions in the hands of the state. This is the meaning of *national* socialism, as opposed to democratic socialism. In national socialism, the objective is centralized control of privately owned

---

17. Nolte, *Three Faces of Fascism,* p. 103. Hitler maintained that "the state is only the means to an end. The end is: Conservatism of race." Cited in Arendt, *Origins of Totalitarianism,* p. 357.

18. J. P. Stern, *Hitler: The Führer and the People* (Los Angeles: University of California Press, 1975), pp. 68–77.

economic activity in the national interest. Democratic socialists believe in public ownership of the means of production as a way of increasing people's control over their own lives.

In the effort to establish national socialism, the Nazis received some preliminary support from the organized labor movement. The key issue was in whose interests this control was to be exercised. It soon became clear that the interests of organized labor were not to be respected, as Hitler moved quickly to destroy the union movement. Those industrialists who did as the Nazis commanded prospered, whereas those who were judged to be unreliable were often deprived of their positions and holdings.[19]

Struggle against enemies becomes the proving ground of the fascist myth. Military aggression is, for this reason, a common feature of many fascist movements. Japan's fascist regime (1941–1944) was headed by a general, Hideki Tojo. Hitler came to power under the sponsorship of Field Marshal Paul von Hindenburg, a hero of the First World War and a symbol of German honor.

The common characteristic of fascist and militarist belief systems is, however, that they identify groups of people as the "enemy." Scapegoating is an inescapable part of ideologies that rely on the myth of a chosen people. As reality deviates from the myth, the tensions that develop feed the fires of anger toward the "enemy." This dynamic in Germany resulted in the passive acquiescence of millions of people, and the direct participation of thousands, in the murder of more than 6 million Jews. Hitler had from the beginning proclaimed his hostility to the Jews, arguing in a letter to President Hindenburg in 1933 that Jews were "an entirely alien body, which has never really become one with the German people."[20] Whatever went wrong in Germany, including its defeat in the First World War, could be blamed on the Jews.

The core of fascism was the *Führer* principle: the *Führer* is the purest manifestation of the moral will of the race.[21] It was with this principle that both Germany and Italy were led into an unreal world where morality gave way to sadistic manipulation and barbaric destruction. The themes fascist leaders used—nationalism and racism—do not lend themselves very well to solving the issues of politics and the economy. In the end, German, Italian, and Japanese

---

19. David Schoenbaum, *Hitler's Social Revolution: Class and Status in Nazi Germany* (New York: Doubleday [Anchor], 1967), pp. 77–158. Schoenbaum points out that "with the demolition of the unions and the introduction of the law on 'The Organization of National Labor,' business exchanged the pressure of the unions for the pressure of the State" (p. 157). Control over managerial decisions was lost to the Nazis.

20. Remak, *The Nazi Years*, p. 147.

21. Stern, *Hitler*, pp. 130–134.

fascist ideologies were little more than justifications of the power of the leader and his party. Fascist doctrines concerning the economy, the role of the state, the position of labor, and the responsibilities of business all gave way to the expediencies of preserving power.[22] Beyond an initial mobilization, the everyday realities of people's lives could not be improved by extolling the virtues of a nation or the superiority of a race.

Fascism in the United States

Although there is a long history of racist, nationalist, and authoritarian political tendencies in the United States, little success has been achieved by any movement identified as fascist. The reason is the difficulty of combining all three elements within the American context. Just as socialists have difficulty organizing class-based politics in a dispersed and diverse population, so fascists have a problem with securing allegiance to one ethnic and racial group among many.

The effort to create a German Bund in the United States modeled on Hitler's National Socialist Party was a dismal failure.[23] Elements of the Ku Klux Klan who organized themselves into the Black Legion, a militant white supremacist corps, were long on mysticism and short on effective political action.[24] The American Nazi Party, under the leadership of George Lincoln Rockwell, never attracted more than a few hundred followers.

More significant are religious extremists who advocate authoritarian solutions to America's various crises and proclaim the innate superiority of Christian —or, lately, Islamic—peoples. Not all of these appeals lead to fascism; it is the mix of religion and authoritarian political solutions that contains the potential for fascist politics. Small groups of "militia" occasionally combine all three elements, and attempt to operate outside the law.

In the words of two scholars who surveyed the entire history of right-wing extremism in the United States, "The American population is still highly vulnerable to political extremism; the American political system is less vulnerable, but scarcely fail-safe."[25] The reason for this vulnerablity is the high level of insecurity in American life. The anxiety and dislocation caused by a fast-paced competitive economy create the environment for scapegoating. Conspiracy theories

22. Arendt, *Origins of Totalitarianism,* p. 404. Cf. Schoenbaum, *Hitler's Social Revolution,* pp. 155–158, and Ivone Kirkpatrick, *Mussolini: A Study in Power* (New York: Avon, 1964), p. 175.

23. Sander Diamond, *The Nazi Movement in the United States, 1924–1941* (Ithaca, N.Y.: Cornell University Press, 1974).

24. Peter Amann, "Vigilante Fascism: The Black Legion," *Comparative Studies in Society and History* 25 (1983): 490–524.

25. Seymour Martin Lipset and Earl Raab, *The Politics of Unreason: Right Wing Extremism in America, 1790–1970* (New York: Harper and Row, 1970), p. 508.

directed at races, ethnic groups, cliques, women, or unpopular leaders provide easy recourse when times are hard and personal circumstances are difficult. The more unstable the environment is perceived to be, the greater the danger of extremism and the more likely it is that unprincipled demagogues will profit from people's need to believe.

The signs of this phenomenon in U.S. political life are many. Demagoguery based on racism, the periodic waves of "Red scares" in which all those who disagree with the prevailing social wisdom are branded as communist sympathizers, and theories of Jewish conspiracies all have a rich history. The mythological character of these episodes is demonstrated by the lack of connection to verifiable evidence. There may have been a small number of believers in communism in positions of influence in the United States in the 1950s, but Sen. Joseph McCarthy never found one of them as a result of his famous investigations. Yet his power over public opinion was enormous, and it was used to destroy the reputations and careers of hundreds of innocent people who were merely accused, without proof, of "anti-Americanism."[26]

Theories of racism or historical conspiracy do not withstand rational analysis. The interpersonal variation in mental and physical ability among people of a given race always outweighs the average differences *between* races.[27] Conspiracy theories lose credibility when large decisions are said to have been involved, because of the number of people that would have had to maintain secrecy. Yet the temptation to resolve the difficulties of modern life by these simple means remains.

In contemporary society, with the complexity of relations among huge centers of economic, political, and cultural power, it is less likely that fascism would resemble its classic form. The channels of communication are far more diverse, the sources of criticism more numerous, and democratic traditions stronger than they were in Western Europe and the Orient in the 1920s and 1930s. Yet Bertram Gross, in *Friendly Fascism: The New Face of Power in America,* argues that a new variety of fascism is on the rise.[28]

This "friendly" fascism achieves much the same result as the classic variety, but the means are different. Rather than employing force, friendly fascism uses the media to divert attention through displays of sex and violence, manipulate feelings through symbolic appeals to patriotism and religion, and shape opinion so as to isolate dissenters. His fundamental concerns are the weakening of dem-

---

26. See Thomas Reeves, *The Life and Times of Joe McCarthy: A Biography* (New York: Stein & Day, 1983), and Walter Goodman, *The Committee: The Extraordinary Career of the House Committee on Un-American Activities* (New York: Farrar, Straus and Giroux, 1968).

27. See Philip Green, *The Pursuit of Inequality* (New York: Pantheon, 1981), Chap. 3.

28. Gross, *Friendly Fascism* (Boston: South End Press, 1980). Cf. Zbigniew Brzezinski, *Between Two Ages: America's Role in the Technetronic Era* (New York: Vintage, 1970).

ocratic attitudes and what he perceives as the decline of effective participation in major decisions by the American people. Gross's scenario for fascism is harder to evaluate than the classic pattern, because the forces at work are by their very nature less visible. The verification of this theory depends on a careful and realistic assessment of the status of people's security and liberties.

Another perspective on the dangers arising from fascism comes from the work of A. James Gregor. In *The Fascist Persuasion in Radical Politics,* Gregor contends that many movements that identified themselves as Marxist should better be conceived of as fascist. He suggests that "Karl Marx would have found very little in the political culture and political institutions of Cuba, China, or Russia that he could identify as Marxist."[29] The symbolism of Marx's class-based revolution has been borrowed to justify the sort of authoritarian statism that fascists advocate directly.

CONCLUSION

The decline of meaningful public involvement in decision making is the universal characteristic of fascism. The Nazis created the illusion of participation through parades and plebiscites. The purpose of this show was the opposite of real participation, as A. F. K. Organski points out:

> Political mobilization serves the double function of disciplining the masses into an attitude of obedience in which non-participation in decision-making is taken for granted and becomes a virtue, and of further disciplining them into an attitude receptive to making sacrifices. At the same time, the attention of the mobilized population is directed away from their grievances and channeled into harmless political activity.[30]

In reality, "classic" fascism meant rule by a tiny group of ruthless demagogues. Nevertheless, the illusion of participation is the subtlest aspect of fascism. By appealing to the need to belong, to be included, and to feel the strength of solidarity, fascism taps a powerful current in people's lives. If, at the same time, it promises deliverance from economic crises and relief from the pressures of modernity, the loss of effective participation is not so obvious.[31] It is the difference between the appearance and the reality of participation in power that is the measure of fascism, whether classic or contemporary.

---

29. A. James Gregor, *The Fascist Persuasion in Radical Politics* (Princeton, N.J.: Princeton University Press, 1974), p. 395.

30. A. F. K. Organski, "Fascism and Modernization," in *The Nature of Fascism,* ed. S. J. Woolf (New York: Random House, 1968), p. 33.

31. Cf. George Mosse, "Introduction: A General Theory of Fascism," in Mosse, *International Fascism,* pp. 1–41.

CONTEMPORARY IDEOLOGIES

PART TWO

CHAPTER NINE

INTRODUCTION TO PART TWO: LIBERATION IDEOLOGIES

It makes sense, I think, to differentiate between liberty and liberation and . . . between the revolutionary actions which secure the first, and the inner emancipation that frees the second. A worldwide new identity, one suspects, eventually will have to liberate itself . . . from the variety of revolutionary patterns by which liberties were first secured, and from their moralistic fervor, puritan or radical.

ERIK ERIKSON
Dimensions of a New Identity (1974)

Liberation refers to freedom from some form of oppression, and it is a central theme of a wide array of movements. In the women's liberation movement, the objective is freedom from sexist discrimination. For those in the black liberation struggle, institutional and personal racism are the oppressors. As the opposite of oppression, liberation points to the removal of abuses of people's rights. Beyond the release from oppression comes the question of the positive meaning of liberation.

What is liberation? Since the mid-1960s, the concept of liberation has taken on several meanings. In this introductory chapter, I will define the basic theme of liberation ideologies and provide illustrations taken from movements of women and minorities. In the next two chapters, on feminism and racial nationalism, the theme of liberation will be developed in more detail and will be related to other aspects of those movements.

It is becoming possible to construct from various examples and sources an ideology of liberation. Because this ideology has taken shape at least as much in practice as in theory, the construction is tentative, subject to several interpretations, and even contradictory. The movement has international dimensions, but we will focus on developments in the United States, where ideas about liberation have been elaborated against the background of conceptions of individual rights and civil liberties and have taken forms that have made a considerable impact around the world.

A VISION OF LIBERATION

Defined negatively, liberation is freedom from any form of oppression. Oppression means exercising power so as to deny people a chance to live and express themselves as they wish. This concept points in the direction of a positive definition of liberation: the full realization of inner potential as an individual or a member of a community free of any constraining uses of power. As straightforward as that definition may seem, there is a tension in liberation ideology between its individualist and communitarian overtones, which will emerge as specific liberation movements are considered.

What would life be like in a fully liberated society? Essentially, people would be accepted on their own terms. Rather than having their existence defined and constrained by people of a different gender, nationality, race, or sexual preference, individuals would make life decisions autonomously or within communities of like-minded, or at least tolerant, people. There would be no unequal treatment or discrimination. Differentiation would be a matter of choice, not a policy imposed by a governmental or social structure.

Obviously, there are a variety of conceptions of a liberated existence, and there are conflicts between them. Emphasis in the Latino community on the values of the traditional family might well conflict with feminist views on expanding the lifestyle choices available to women. To resolve the conflicts on paper would be meaningless, because they are very real in practice. What can be done is to assemble a composite view of liberation by identifying sources of oppression and examining what life would be like without those limitations.

The cardinal value of liberation ideology is *equality*. However, equality means something different in liberation ideology than it means in socialism or classical liberalism. Socialists want to extend equality by democratizing the control of the means of production; for classical liberals, equality centers on due process under the law.

Liberation movements have included these approaches to equality. They have also added meanings having to do with limiting practices of power that constrain people's prospects for advancement, undermine their sense of identity, and repress the expression of alternative cultural styles. Liberation ideology has broadened the meaning of "equal treatment" in confronting cultural practices and informal exercises of power that limit people's freedom.

Liberation movements have developed an understanding of power structures that goes beyond governmental institutions. The experience of victimization at the hands of employers, social workers, and neighbors, for example, makes clear that the most telling forms of power are sometimes outside the government and beyond the reach of conventional politics.[1] Liberation movements have had to devise ways of confronting these inequities at their sources in social customs, habits, and informal structures of power. This wider conception of power and of politics is part of the value gained from studying liberation ideologies.

A second dimension of liberation revolves around the question of *identity*.[2] The concept of identity has an intuitive meaning for most people: it refers to a sense of who we are that gives continuity and meaning to our daily experiences. It is tempting to think of identity as self-created, as if we can assume whatever identity we choose. Yet in the course of everyday life it is readily apparent that identity is not something we simply present to the others around us. We rely on the reactions of others to make sense of our identity. Even the most determined "individualist" depends to some extent on public recognition of the role that he or she is playing.

A secure sense of identity really involves a transaction between the self and others in one's surroundings. Thus, the identity transaction has an element of power in it. If we are constrained by negative identities associated with our ethnicity, gender, race, or class, there are serious limits to our ability to achieve a desirable sense of identity. On the other hand, communities generate preferred identities that serve useful social purposes: the nurturer, the hard worker, the hero, the scholar. Communities also stigmatize identities that create problems: criminals, molesters, drug abusers, and so on.

Consequently, power over identities is shaped by a third dimension of the problem of liberation, *culture*. Cultures organize myths, roles, symbolic expressions, and ways of providing goods and services so as to achieve some kind of liv-

---

1. For an examination of these informal sources of power, see Murray Edelman, *Political Languages: Words That Succeed and Policies That Fail* (Madison, Wis.: Institute for Research on Poverty Monograph, 1977).

2. See Chap. 12. Cf. Kenneth R. Hoover *et al.*, *The Power of Identity: Politics in a New Key* (Chatham, NJ: Chatham House/Seven Bridges, 1997).

able social environment for communities of people. Although we usually think of political power as having to do with the distribution of income and wealth or of health care, education, and transportation, it is also involved in the exercise of cultural influences over the formation of identity and the definition of roles that can be played in the society.

The intricate interplay between individual aspiration and community need forms the matrix from which identities emerge. Communities and nation-states typically achieve the greatest concentration of power when they are able to lay claim to the most essential processes of identity formation.

Totalitarian regimes seek to do this by gathering all the forms of political, economic, and cultural power in the hands of the state. Traditional conservatives, although recognizing that authoritative cultural institutions are important, have sought to limit the concentration of this sort of power in any one institution. Classical liberals have opposed the concentration of power over people's beliefs and feelings through constitutional government, protections of civil liberties, and the ideal of due process of law. These protections have had to compete with powerful tendencies in the other direction: concentrations of economic power, racism, sexism, class discrimination, and other exclusionary attitudes. This interaction of governmental power, identity formation, and cultural role structures provides the backdrop for the development of liberation ideologies.

LIBERATION: A SUMMARY

At the beginning of this chapter, liberation was defined as "the full realization of inner potential as an individual or a member of a community free of any constraining uses of power." This definition is intended to point to a difference between individualist and communitarian understandings of liberation. The key issues posed by the liberationist vision are two: the achievement of meaningful levels of choice for all individuals in the society and a consciousness of the role of solidarity, family, and community in human development. The first step for both the individualist and communitarian versions of liberation is the identification and elimination of sources of oppression. As we will see in the following chapters, the second step is more complicated: the working through of a positive conception of liberation that makes sense of relations with society.

Although there is a certain clarity and simplicity to arguments over wealth or property rights, for example, the politics of liberation is necessarily a more complex and difficult matter. In the remaining chapters in Part Two, we will see how this movement has developed through approaches to problems of sexism, racism, and the environment. Chapter 13 will place liberation ideologies in the context of theories of human development and will suggest some ways of summarizing what has been learned in the twentieth century about ideology and politics.

CONCLUSION

There is a general pattern to the history of liberation movements in the American context. The crucial ideas, whether directed toward minorities' or women's status, show some interesting similarities. Equality has been the guiding value through a progression of steps beginning, first, with arguments for civil rights, then cultural consciousness raising, then political and economic power.

These three phases overlap broadly and are different in each movement. Although a thematic history of the ideas is possible, it must be remembered that, in practice, each group has a spectrum of opinion. There are conservative as well as liberal blacks, moderate and radical Hispanics, and socialists as well as capitalists in all these movements. In the next two chapters we will be tracing the ideas of leaders and thinkers within each movement that have contributed to forging a new meaning for liberation. These ideas have influence well beyond their origins. They have contributed to the increasing power of the idea of liberation in American politics. Two of these movements illustrate the struggle most clearly: women's liberation and black nationalism.

CHAPTER TEN

GENDER AND IDEOLOGY

SARA WEIR

In a sense, feminism has always existed.

Certainly, as long as women have been subordinated, they have resisted that subordination.
Sometimes the resistance has been collective and conscious; at other times it has been
solitary and only half–conscious, as when women have sought escape from their socially
prescribed roles through illness, drug and alcohol addiction, and even madness. Despite the
continuity of women's resistance, however, only within the last two or three hundred years
has a visible and widespread feminist movement emerged that has attempted to struggle in
an organized way against women's special oppression.

ALISON M. JAGGAR
Feminist Politics and Human Nature (1988)

Throughout history, feminist scholars have focused primarily on similarities and differences between men and women. More recently, the focus has shifted, looking not just at relationships between men and women, but also at the differences among women. Examples of these differences include the cleavages created by factors as varied as race, ethnicity, class, and sexual identity. Thus, authors like Alma Garcia and Patricia Hill Collins note that commitments to racial identity and struggles to overcome discrimination often lead to women of color having more in common with men of color than with white women.

As was discussed in Part One, a number of ideologies emerged beginning in the seventeenth century with the Age of the Enlightenment. Early feminist thinking both parallels and critiques these ideologies. For our purposes, we will

155

contrast and compare liberal, Marxist, and radical approaches. We will also examine contemporary tensions within the feminist movement, focusing primarily on differences among women.

VISIONS OF LIBERATION IN THE HISTORY OF FEMINISM

The literature on the relationships between gender and power does indeed deal with the classic issues of individual preference versus community control, often conceived as the tension of liberty versus order, and of the struggles over equality and inclusion. These questions of power, and of the capacity of dominant groups to define the experiences of others, are also central to the postmodern critiques discussed later in the chapter.

During the 1960s and 1970s, feminists raised questions regarding the scope of politics and the boundaries between public and private life. With slogans such as "The Personal Is Political," they forced lawmakers to recognize issues such as domestic violence as public, rather than private, problems. They also worked at extending basic legal rights to divorce, and to credit for women independent of their male partners. These debates about the scope and nature of politics, however, continue to divide feminist scholars and their critics even today.

According to Alison Jagger, "Liberation is the correlate of oppression. It is release from oppressive constraints."[1] Liberation expands the range of issues that are considered to be political. In this respect, the concept of liberation provides a theme that will help us trace the ideological meanings of feminist thought in particular.

All modern feminist theories offer the promise of liberation. They are theories of change, and the social movements that are organized around them challenge the status quo. What many people do not realize is that beyond this common point of agreement about oppression of women and the need for liberation and change, feminist theories differ fundamentally. Like the classical ideologies they mirror and challenge, each offers a unique understanding of the oppression women face, strategies for overcoming that oppression, and a vision of the "good society." Thus several people might describe themselves as feminists but disagree fundamentally about the problems women face and the means for overcoming them.

A comparison of three modern feminisms—liberal, Marxist, and radical—illustrates the nature of these differences. For this reason the discussion of feminism will focus not on a single vision, but on three distinct visions, coming from the modern theoretical literature. This discussion is followed by the introduction

---

1. Alison Jaggar, *Feminist Politics and Human Nature* (Totowa, NJ: Rowman Littlefield, 1988), p. 6.

of a newer critical approach, favored by many contemporary feminist thinkers, postmodern feminism. Postmodern feminists challenge " . . . the dualistic categories of public/private or nature/culture." Focusing on concepts such as identity and difference, these thinkers and critique "deconstruct" all modern theories.[2] Before looking more closely at the theoretical origins and characteristics of several feminist theories, we will examine feminism as a basis for social movements in the United States.

A BRIEF HISTORY OF ACTIVISM IN THE UNITED STATES: THREE WAVES OF FEMINISM

Upon examination, social movements organized around feminism and women's issues in the United States can be divided into three historical periods or waves of activism. These waves bring together and illustrate the relationship between feminist theories and movements for social and political change. As we enter the twenty-first century, many feminists argue that we have entered "the age of the third wave of feminism(s)."[3] The principal goal of the first wave of feminism was formal, legal equality for women. The first wave of women's activism was organized primarily around tenets of classical liberalism, and the argument that, with proper education and training, women were as capable of rational thinking as their male counterparts. This movement began in the late eighteenth century with the writings of Mary Wollstonecraft (1759–1797), and culminated in the amendment of the Constitution of the United States to extend voting rights to women.

The greatest gain of this early period of activism was the passage of the nineteenth Amendment. The women's suffrage movement called for the extension of the rights of citizenship to women. Through pressure on politicians and nonviolent protests, activists such as Susan B. Anthony (1820–1906) and Elizabeth Cady Stanton (1815–1902) overcame the opposition of conservative forces to broaden the scope of citizenship in the United States.

It was white, middle- and upper-class women who gained the most from the first wave of feminist activism. The suffrage movement did little to address the economic hardships faced by many poor women and women of color, nor did it address the discrimination encountered by most women in everyday life. After the suffrage movement, women made some gains in their efforts to be included in public life. It was not, however, until the post-World War II period that women once again organized viable, broad-based social movements.

---

2. Barbara Arneil, *Politics and Feminism* (Malden, MA: Blackwell Publishing, 1999), p. 186.

3. *Ibid.*, p. 153.

A breaking point between the first and second periods of women's activism comes with the publication of Simone de Beauvoir's *The Second Sex*. Barabara Arneil observes that de Beauvoir embraces the first wave (classical liberal) beliefs of "humanism, equality and reason," yet moves beyond these beliefs to focus on distinct categories of feminism characteristic of second wave thinking.[4] Examples include radical feminism and other types of "hyphenated" feminisms.

One of the most important features of second wave feminism was the recognition that power is found in private as well as public life, and that for many women it is oppression in the private sphere that in fact harms them the most. The popular political slogan of the day, "The Personal is Political," reflected the newfound importance of exploring the exercise of power in a variety of settings. As Arneil concludes, "Each of the different forms of feminism developed its own ideas about how to break through this oppression of women in the private sphere."[5]

Second wave political strategies focused on such diverse issues as the Equal Rights Amendment to the United States Constitution, consciousness-raising groups for women, abortion rights legislation and litigation, and affirmative action. It was a time of great gains, but once again these gains primarily reflected the interests of white, well-educated women. The 1980s and 1990s saw increasing criticism of traditional organizations such as the National Organization of Women (NOW) by women whose needs were not addressed during this second period of activism.

Third wave feminism moves away from the practice of categorizing feminisms as reflections of existing western political theories. Drawing instead upon a number of identities, third wave feminists are less concerned about internal consistency than first and second wave feminists. Arneil illustrates this departure from modern thinking with the following example: ". . . a lesbian feminist might simultaneously defend the right of privacy (traditional liberal tenet), the social constructedness of identity (post-modern tenet) and materialism as the basis of political power (socialist tenet)."[6]

Third wave feminism makes room for a number of voices, hopefully including many of the women who were marginalized by limitations set forth in second wave thinking. Drawing upon postmodern theories, as well as the authenticity of differing personal experiences, these contemporary visions offer a rich source of new thinking about liberation. As social movements emerge, we can expect that

---

4. *Ibid.*, p. 163

5. *Ibid.*, p. 165.

6. *Ibid.*, p. 153.

they will be based on more than gender. Instead, they will combine and reflect ever more complex realities of racial, ethnic, sexual, and class difference. To understand more clearly how and why these periods of women's activism appeared, we need to look more carefully at their origins in classical liberalism, reform liberalism, Marxism, and postmodern movements and theories.

ORIGINS: LIBERAL FEMINISM

In classical liberalism, all individuals are perceived as unique and distinctive. The state is based not so much on an image of a uniform human nature, as on the need to have a rational basis for resolving conflicts between individuals. Liberalism was born in an age of great conflict fueled primarily by religious and economic differences.

While classical liberal ideology was, during the Enlightenment, a revolutionary departure from the feudal systems that preceded it, its focus on citizenship and individual rights did not extend to women. Like other classical liberals, those feminists who advocate liberal positions do not attempt to resolve all questions of gender-based differences. Instead, their strategies for overcoming oppression focus on equality before the law and the inclusion of women in public life.

In the eighteenth century, women (along with many other groups in society) were not considered to be capable of rational thinking and thus were not accorded even the most fundamental rights of citizenship. For example, in 1787 the U.S. Constitution effectively excluded all women from citizenship. During this period of time, women were viewed as property and, as such, had few civil rights—the right to vote, to own property, and to make decisions about marriage and divorce were the domain of free white men only. Early liberal feminists attempted to demonstrate that women were indeed fully capable of rational thinking and therefore should be extended the rights of citizenship accorded to free men.

Among the best-known early feminists to make claims about women's nature and rationality is Mary Wollstonecraft (1759–1797). In *The Vindication of the Rights of Women* (1792), Wollstonecraft presents the first sustained argument for women's equality to be published and widely read. A member of the most intellectually revolutionary literary circles of her time, Wollstonecraft used her position to argue for the education of women and to criticize popular thinkers of the time such as Rousseau and Milton.[7] She believed that until women could acquire reason, morals, and experience on the same terms as men, neither sex would

---

7. Mary Wollstonecraft, *Vindication of the Rights of Women* in *The Norton Anthology of Literature by Women,* Sandra M. Gilbert and Susan Gubar, eds. (New York: W.W. Norton and Company, 1985), pp. 135–160.

achieve its full potential. According Wollstonecraft, sexism is debilitating to men because it allows them to gain from oppression rather than from their own efforts. Sexism undermines women because it removes the means of self-improvement.

Liberal feminists of the nineteenth and twentieth centuries recognized that women were oppressed in many areas of their lives. Their strategies for change, however, focused primarily on bringing about changes in the legal system, expecting that formal equality would lead to wide-ranging equality or rights.

In the United States the longest, and in the view of liberal feminists, most important struggle for legal equality and inclusions was the women's suffrage movement. Led primarily by Susan B. Anthony and Elizabeth Cady Stanton, this movement emerged from the Abolition and Temperance Movements. Women like Anthony, Stanton, and many others were active in the movement to abolish slavery. It was their exclusion from meetings and leadership positions that led them to organize a series of meetings on the rights of women. The most historically famous of these gatherings was held in Seneca Falls, New York, in 1848. "The Declaration of Sentiments," produced by the conference called for broad political and social rights for women. By using language that paralleled the United States Declaration of Independence, this document served as an important statement of the emerging movement for equal rights for women.[8]

The movement struggled with only minor successes into the twentieth century. Finally, a number of factors, including the strength of the Progressive movement (see Chapter 5), the unifying of two rival political factions to form the National American Women's Suffrage Party, and the intensifying of highly visible political protests led in 1920 to the passage of the nineteenth Amendment to the United States Constitution. Women's suffrage was the major success of the first wave of feminism in the United States, but other civil rights were also gained during this time.

Active among the supporters of women's suffrage were many middle-class women of African American descent. Best known among them are Sojourner Truth (1797–1883) and Ida B. Wells (1863–1931). In 1851, Truth made her now famous, "Ain't I A Woman?" speech, calling on those supporting suffrage to include full citizenship for enslaved people as well.[9] Ida B. Wells, a longtime social

---

8. For further information on the Women's Suffrage movement, see "Not for Themselves Alone: The Story of Elizabeth Cady Stanton and Susan B. Anthony," a documentary film by Ken Burns and Paul Barnes, 1999.

9. Sojourner Truth, "Ain't I A Woman?" in *The Norton Anthology of Literature by Women,* Sandra M. Gilbert and Susan Gubar, eds. (New York: W.W. Norton and Company, 1985), p. 253.

activist and journalist was the President of the Alpha Suffrage Club in Chicago. The Alpha Club was among the first black women's groups organized in support of suffrage. Although Wells worked closely with Susan B. Anthony and Elizabeth Cady Stanton, Stanton and others were willing to sacrifice suffrage for African American women if it would bring the support of southern politicians to the cause of suffrage for white women. During the first wave of feminism, this willingness to exclude some on the basis of race set the stage for many of the tensions and criticisms expressed today about mainstream women's groups by many women of color.

Patricia Hill Collins describes a rich tradition of activism among African American women in this country. In 1831, African American intellectual Maria Stewart became the first American woman of any race to lecture in public on political issues, as well as the first to distribute notes from her lecture to those in attendance.[10]

Indeed, Collins develops what she calls "Black Feminist Thought." Citing goals that only sometimes intersect with those of white women, Collins develops a theory based on the core themes of overcoming racism and sexism, self-definition to overcome negative stereotypes, the interdependence of experience and consciousness, and the relationship between thought and action.[11] Her work moves beyond the liberal feminist vision of a "good society" to draw upon all of the types of feminism discussed in this chapter.

Second wave liberal feminists (1960s–1980s) have used the language of reform liberalism to argue for the right to the vote, for equal rights of property ownership, and for equal employment opportunity. The inclusion of gender as a protected category in the 1964 Civil Rights Act has opened a door for the passage of additional legislation pertaining to women. One example of this is the 1972 passage of Title IX, which mandates greater funding for women's sports at public schools and colleges.

Contemporary liberal feminist challenges are wide ranging. Liberal feminists use litigation strategies to force greater protection of individuals. Recent Supreme Court decisions regarding sexual harassment have extended and clarified the protection the law affords. These advances include identifying clearer legal definitions of sexual harassment, which is viewed under the law as a form of workplace discrimination. In addition, abortion rights continues to be a highly contested issue both within the feminist community and among the general population.

---

10. Patricia Hill Collins, *Black Feminist Thought: Knowledge, Consciousness and the Politics of Empowerment* (Boston: Unwin Hyman, 1990), p. 3.

11. *Ibid.,* Chapter Two.

ORIGINS: MARXIST FEMINISM

Marxism, as much as liberalism, is a product of modernism. Although Karl Marx's writings are critical of capitalism as a system of production, he believed his alternative, communism, was scientific in nature and that it offered a universal explanation of the distribution of power in society. Grounded in "historical materialism," this explanation is the basis of a social and economic theory rivaling classical liberalism.

As was discussed in Part One, Marxism, like other forms of socialism, begins with an analysis of material production. Marxism focuses on the groups and relationships that emerge from economic production and the capacity of people to work. Liberalism, by contrast, focuses on individuals exercising their capacity to reason, to explain the existence of government.

Barbara Arneil observes: "Production and the conflicts which emerge as a result of the different relationships groups of people have with the means of production, lies at the heart of both history and politics, properly understood, according to Marx."[12] The "groups of people" described above would, according to Marx, be organized in social classes. The two classes that are central to Marx's critiques of capitalism are the capitalist class (or *Bourgeoisie*) and the industrial working class (or *Proletariat*). Other important tenets of Marxism include a class analysis of society, an examination of the historical divisions of labor leading to class conflict, a vision of human alienation under capitalism and a belief in the communal ownership of property and productive resources.[13]

All socialist and Marxist feminists focus on economic inequality as a source of political inequality, but specific critiques tend to be based on one of the tenets of Marxism. Some Marxist feminist theories involve challenges to existing class relationships, especially as they create a double oppression for women—one based upon her class position and one based upon gender and discriminatory practices within family structures. An orthodox Marxist feminist would argue that gender-based inequalities are a product of the capitalist period. Thus, when capitalism is overthrown by socialist revolutions (to be followed by communism), women will be liberated to stand as equals in a classless society.

In sum, Marxist feminists are critical of liberalism and the possibility of political equality leading to economic or social equality for women. Specific feminist criticisms, as well as their visions of the "good society," are as diverse as the many tenets of Marxism. Marxism and other socialist theories serve as a basis, and a point of criticism, for the radical theories that emerged in the 1960s with the "Second Wave" of feminist activism.

---

12. Arneil, *Politics and Feminism*, p. 138

13. *Ibid,* p. 138–140; *The Communist Manifesto* in Robert Tucker, ed. *The Marx-Engels Reader,* 2nd ed. (New York: W. W. Norton, 1978).

ORIGINS: RADICAL FEMINISM

Radical feminism emerged out of the social movements in post-World War II America. Frustrated by gender-based discrimination in the civil rights and anti-war movements, many women activists became convinced that neither liberal nor Marxist visions of the good society would lead to true equality for women. While these views were not new, the clarification and development of the concept of "patriarchy" as a structure independent of, and yet intimately entwined with other forms of oppression against women, and the focus on women's biology as a tool for liberation, set radical feminism apart from the socialist and psychological elements it emerged from.

According to Alison Jaggar, radical feminists define patriarchy as a system of male domination, based upon the sexual assignment of roles in private and public life to women and men, respectively. Radical feminist strategies for overcoming oppression focus on overcoming gender-based social inequalities created by patriarchy, as well as moving beyond "female" and "male" to the concept of gender.[14] Gender assumes that sex roles are socially constructed, thus there are many possible identities beyond the duality of male and female.

A variety of strategies for overcoming patriarchy emerged during this period. Examples include consciousness-raising groups for women and many other sexually separate activities. The power of lesbian separatist movements that gained strength in the 1960s is still felt today. Although the understanding of what constitutes oppression is different for radical feminists than it is for liberal and Marxist feminists, they share a belief in the universality of women's oppression. Later radical thinkers, such as Adrienne Rich, move beyond the traditional confines of duality and universality to recognition of "the complexity of women's experience of domination."[15] These thinkers set the stage, in America, for the third wave of feminism; one that rejects universality and duality in favor of difference and multiple identities.

ORIGINS: POST-MODERNIST FEMINISM

As previously discussed, many contemporary feminists hope to avoid the kind of hyphenated subordination that terms like "post-modern feminism" suggests. The focus of this current wave of activism might best be illustrated by the theme of the 1995 United Nations Conference on Women, "Seeing the World Through a Woman's Eyes."[16] Third wavers challenge the common beliefs in all grand polit-

---

14. Jaggar, Chapter Five.

15. Jaggar, p. 118.

16. Arneil, *Politics and Feminism,* p. 154.

ical theories. In the place of theory, many scholars use a variety of methods, including the analysis of language and texts, and deconstruction of theories, to reveal underlying power relationships. No single research method is commonly adhered to, thus the voices of many people marginalized by traditional academic and social discourse are allowed to emerge in their own right.

Most important among these marginalized voices are those voices of women of color and others whose life experience is shaped by multiple identities, i.e., mother, worker, Chicana, lesbian, immigrant, etc. Post-modern thinking allows and encourages the recognition of their diverse positions in society. Within the third wave there are criticisms of past theories, but we are beginning to see the emergence of feminist writings that are also *reconstructive*.[17] Areas where the scholarship is emerging, including feminist legal studies"[18] and a focus on lesbian identity, including "Queer Theory." Excitement and complication emerge in the third wave of feminism, when the traditional structures of theory are set aside. In their respective works, third wave thinkers reflect the complications of attempting to overcome dualistic thinking.[19]

CONCLUSION

Historically, feminist movements have embraced both theory and practice to overcome the oppression faced by women. The changes that come about as a result of women's liberation benefit each member of society, not just women. From the formal equality espoused by first wave feminists to the current focus on identity and difference, feminist theories, and the critical debate they engender, continue to be important catalysts for social change and to reflect the cutting edge of social thought at any given time.

17. See, for example, Nancy J. Hirschmann and Christine Di Stefano, eds., *Revisioning the Political: Feminist Reconstructions of Traditional Concepts in Western Political Theory* (Boulder, Colo.: Westview Press, 1996).

18. Susan J. Hekman, *Moral Voices, Moral Selves: Carol Gilligan and Feminist Moral Theory* (University Park, PA: Penn State University, 1995), p. 161.

19. See, for example, the works of Donna Haraway, Trinh T. Minh-ha and Gloria Anzaldua, Iris Marian Young and Patricia Hill Collins.

CHAPTER ELEVEN

RACE AND NATIONAL LIBERATION

VERNON JOHNSON

*The most powerful as well as creative results of
the nationlist imagination in Asia and Africa are posited not on an identity, but rather on a
difference with the modular forms of the national society propagated by the modern west.*

PARTHA CHATTERJEE

Racial inequality is a major form of human inequality not addressed in the classical treatments of ideology. But the major proponents of every ideology discussed in this text held definite views regarding the inferiority of non-Europeans. And wherever we have seen attempts to put those ideologies into practice, racism has been manifested in their implementation.

The world in which political ideologies grew up was the world of Western civilization. To say Western is to say European, and white. It was a world that accrued increasing power to itself vis-à-vis the rest of the planet from the fifteenth century onward. Thus, the two dimensions of the ideological spectrum that we have employed throughout the text, those of difference/similarity and power/freedom, have been combined in the service of racial domination and the pursuit of racial liberation. The major themes of world history from the sailings of Columbus to the present have been the expansion of Western European influence and control across the globe, the attitudes of Europeans toward "the others" they encountered, and the responses of "others" to that European expansion.

The thing that steadily separated Europe from the rest of the world over those centuries was the scientific revolution and its increasing application of scientific knowledge to control over nature. It was the application of scientific knowledge to navigational technologies that allowed Europeans to travel and trade globally. And it was also the superior application of scientific know-how that spawned the military technologies that came to be the core of European dominance in every corner of the world.

THE VISION OF WHITE SUPREMACY

Although the process developed unevenly from place to place, by the seventeenth century the almost universal European response to contact with non-Europeans was white supremacy: the idea that white Europeans were biologically and culturally superior to the inhabitants of the rest of the world. As Paul Gordon Lauren documents in his *Power and Prejudice,* biology and anthropology were instrumental in reinforcing cultural racism with a racism based in science. The Swedish naturalist Carol von Linnaeus published *Systema Naturae* in 1735 detailing a hierarchy of the races with whites at the apex and blacks at the bottom next to the subhuman category of "monstrous."[1] The renowned German physiologist Johann Friedrich Blumenbach is often credited with founding the discipline of anthropology. He "introduced the term Caucasian" in 1775, and in his own typology averred that "the white color holds first place," while the other races were "merely degenerates from the original."[2] A century later, the great Charles Darwin himself contributed to scientific racism. Although the overtly racist principles of social Darwinism were heralded by others, the seeds of the doctrine could be found in Darwin's own work. In his *Descent of Man* (1871), Darwin predicted that "the civilized races of man will almost certainly exterminate and replace the savage races throughout the world."[3]

Philosophy and ideology were not immune from modern intellectual racism. In relationship to the themes running through this text, nearly all Western ide-

---

1. Paul Gordon Lauren, *Power and Prejudice: The Politics and Diplomacy of Racial Discrimination,* 2nd ed. (Boulder, Colo.: Westview Press, 1996), p. 21.

2. Ident.

3. Charles Darwin, in "The Descent of Man and Selection in Relation to Sex" (1871) in Lauren, *Power and Prejudice,* p. 37.

ologies have thought that the differences between Europeans and others were more important than their similarities. And freedom, for ideologies that promoted it, was something Europeans might realize; but others were subject to European authority. For ideologies based in authoritarianism, the primary concern was collective white authority over non-whites.

One might expect Enlightenment thinkers, who were generally concerned with ending oppression and any barriers to the fulfillment of human potential, to be more enlightened with regard to matters of race; but for the most part, they were not! The Scottish philosopher David Hume exclaimed that "there was never a civilization of any other complexion than white, nor even an individual eminent either in action or speculation."[4] Voltaire believed that as a result of the hierarchy of nations, Negroes are thus slaves to other men."[5] The classical liberal philosopher John Locke, who was read by most of the American founders, invested in the slave trade and was an apologist for slavery.[6]

Struggling as they were to create a new world in the North American wilderness, it is not surprising that founders themselves held similar views. Thomas Jefferson, one of the more liberal of the founders, wrote that blacks "are inferior to whites."[7] Socialist thinking has not been immune to white supremacist thinking. Karl Marx himself was generally disparaging in his remarks toward non-European societies. He saw in the long and glorious history of the Indian subcontinent "semi-barbarian, semi-civilised communities" which had "no history at all" prior to British conquest.[8] There were always countering views upholding the essential humanity and dignity of people of color, but the point here is to simply illustrate the way in which white supremacist views were very influential in the mainstream of Western political thought.[9]

The white supremacist views of Europeans made their way into the institutions of government in two major ways. Most Africans, Asians, and natives of the Americas became associated with white supremacist government through the colonial systems of one or another of the great European powers. Only a com-

---

4. *Ibid.,* p. 22.

5. *Ibid.,* p. 22.

6. For an extended discussion of Locke's complicated views on racial slavery, see James Farr, "So Vile and Miserable an Estate: The Problem of Slavery," in Locke's *Political Theory,* May, 1986.

7. Michael Omi and Howard Winant, *Racial Formation in the United States: From the 1960s to the 1980s* (New York: Routledge, 1991), p. 183.

8. See Marx, "On Imperialism in India," p. 581, and "The Future Results of British Rule in India," p. 583, both in Robert C. Tucker, *The Marx-Engels Reader* (New York: W. W. Norton and Company, 1972).

9. See Lauren, *op. cit.,* for a portrayal of debates about race in Western societies since 1492.

paratively small number of whites were required to actually live among the natives. Colonial administrators, some military forces, and metropolitan capitalists might live in the colonies, normally on a temporary basis. In every instance Europeans lived separately from the natives, and were party to a different constellation of rights and obligations before the law. The object of the colonial system was to subject territories and peoples to European overlordship in order to extract wealth.

By the late nineteenth century, when the last great surge of colonization was taking place, liberal and socialist ideas were contending for the hearts and minds of European publics. Both ideologies talked about the rights of man in universal terms, and to that extent, were sympathetic to the plight of the colonized. But in order to rationalize the denial of self-government to the colonized, new ideological twists were devised. The French and the Portuguese heralded their "civilizing mission" in Africa and Asia. They argued that they were in the colonies to extend the virtues of French, or Portuguese civilization to the colonials. The British acknowledged that they were trying to civilize the natives, but lamented their cultural backwardness. Instead of the glory of the civilizing mission, the British cited the uncertainties of the "white man's burden" in the colonies.[10]

A second kind of colonialism could be found where hospitable climates and abundant natural resources compelled large numbers of Europeans to settle in colonial countries. These "white settler colonies" featured sweeping expropriations of the land from natives, some of the most brutal forms of native labor exploitation, rigid social segregation of the races, and the nearly complete denial of native political rights within the governing white political system. The United States, Canada, Australia, New Zealand, Algeria, and Rhodesia were some of the more prominent of these white settler colonies.

THE EMERGENCE OF RACIAL NATIONALISM

In the first decade of the twentieth century, European countries, or their descendents, governed approximately 85% of the world's people and its territory. But the same military-industrial power that had allowed white nations to rule the world soon undermined the continuing efficacy of that rule. The human tragedy of World War I, ironically, unleashed ideological forces that led to decolonization. The causes of the war are beyond the scope of this chapter. But after the first two years of fighting, the terrible loss of life had caused all sides to be reluctant to attack. After much prodding, the United States was finally convinced to enter the

---

10. Regarding the colonial ideologies of the different European powers, see Robert O. Collins, *Problems in the History of Colonial Africa, 1860–1960* (Englewood Cliffs, N.J.: Prentice-Hall, 1970).

war on the side of Great Britain, France, and Russia. But American President Woodrow Wilson would only enter the war if his country could place its stamp on the configuration of the post-war global order. Like most Americans, President Wilson found European struggles over power and empire immoral. He sought to end war and imperialism after the war was over. Wilson called for the creation of a League of Nations to pursue collective security among states. One of the pillars of his plan was allowing self-determination of the many national groups laboring under the yoke of various European empires.

Immediately, after the war, several new European states were created out of the ashes of the German, Austro-Hungarian, and Ottoman and Russian empires.[11] The non-European colonies of Germany, and former Ottoman holdings in the Middle East, were placed under the League of Nations Mandate. That system placed former colonies under the rule of victorious powers, either Great Britain or France, for tutelage along the path to self-governance. But the discourse on self-determination that was propagated by Wilson could not be contained within European borders. Africans and Asians from the colonies were studying in Europe during the war. Many others had received missionary educations at home. These people followed the events of the war and listened to Wilson's words with great interest. The language of self-determination had been pitched in universal terms, and peoples from Africa and Asia thought it might pertain to them, too. From the Peace of Versailles on, movements for self-determination rose up across the colonial world. In every case, they took nationalism as their ideology.

In most cases these colonized areas were hardly nations. They had been configured according to the interests and limits of the several colonial powers. They usually contained within them a diversity of ethnic and religious groups. They would expend a great deal of energy over the rest of the century determining what it meant to be a member of their nations in a positive sense; *but all third world nationalist ideologies have been against colonialism and the system of white supremacy that came with it.*

In the white settler colonies, the penetration of the Wilsonian discourse led to calls for "racial equality."

In settler colonies that remained a part of a European empire, ruling whites had usually achieved a level of self-government by the 1920s. As they witnessed the growth of native nationalist movements in neighboring countries, whites usually came up with ideologies that would permit educated and middle class natives to vote, while the masses continued to be denied. In this way, whites could be the majority of the electorate and still have things their way. These innovations always

---

11. Yugoslavia, Albania, Austria, Hungary, Turkey, Poland, Czechoslovakia, Finland, Romania, Bulgaria, Latvia, Lithuania, and Estonia.

ultimately failed. Natives responded by pursuing more radical strategies in these cases as well. Revolutionary nationalism heavily influenced by Marxism was the typical ideological progression here, tied to an armed guerrilla insurrection intending to dislodge white rule.

Some of the settler colonies, such as the United States, Australia, and South Africa, were already independent by World War I. Movements among natives and other people of color in these "post-white settler colonies" to gain equality before the law met resistance from whites.[12] This caused large numbers of people of color to become frustrated and impatient with the pace of change and the continuing indignities heaped upon them. They began to develop ideologies of cultural and racial nationalism to foster a sense of pride and esteem in who they were. These more radical ideologies were usually accompanied by more aggressive political strategies for bringing about social change.

In the colonies, settler colonies and post-settler colonies alike, a major component of nationalism among peoples of color has been liberation from the institutions of white supremacy. The next section describes the features of some prominent cultural and racial nationalist ideologies.

CULTURAL NATIONALIST IDEOLOGIES OF PEOPLES OF COLOR

Anti-Colonial Nationalisms

In the twentieth century, the major parts of the world remaining under European direct rule were nearly all of Africa, south and southeast Asia, and parts of the Middle East. It was in these regions that the Wilsonian discourse on self-determination ramified after the Peace of Versailles in 1919. In each of these regions, we see movements for national self-determination that employ some kind of cultural or racial argument as part of their reasoning about the need for independence. Colonialism, in denying the capacity for self-government, was viewed as a fundamental abridgement of the rights of man. In analyzing the *raison d'etre* for their colonization, the nationalists analyzed the impact of the civilizing mission on the mindset of their countrymen and women. Becoming civilized entailed rejecting one's native culture and becoming as much like the Europeans as possible. However, the economic and educational opportunity structure of colonial systems was not set up to offer large numbers of the natives a chance to become civilized in the white man's terms. Those economies, as we said earlier, were geared toward the extraction of wealth and the subjection of

---

12. "Post-white settler colonial situation" is Ibbo Mandaza's phrase, in Mandaza, ed., *Zimbabwe: The Political Economy of Transition, 1980–1981* (Harare, Zimbabwe: Jongwe Press, 1987).

natives toward that end. Besides, the very notion of a civilizing mission presumed that native cultures were uncivilized, unsophisticated, and, in general, had nothing of value to offer a modernizing and industrializing world. Under the weight of these ideas and the demonstrated physical superiority of European technology, colonial natives experienced a collective loss of self-esteem and pride in their cultures.

The first job of colonial nationalists was to resurrect their peoples from the psychological and ideological burden of white supremacy. When people believed in themselves and the worth of their cultures, they might then acquire the confidence to mobilize politically to achieve their independence. Along with being against colonial white supremacy, nationalist thought was concerned with fabricating a nation and a national idea from what frequently were a multiplicity of cultural groups within the colonial territory. It is for this reason that the racial critique of colonialism became so crucial. The racism and experience of indignities at the hands of whites was the main thing colonized peoples had in common. It was also the starting point for nation-building, which involved the creation of new institutions after colonialism, but more immediately, *the social construction of the myth of a nation in the late colonial period.* Let us now turn to the differing ways that colonial nationalists pursued their ideological project.

The archetype for anti-colonial nationalist movements in the twentieth century was that of India. The Indian Congress Party founded in 1885 was the driving force for the movement. By the 1920s, Congress was clamoring for independence from the British Empire under the leadership of Mohandas (Mahatma) Gandhi and Jawaharlal Nehru. The Indian subcontinent was home to a proud civilization based around the Hindu religion. The country subsequently became a crossroads for the religious, cultural, and political developments of southern and western Asia for more than four thousand years. Since the sixteenth century, India had suffered under foreign rule, first by the Muslim Mughals, and from the late eighteenth century, at the hands of the British. Through all of the ebbs and flows of history, however, India retained a sense of national unity, while also developing a tradition for tolerance of cultural and religious pluralism, and political decentralization of power.

Indian nationalism actually begins in the realm of culture, a generation before the formation of the Congress Party. Indian nationalists developed the idea that in response to Western modernity there were two domains to consider: the outer and the inner. Indian political philosopher Partha Chatterjee nicely delineates the difference between the two.

> "The material is the *domain of the outside,* of the economy and of statecraft, of science and technology, a domain where the West had proven its superiority and the East had succumbed. In this domain, then, Western superiority had to be

acknowledged and its accomplishments carefully studied and replicated. The spiritual, on the other hand, is an *inner domain,* bearing the essential marks of cultural identity."[13]

Indian cultural nationalism was expressed through the print media, the arts, education, and the orientation toward the family. Chatterjee goes on to posit that in this inner domain, "the nation is already sovereign, even when the state is in the hands of the colonial power."[14] Chatterjee points out that the distinction between the inner and outer domains is characteristic of many third world countries striving to create a sense of nationhood. Under the intellectual and spiritual guidance of Gandhi and Nehru, the nationalist movement elaborated upon the distinction between the two domains. To the charge that the West was civilized and India was not, Gandhi countered that India too was civilized. It was just different. From Greece and Rome, to the twentieth century, the West had seen a series of civilizations that had come and gone, while India had weathered many historic influences, yet remained India. For Gandhi, the West was materialistic, acquisitive, competitive, and individualistic and in the end required immoral behavior to achieve success. On the other hand, India was spiritualistic, unconcerned about acquiring wealth, communitarian, and moral.[15] Nehru added that while India had a penchant for stability, the technological drive of the West induced ceaseless change. And, for all of its creativity, the military-industrial competition between the great Western powers threatened to destroy the whole of humankind.[16]

Buttressed by a sense of self-worth that grew out of an ancient and high civilization, Indian nationalism was more cultural than racial, and more anti-Western than anti-white. And because there was a grand Indian tradition that could be looked back to, it could seek to modernize the state and the economy to harness the magic of Western material power, and use those same material forces to insulate the inner cultural and spiritual domain from Western contamination. Gandhi's belief in the superiority of spiritual power over material force informed his notion of "satyagraha," or passive resistance. This became Congress's strategy of nonviolent civil disobedience against British rule, which led to decolonization of India in 1947.

The Gandhian strategy of passive resistance became the model for movements against colonialism across Asia and Africa from the 1920s to the 1960s

---

13. Partha Chatterjee, *The Nation and Its Fragments: Colonial and Postcolonial Histories* (Princeton, N.J.: Princeton University Press, 1993), p. 6.

14. Ident.

15. Mohandas K. Gandhi, "Indian Home Rule," in Paul E. Sigmund, ed., *The Ideologies of the Developing Nations* (New York: Praeger, 1972), pp. 112–113.

16. Jawaharlal Nehru, "The Discovery of India," in Sigmund, ed., *op. cit.,* pp. 132–133.

(and even into the 1980s if one includes the anti-apartheid struggle in South Africa). Most countries emerging from colonialism, however, did not have a coherent cultural tradition upon which to build a modern nation. Nevertheless, they employed the inner/outer domain strategy to undertake the social construction of nations where colonialism had thrown disparate peoples together. Africa was particularly afflicted by this problem of excessive cultural pluralism. Anti-colonial African nationalists responded to this situation by positing an overarching civilizational unity that bound Africans regardless of their parochial affinities.

There were two broad tendencies in this effort to construct a unified African civilization. One was African Socialism. African Socialists, generally, argued that traditional Africa exercised socialist values, albeit in a preindustrial setting. Kwame Nkrumah (1909–1972), the first president of independent Ghana in West Africa, maintained that traditional African societies held the values of egalitarianism, humanism, and communalism.[17] *Humanism* is the idea that each individual has dignity and self-creativity, which the social order ought to uphold. *Egalitarianism* means that individuals are viewed as equals in their humanity. *Communalism* is a political and economic system in which the labors of individuals are dedicated, primarily, to the collective or communal welfare. Taken together, these values can be seen as a socialist value system.

As preindustrial economies living near the subsistence level, it is possible that most traditional African societies probably did operate, roughly, according to the principles Nkrumah identified. But over the centuries, as Nkrumah also points out, Africa was also ravaged by Islamic and European conquests. As African countries sped toward independence, therefore, they were racked by what Nkrumah called a crisis of conscience. That crisis issued from the presence of three Africas in the hearts and minds of its people as they were arriving at independence: traditional Africa, Islamic Africa, and Euro-Christian Africa. For Nkrumah, many Africans were conflicted, because of their adherence to parts of each of these three great traditions. And he would say that by the time independence was approaching, nearly all Africans were affected by at least two of them. The challenge for governments in newly independent African states was to fabricate a national myth that would advance traditional African values, and synthesize them with Islamic and Euro-Christian beliefs and values through the modern state.

A more explicit racial orientation can be found in the philosophy of "Negritude" put forward by Léopold Senghor (b. 1906), the first president of the

---

17. Kwame Kkrumah, *Consciencism; Philosophy and Ideology for Decolonization* (New York: Monthly Review Press, 1970), Chapter 3; see also the writings of Julius Nyerere, *Ujama—The Basis of African Socialism,* in Sigmund, ed., *op. cit.,* pp. 299–305.

West African country of Senegal. Against the dehumanization of colonial subjection, Senghor declared a Negro-African humanity. In his schematic, white humanity achieves its rationality through analysis, and in doing so separates itself from other humans and nature. This sets off a competition between humans as individuals and human communities, which is ultimately dehumanizing for all. In contrast, black humanity becomes rational through intuition and feeling. In feeling for "the other" Negritude suggests harmony and oneness with other humans, and nature. His thorough-going humanism leads Senghor to aver that socialism is a superior political and economic system to capitalism. This warmth of feeling for humanity is the black world's contribution to a future planetary civilization.[18]

From the Arab world we get a portrait of psychological crisis parallel to what Nkrumah sees in Africa in the writings of Gamal Abdel Nasser, who was the President of Egypt from 1956–1970. He observes the fact that, as a crossroads of the world since ancient times, Egypt has been influenced by many great civilizations, but has also been the object of many conquests. Nasser himself led a military coup in 1952 to rid Egypt of a monarchy that was a puppet of Great Britain. He perceived that centuries of being buffeted around by successive imperialists had left the Egyptian people unstable and lacking in self-esteem. Moreover, the history of the entire Middle East and North Africa had witnessed a similar set of experiences. Therefore, these Arab peoples constituted a nation for Nasser. Arab nationalism was cemented by a shared Arabic language, a culture based upon the traditions of Judaism, Christianity, and Islam, and a political orientation based upon the region's strategic importance due to its geographic position and its oil wealth.

Arabism was only one of what Nasser called the three circles composing the Arab nation. The second circle was the continent of Africa. Referring to the Arab world as "the guardians of the Continent's northern gate," he argued the struggle for decolonization south of the Sahara was intertwined with the Arabs' own quest for self-determination. The third circle was the Islamic world. Nasser also saw all Muslim countries from North Africa to Southeast Asia as united in their faith, and in their common aspiration for self-determination as Muslim nations.[19]

In differing ways across the world that was moving from colonialism to independence we see leaders reaching for a formula to dismantle the ideological edifice of European supremacy, and simultaneously, construct a positive national identity out of the cultural disarray bequeathed to them. In most cases, colonized countries gained independence after a period of nonviolent political agitation

18. Leopold Senghor, "What Is Negritude?" in Sigmund, ed., *The Ideologies...*, pp. 250–252.

19. Nasser, "The Philosophy of Revolution," in Sigmund, ed., *The Ideologies....*, pp. 150–156.

convinced the colonizers of the seriousness of their claims. In colonies where there were significant numbers of white settlers, however, the scenario was frequently different.

Anti-Settler Colonialism

Whites in the settler colonial world were politically enfranchised in the twentieth century. In British settler colonies, representative government was usually extended to whites only, sometime between the 1920s and 1950s. In Portuguese and French Africa, whites participated in metropolitan representative institutions. This disparity in political rights only increased native hostility toward the system. In response to the global discourse on self-determination, settler colonies fabricated ideologies attempting to illustrate the legitimacy of the colonial order. In elaborating the rationale for continuing colonialism those ideologies were also required to account for the racial inequality of the system.

Typical of British Africa was the white response in Central Africa. From the 1920s, settlers in Southern Rhodesia had held "responsible government," a system which gave them virtual autonomy in domestic affairs and excluded Africans from participation. In the 1930s Southern Rhodesian Prime Minister Godfrey Huggins began to call for amalgamation of Southern and Northern Rhodesia and Nyasaland into a federation that might eventually gain full independence from Great Britain. Huggins envisioned a system of "racial partnership" in the new polity. That partnership, according to Huggins would be akin to that "between 'a horse and rider' in which African beasts of burden would be ridden by European riders toward economic development and prosperity."[20] On the basis of that understanding, the Central African Federation was launched in 1953. The Federation was unstable from the beginning. In order to legitimize the notion of racial partnership, the small but growing African middle class was to be extended voting and broader political rights, while the masses continued to be disenfranchised. Against the backdrop of growing African nationalist movements in all three territories, the federal franchise law passed in 1958. In a polity where 95% of the people were African, only 7% of eligible voters were African.[21] This was the best that British settlers were prepared to offer in terms of racial partnership.

In the early 1960s, the federation collapsed as African nationalists led Northern Rhodesia and Nyasaland to independence. However, in the south settlers were a larger percentage of the population and more firmly entrenched. They declared their

---

20. In Vernon Johnson, *Coalition Formation and Social Revolution in Ethiopia and Zimbabwe,* Ph.D. Dissertation, Pullman, Wash.: Washington State University, 1985, p. 93 n.

21. *Ibid.,* pp. 89–105.

independence from Great Britain unilaterally in 1965. Africans replied by forming two separate guerrilla movements: The Zimbabwe African People's Union (ZAPU) and the Zimbabwe African National Union (ZANU). Each adopted a strategy of pursuing armed struggle to achieve majority rule in 1965. ZAPU had been the main nationalist party until 1963, when a split along ethnic lines occurred. But the unified nationalist movement had developed a racial consciousness vis-à-vis white supremacy under a succession of political parties by the 1950s. The African National Congress, a forerunner of ZAPU, called for "national unity . . . in true partnership, regardless of race, colour or creed" in 1957.[22]

The revolutionary nationalism articulated after 1965 had several components typical of guerrilla ideologies worldwide after 1945. Along with the commitment to *armed struggle* came the adoption of *socialism* as a long-range goal for the future post-revolutionary society. The *mobilization of the rural peasant masses* was undertaken to prosecute the war. That mobilization had to be stimulated by politicizing the peasants' consciousness of their racial oppression. Revolutionary guerrillas tried to create *liberated zones.* These are areas in the countryside where their popular mobilization prevents the colonial state from governing effectively. In those liberated zones, the guerrillas usually attempted erect *embryonic state-like institutions.* In other words, they begin to govern themselves.

A big key to the success of such movements is their ability to gain important *international supporters* by relating global standards regarding human rights to their struggles. During the Cold War, the Soviet Union was eager to support anti-colonial revolutions in the Third World because they saw opportunities to increase their influence at the expense of the West. This was especially true if those movements espoused socialism. But another crucial source of support for anti-colonial guerrillas was sectors of the public in Western countries themselves. The guerrilla movements had offices in many of the major Western capitals and became expert at mobilizing public backing, and even legislative support around their quest for self-determination. Comprehensive global economic sanctions were imposed on Rhodesia under the United Nations in 1968.

The combination of guerrilla insurrection, arming by the Soviet bloc, and diplomatic isolation from the entire world placed tremendous pressures on settler colonial regimes. It is important to recognize the central role of ideological forces in bringing these changes: revolutionary nationalism in compelling the colonized to uprise, and the ideology of human rights in forging the global alliance that ultimately brought white supremacist regimes down.[23]

---

22. Nathan Shamuyarira, *Crisis in Rhodesia* (London: A. Deutsch, 1965), p. 46.

23. This argument about the role of ideology and international actors is made fully in Vernon D. Johnson, "The Structural Causes of Anticolonial Revolutions in Africa," *Alternatives,* No. 18, 1993, pp. 201–227.

Post-Settler Colonial Nationalism

Many countries originated as white settler colonies and were able to achieve political independence without dismantling white supremacy. Because Great Britain had the world's largest and most successful colonial empire, it is not surprising that practically all of these *post-white settler colonies* are in former British colonies. The United States and the Republic of South Africa illustrate this phenomenon. Both of these countries gained independence before World War I, that is, prior to the impact of Wilsonian norms of human rights on global society. As we have shown above, that was a time in which the ideology of white supremacy was everywhere ascendant. Neither the founders of the United States, nor South Africa experienced significant pressures for racial equality as they were structuring their constitutions. However, those pressures became manifest in the two as independent countries.

The United States had been independent from Britain for nearly 150 years by the time of the Peace of Versailles. It was already the richest and most powerful country in the world, and arguably, the most politically stable. It had a long history of institutionalized white supremacy beginning with the dispossession of the native populations and the enslavement of blacks. But it had also incorporated successive waves of European immigrants into the white population since independence, making whites, by far, the majority of the population. This vast white majority placed the United States in a less vulnerable position, culturally and politically, than some of the countries we have discussed, thus far. While pushing its racial minorities to the margins of society, it had successfully inculcated the myth of liberty and limitless individual possibilities into white population.

The issue of racial equality had emerged in the U.S. at the time of its Civil War in the 1860s over the question of what to do about its black population now free from slavery. Though blacks were initially given full citizenship and the right to vote, the entrenched racism of whites caused a reinterpretation of post-Civil War amendments and laws that allowed for a reconfigured white supremacy. The *Plessy v. Ferguson* U.S. Supreme Court decision of 1896 codified the doctrine of "separate but equal" access to public accommodations, education and housing as the American way of life. The separate but equal doctrine was rigidly enforced in the eleven states that had formed the Confederacy during the civil war. But it is important to realize that physical and social segregation from whites and inferior educational and job opportunities were the norm for people of color throughout the country until the 1960s.[24]

---

24. For a discussion of institutionalized white supremacy with regard to all non-whites in America, see Ronald Takaki, *A Different Mirror: A History of Multi-Cultural America* (Boston: Little, Brown and Company, 1993).

In the fifties and sixties, a powerful civil rights movement led to the transformation of the American political system into one that legally supported racial equality. The ideology of that movement was termed *racial integration*. The earliest breakthrough was *Brown v. Board of Education of Topeka Kansas,* a U.S. Supreme Court decision in 1954, which ended legal school segregation and undermined the logic of segregation in other areas. Over the next decade, the civil rights movement led by Dr. Martin Luther King, Jr., precipitated the passage of the Civil Rights Act of 1964 and the Voting Rights Act of 1965. These laws led to the mass enfranchisement of blacks, Latinos, and many Asian and Native Americans, as well as sweeping changes in daily American life regarding matters of race. But the movement to bring racial equality had taken its toll. Civil rights workers in the American South were routinely harassed, intimidated, and sometimes physically assaulted. Some even lost their lives. Many of the young African American civil rights workers became radicalized, losing faith in the political system and the humanity of white Americans in general. In 1966, they began to call for *Black Power,* the establishment of separate political, economic, educational, and cultural institutions for African Americans. The seminal work in articulating the vision for Black Power was the text of the same name written by activist Stokely Carmichael and political scientist Charles V. Hamilton. Their argument revolves around what they called the "three myths" of coalition politics.[25] The first myth was that the interest of black people and liberal white groups could ever coincide. The second was that viable coalitions could be formed between the economically and politically powerful and those who are economically and politically weak. Finally, they held that it was a myth to believe that political coalitions are sustained on the basis of morality.

Carmichael and Hamilton's cynicism stemmed from the experience of the Student Nonviolent Coordinating Committee (SNCC) in working with the Democratic Party. At the 1964 Democratic National Convention, SNCC sought to get the integrated Mississippi Freedom Democratic Party (MFDP) seated instead of the all-white Mississippi regulars. After many liberal constituencies in the party had agreed to support the MFDP, they abandoned it under pressure from President Lyndon Johnson. This proved to SNCC members that black-white political coalitions were untenable, and that black people needed to create their own political and economic institutions.[26]

---

25. For a discussion of the "three myths" and the experience of the Mississippi Freedom Democratic Party, see Stokely Carmichael and Charles V. Hamilton, *Black Power: The Politics of Liberation in America* (New York: Vintage Books, 1967).

26. See Alphonse Pinkney, *Red, Black, and Green: Black Nationalism in the United States* (New York: Cambridge University Press, 1976); and John McCartney, *Black Power Ideologies: An Essay in African-American Political Thought* (Philadelphia: Temple University Press, 1992) for detailed discussions of black nationalism in the U.S.

This aspiration for *racial separatism* was mirrored in Latino communities in the *Chicano movement*.[27] And Native Americans, who had always had institutional separatism with their treaty rights, began to voice their claims around tribal sovereignty more loudly. Ironically, once the genie of racial equality was let out of the bottle, people of color were not satisfied with legal equality and the integration of public accommodations. They wanted rapid redress for grinding poverty, deplorable living conditions, second-class educational opportunities and the continuation of widespread economic and social discrimination. When change came slowly, radical nationalisms of people of color emerged. They made demands that might lead to the dismemberment of the U.S. as a territorial entity, or the abandonment of the values upon which the nation had been built.

These radical nationalisms took two trajectories: cultural nationalism and socialist nationalism. Many *cultural nationalists* sought secession of a part of the U.S. and the creation of a new state for their group. Organizations like the Nation of Islam and the Republic of New Africa saw the Southeast as the historic African American homeland since the times of slavery. Under its leader, Elijah Muhammad, the Nation of Islam saw territorial separation as a long-term goal. More immediately, it sought self-reliance in the spheres of religion, economics, and education. The Nation is a religious sect melding principles of black nationalism with Islam. Its adherents believe that white people are a devil-race created by a mad scientist on an island in the Aegean Sea. The fall of the white race is supposed to be imminent, but presently they are thought to be too powerful too defeat. Therefore, black Americans are implored to form their own businesses to develop economic self-sufficiency, and establish their own school systems to provide their children with a positive self-image and also a laboratory where the troops for the coming racial confrontation can be socialized.

The Republic of New Africa, led by Imari Obadele, incorporated views similar to those of the Nation of Islam in terms of economic and educational self-reliance, but it articulated a more aggressive political strategy. After acquiring land in Mississippi in 1972, Obadele declared the inception of the Republic and called for a United Nations-sponsored plebiscite giving African Americans three choices: remaining a part of the U.S., emigrating back to Africa, or establishing a separate homeland in the United States. The Republic of New Africa wanted the southern states of Louisiana, Mississippi, Alabama, Georgia, and South Carolina for a new country for African Americans. Obadele also supported guerrilla warfare against the U.S. to achieve national self-determination.[28]

27. On Chicano separatism, see Alfredo Mirande, *The Chicano Experience: An Alternative Perspective* (Notre Dame, Ind.: University of Notre Dame Press, 1985), p. 75. For the emergence of the Native American political voice, see Alvin Josephy, *Now That the Buffalo's Gone* (Norman, Okla.: University of Oklahoma Presss, 1984).

28. In McCartney, *op. cit.,* pp. 178–180.

Mexican American cultural nationalists have also called for territorial secession. The northern third of the original state of Mexico was incorporated into the United States as a result of the Mexican War, after 1848. Although the Treaty of Guadalupe Hidalgo ending the war guaranteed the protection of Mexican property rights in the newly acquired lands, much land was lost to white Americans by legal maneuver and outright expropriation. There was a great deal of unrest in the American Southwest in the period between 1848 and World War I. In 1915, Mexican American radicals adopted "the Plan de San Diego," which "outlined a military revolt which would lead to the creation of an independent nation in the territory acquired by the U.S. during the Mexican War."[29] In the 1960s, infuriated by tales of lost lands among rural Mexican Americans in New Mexico, Reies Lopez Tijerina formed the Federal Alliance of Land Grants. The "Alianza" initially pegged its hopes for the return of lands on the Treaty of Guadalupe Hidalgo, but later called for their recapture "by any means necessary." In 1969, another Mexican American activist, Rodolfo "Corky" Gonzales, declared the Southwest "Aztlan," the historic homeland of the Chicano people.[30]

Instead of pursuing a secessionist strategy, *socialist nationalists* sought a multiracial socialist alliance to overthrow the American capitalist system. The most famous revolutionary nationalist organization in the U.S. was the Black Panther Party for Self-Defense. The Party was founded in Oakland California in 1966 by Huey P. Newton and Bobby Seale to counter the police brutality so commonplace in African American communities. Panthers patrolled the black communities of Oakland watching police during arrests to see if those arrested were denied their constitutional rights. They typically carried guns and lawbooks. In 1967, the California Legislature introduced a bill to ban the carrying of loaded weapons in urban areas. The Black Panthers traveled to the state capitol, barged in on the legislature and read Executive Mandate One opposing the legislation. They made international news and chapters were formed across the country almost overnight.

Although they made headlines with acts of daring, the Panthers also believed in the philosophy of self-reliance of cultural nationalist groups. They established a number of community services, including free breakfast programs for schoolchildren, health clinics, free clothing outlets, and a Peoples Sickle Cell Anemia Research Foundation.[31] At the same time, Huey Newton advanced an ideology of intercommunalism as a strategy for revolution. In its basic outlines, intercommunalism was similar to a number of revolutionary nationalist ideologies

29. Mirande, *op. cit.,* pp. 74–75.

30. *Ibid.,* pp. 3, 75.

31. Sickle cell anemia is a blood disease found disproportionately in black people.

employing a race/class analysis to devise a strategy for transformation in the U.S. According to this doctrine, African Americans were a colonized nation within the U.S., but their oppression, like that of nations of color the world over, was due to international capitalism. International capitalism represents reactionary inter-communalism for Newton. Revolutionary intercommunalism would ensue, when communities everywhere uprise, overthrow capitalism, "seize the means of production and distribute wealth in an egalitarian way to the communities of the world."[32] Since capitalism was also the real enemy in the United States, and black people were a minority, intercommunalism there meant building an alliance between white revolutionaries and revolutionaries of color to overthrow the government.

The Black Panthers are perhaps the most interesting nationalist movement in the United States during the 1960s and 1970s. Although we have placed them in the socialist nationalist category, their community service programs were geared toward self-reliance in a manner similar to cultural nationalist groups we have discussed. It is no wonder that they captured the imagination of large numbers of black and white youth in their heyday.

CONCLUSION

Nationalist ideologies among the peoples of color of the world have been responses to ideologies of white supremacy emanating from the European world. White supremacy portrayed non-Europeans as different in a way that marked them as inferior. In doing so white supremacy justified power over societies of color everywhere and the denial of their freedom. Nationalists from the world of color have accepted the demarcation of difference and sought to derive a positive sense of dignity and self-worth from it. They have also striven to use nationalism to mobilize their countrymen and women to assert the power of self-determination in politics and in cultural life.

We have discussed nationalism as it pertains to peoples of color, but it is important to recognize the power of nationalist ideas amongst peoples the world over. Leon Baradat has declared that "nationalism is the most powerful political idea of the past several hundred years."[33] The great states of the North Atlantic world that have dominated political, economic, and scientific developments of the modern era were all able to harness the natural and human potential of their lands on the basis of nationalism. It was the stresses of nationalist competition in

---

32. Huey P. Newton, *To Die for the People* (New York: Random House, 1972), p. 32.

33. Leon P. Baradat, *Political Ideologies: Their Origins and Impact,* 5th ed. (Englewood Cliffs, N.J.: Prentice-Hall Publishers, 1994), p. 43.

Europe that caused Fascism and the terrors it unleashed upon humanity. Liberalism and socialism, the other great political doctrines of modernity, have each been worked out in national political contexts. Without nations organized into states, they could not have been effectively put into practice.

Even as liberalism appears ascendant in the twenty-first century, bringing with it urges toward internationalization, nationalism remains a potent force. The breakup of the Soviet Union and Yugoslavia was due to resurgent nationalist sentiments. The creation of Scottish and Welsh Parliaments in Great Britain and the Quebec movement in Canada are examples of the impact of micronationalist projects in the Western world. As powerful as liberal ideas seem at the beginning of the new millennium, the idea that people can achieve both freedom and empowerment through celebrating difference seems as tenacious as ever. Some notion of cultural affinity is the basis of all nationalisms. Humans are social animals even as they are each unique individuals. Nationalism plays to a profound urge in human beings for collective security. This is not a bad thing in and of itself. We can only hope that in the rush for collective security, humans do not perpetrate more of the horrible crimes against humanity we have witnessed in the twentieth century.

CHAPTER TWELVE

ENVIRONMENTALISM

JOHN MILES

The system of the commons we now live under
separates power and responsibility. It is an unstable state. If we want civilization to survive,
and if we are unwilling to go back, then we must go forward. We must take the next step in
evolution and bring power and responsibility together once more, this time in the community.

GARRETT HARDIN
Exploring New Ethics for Survival

We must acknowledge both the centrality and the limits of our self–interest. One can
hardly imagine a tougher situation.

WENDELL BERRY
Home Economics

Everyone lives in the environment. Most take for granted that their needs and wants can be met by the unlimited resources of planet earth. Some may wonder whether the limitlessness of these demands can be matched by limitless natural resources, but they are reassured that if Mother Nature's cupboard becomes bare, technology will develop an alternative and all will be well.

Then there are the environmentalists, that group of worriers who seriously doubt that nature can provide all that is needed and wanted by an ever-growing human population. These people suggest that nature has limits, that there is a carrying capacity or limit to how many humans can live on the planet. They argue that humans must limit the growth of their population, their economies, and their demands. If they do not, the consequences may be dire, such disasters as famine, pestilence, or at least reductions in the quality of human life.

Environmentalists call for constraint and restraint, for adaptation to environmental limits. They call for sustainability, an approach to living on the planet that does not foreclose on the options of future humans. They want to limit human reproduction, conserve Earth's biological diversity, restrain the release of toxic byproducts of human enterprise into the environment. They strive to protect Earth's beautiful places and its wondrous creatures, all the while providing for the needs of the current human generation, wherever on the earth they may be, and assuring such provision for future generations. In short, environmentalists call for human society to adapt to environmental constraints, to limit its consumption of resources and its growth to sustainable levels.

THE ENVIRONMENTAL CHALLENGE)

How can this be achieved? The current situation, at the turn of the century and millennium, is far from this environmentalist goal. The drive for sustainability must, it seems, begin with limiting population, for every additional human adds to the species' stress on nature. Those in the high-consumption developed world add greater stress than in other areas. A recent "medium-fertility" population scenario from the United Nations projects stabilization of fertility rates by 2055 leading to a global population of 9.4 billion by 2050, 10.4 billion by 2100, and 10.8 billion by 2150.[1] These figures compare to a population of 6 billion at the turn of the millenium. Such projections assume that current fertility rates will decline, and this will not happen on its own. Decisions to bring them down will be required, and if the current debates over population control are any indication, these will be difficult decisions to make.

Any description of the challenge of achieving environmental sustainability begins with population because human consumption of resources and impacts on natural systems are the foundation of all environmental problems. The list of problems humans visit upon their environment is very long and, of course, varies geographically around the earth. Global problems include loss of biological diversity, climate change, stratospheric ozone depletion, soil loss, depletion of protein sources such as fisheries, and depletion and pollution of freshwater supplies, to name a few. In the U.S., air pollution continues to be a problem with advances in auto emission controls being overwhelmed by the sheer number of vehicles and miles driven. Waste continues to be generated in vast amounts, posing great

---

1. UN Secretariat, Population Division, *Population Newsletter.* New York: Department of Economic and Social Affairs, No. 65 (June 1998), p. 2

challenges for safe disposal. Land development encroaches upon wetlands, farmlands and other highly productive ecosystems. Freshwater aquifers are consumed and contaminated in many areas. The list goes on.

Forecasting the future is difficult, and forecasts based on linear projections are often wrong, but evidence is very compelling that unless some major changes are made in the way people live upon the earth, the future will be grim for many. For example, the first eight months of 1998 were the warmest on record, a situation attributed by many scientists to global warming to which humans are contributing. Higher temperatures mean more energy driving the climate system, and this contributed in 1998 to serious flooding in China that killed an estimated 2,500 people and displaced 56 million. Monsoon rains in Bangladesh left 21 million homeless that year. A hurricane left destruction on an unprecedented scale in Nicaragua and Honduras. Forty-five countries were stricken with record droughts. Human suffering from all of this was immense.[2] The goal of the environmental movement is often described as "saving the planet," yet no doubt the planet will continue to function regardless of what humans do to it. The challenge really is to "maintain or improve the quality of human life" upon the foundation of a healthy planet.

Each year the Worldwatch Institute produces a report on the state of the world, and in the "Millennial Edition" of this report Lester Brown captures the challenge very succinctly. He writes:

> As we look forward to the twenty-first century, it is clear that satisfying the projected needs of an ever larger world population with the economy we now have is simply not possible. The western economic model—the fossil-fuel-based, automobile-centered, throwaway economy—that so dramatically raised living standards for part of humanity during this century is in trouble. Indeed, the global economy cannot expand indefinitely if the ecosystems upon which it depends continue to deteriorate. . . . The challenge is to design and build a new one that can sustain human progress without destroying its support systems and that offers a better life to all.[3]

How might this be done? First, says Brown, we must take responsibility for future generations. We must cooperate globally, reducing international inequalities and tending to the needs of developed and developing, rich and poor nations alike. An "ethic of sustainability" will be necessary, and this ethic will require a "sea change" in economic thinking. The "haves" will have to share with the "have-nots."

---

2. See Lester R. Brown, Christopher Flavin, Hilary French, et al., *State of the World 1999* (New York: W. W. Norton & Co., 1999).

3. Brown, *State of the World 1999* (p. 4).

The goal will be sustainable development, a concept defined by the World Commission on Environment and Development as "development that meets the needs of the present without compromising the ability of future generations to meet their own needs."[4] Such development requires thinking about nature, human nature, and economic activity in new ways. The assumption that nature has an infinite capacity to satisfy infinite human needs and wants must be rejected. Development cannot be built on levels of consumption that deplete irreplaceable resources and damage the fabric of natural systems upon which humans depend for ecological services. This change in thought requires a compelling vision of the future that motivates people to contemplate and ultimately accept such significant change. Environmentalists have attempted to offer such a vision.

VISIONS OF A SUSTAINABLE ENVIRONMENT

The visits of the Apollo astronauts to the moon in the late 1960s were remarkable moments in human history. The technological achievement of getting there was astounding, but so too was the vision of earth across the stark, lifeless face of the moon. Astronaut William Anders said of the view, "The Earth looked so tiny in the heavens that there were times during the Apollo 8 mission when I had trouble finding it. . . . I think that all of us subconsciously think that the Earth is flat or at least almost infinite. Let me assure you that, rather than a massive giant, it should be thought of as [a] fragile Christmas-tree ball which we should handle with care."[5]

Anders and other Apollo astronauts could see in clear and dramatic fashion that the earth was finite. They could understand their dependence upon it for life support more dramatically than anyone before in human history. This vision of the earth from space was one of the sparks of the environmental movement that emerged in the late 1960s. The vision brings into focus what it would mean to "handle with care" this planet upon which humans depend. Features of a sustainable "spaceship earth" would include, among others, the following:

- A human population stabilized at a level at which basic needs of all people could be met without depleting the earth's resources and thereby reducing options for future generations.
- An economic system that provides opportunity for meaningful work, that reduces poverty, that does not subsidize environmental harm but rather taxes it, and that promotes equitability within and between countries.

4. World Commission on Environment and Development. *Our Common Future* (New York: Oxford University Press, 1987), p. 43.

5. Oran Nicks, *This Island Earth* (Washington, D.C.: NASA, 1970).

- A high level of human cooperation that aims for sustainable development throughout the world by elevating environmental protection from its status as a poor relation in the international economic policy arena.[6]
- An "eco-industrial revolution" which reduces consumption of materials by increasing the efficiency of their usage; achieves energy efficiency by reducing energy use per unit of output; and develops and sells in a free market a technology that addresses environmental problems and generates more service to people with less harm to the environment.
- A global community that recognizes the need to conserve nature, including land, air, water, soil, and biological diversity, and that strives to maintain (and when necessary restore) the ecological health and viability of natural systems such as forests, grasslands, wetlands, surface waters, and coastal lands.
- A system of renewable natural resource usage that brings rates of harvest into line with rates of regeneration.
- Lifestyles in modern communities across the world that are simple in means and rich in ends, which achieve satisfaction and fulfillment at low levels of consumption of resources.
- Societies that value and therefore preserve the beauty, wildness and diversity of natural communities and provide ways for people to experience this nature.

This is not a utopian vision of a world in which all problems are solved, but of a world that addresses basic needs of people and assures long-term maintenance of the natural world upon which all people depend. Parts of this vision are achievable by technological innovation, whereas others require major changes in the way people relate to each other. They require changes in how the people in developed countries define quality of life. Measuring the quality of life by how much one has as compared with someone else, and the pressure for ever more material consumption that this competition generates, is a threat to sustainability.

The American writer Scott Russell Sanders describes this vision on a more personal level. "If we are to survive on this planet," he writes, "if we wish to leave breathing room for other creatures, we must learn restraint, learn not merely to will it, but to desire it, to say *enough* with relish and conviction."[7] Hunting for hope to assuage his teenage son's hopelessness and pessimism, Sanders finds it in

---

6. David Malin Roodman, "Building a Sustainable Society" in Brown et al., *State of the World 1999*, p. 177.

7. Scott Russell Sanders, *Hunting for Hope: A Father's Journey* (Boston: Beacon Press, 1998).

wildness, family, fidelity, skill, simplicity, and beauty. He finds it in a lifestyle that does not waste and destroy nature. He sums up the vision in the following way:

> Because we have achieved an extraordinary power to impose our will upon the earth, we bear a solemn obligation to conserve the earth's bounty, for all life. This means we should defend the air and water and soil from pollution and exploitation. It means that we should protect other species and preserve the habitats on which they rely. For our own species, it means we should bring into the world only those children for whom we can provide adequate care, and then we should provide that care lovingly and generously. Since we carry on the work of Creation through acts of inquiry and imagination, we should safeguard the freedom of thought and expression. Since every single one of us may contribute to the growth of consciousness, we should work to guarantee every human being the chance to develop his or her potential.[8]

Sanders envisions a world where humans, with their exceptional power and creative potential, use it to assure survival of nature not at *the expense of* human potential but to *realize* that potential. In his personal style, he writes of sustainability. He is an environmentalist in the sense defined in this chapter.

HISTORY OF ENVIRONMENTALISM

The term "environmentalism" appeared in the late 1960s in reference to a social movement in the U.S. that addressed a set of problems involving the natural world and human impacts upon it. The roots of the movement can be traced back more than a century in American history to stirrings in the minds of writer Henry David Thoreau and scholar-diplomat George Perkins Marsh. They introduced intellectuals in the 1860s to new views of the relationship of humans to nature. They began to think ecologically (though that word had yet to be coined when they wrote), to examine the ways human activity affected the natural world, and to see the ways that the natural world in turn affected human activity. Thoreau and Marsh suggested that some of the problems faced by human communities could be directly related to the way those communities treated nature, and that more care should be exercised not to damage nature.

Thoreau and Marsh stimulated others to think about this, and in the late nineteenth century in America the conservation movement emerged. By this time, there was serious concern that at the rate loggers were cutting trees, and hunters were killing animals, the nation would run out of timber, and the landscape would be devoid of wildlife which many loved to hunt or to contemplate.

---

8. Sanders, *Hunting for Hope,* p. 168.

There was concern that timber cutting would damage the quantity and quality of water upon which cities and towns depended. Water would run off the hillsides taking soil with it, thus damaging agriculture. Another branch of the movement sought to preserve beautiful natural areas where people could study nature and be inspired by its sublime beauty. They fought to establish national parks.

Historians have noted that conservation focused on *efficiency, aesthetics,* and to a lesser degree on *equity.* Efficiency meant that they wanted to ensure that natural resources were used wisely and not wasted. Gifford Pinchot, first chief of the Forest Service and adviser to President Theodore Roosevelt, sought to ensure that natural resources would provide "the greatest good for the greatest number over the longest time." Aesthetics meant that the unique and beautiful places in the American landscape would be saved from development and protected for the enjoyment, inspiration, and education of generations of Americans. Equity meant that the benefits of natural resource development would not be controlled by the rich but would be distributed broadly to the American people.[9]

The conservation movement, which was in place from 1890 to 1970, organized to achieve these goals in several ways. Political leaders like Pinchot found positions in government from which to push their agendas and achieve their goals. "Radical amateurs" like John Muir wrote persuasively in the popular media of their day, and organized like-minded conservationists in nongovernmental organizations like the Sierra Club.[10] Activists lobbied for and achieved the creation of governmental agencies, convincing Congress to establish the Forest Service, National Park Service, Fish and Wildlife Service, and others. Laws were passed and regulations promulgated to protect wildlife during key reproductive periods, to regulate uses of forest and rangeland, and to protect beautiful and important natural areas. The conservation movement was strongest during the administrations of Theodore Roosevelt (1900–1908), Franklin Roosevelt (1932–1945), John F. Kennedy (1960–1963), Lyndon Johnson (1964–1968), and William Jefferson Clinton (1992–2000).

The conservation movement was concerned with avoiding depletion of natural resources. It was concerned about forests, parks, wilderness, and wildlife, and it achieved much. In the period after WWII, however, the nature of the problems that concerned American conservationists began to change. They remained concerned about forests, parks, and wilderness, but their attention was also drawn to problems of pollution, environmental degradation, and ecological disruption. The

9. Martin V. Melosi, "Equity, Eco-Racism, and the Environmental Justice Movement," in J. Donald Hughes, Ed. *The Face of the Earth: Environment and World History* (Armonk, N.Y.: M. E. Sharpe, 2000), pp. 47–75.

10. Stephen Fox, *John Muir and His Legacy: The American Conservation Movement* (Boston: Little, Brown and Company, 1981).

massive industrialization of WWII and continued industrial growth in the post-
war period resulted in increased air and water pollution that began to attract
public attention. Nuclear tests were conducted in the most remote parts of the
world but radioactive isotopes in fallout turned up in the tissues of animals and
even people thousands of miles from the test sites. A science writer named Rachel
Carson wrote a book, *Silent Spring,* about what she called "biocides" that became
a bestseller and generated a storm of controversy about the safety of technologies
that many had come to take for granted as progress. Concerns were increasingly
raised about the "side effects" of benign activities, some of which were revealed
to be threats to human health and welfare. The space program sent Anders and
others to the moon, and the perception of earth as an unlimited resource to satisfy unlimited human wants was severely shaken.

Out of this came environmentalism, a movement that rapidly became global
when, in 1972, the United Nations Conference on the Human Environment was
convened in Stockholm, Sweden. The aims of the meeting were to identify aspects
of environmental problems that required international cooperation, to help developing nations develop without adding to environmental problems, and to decide
how the United Nations could help address these problems. Delegates agreed on
a long list of principles and set up the United Nations Environment Programme.
An unofficial "Environmental Forum" convened at the Stockholm meeting led to
a network of nongovernmental organizations (NGOs) working on environmental
problems that grew to thousands worldwide in the decade after the meeting.

The meeting revealed that environmentalism was becoming politically more
acceptable and governments beyond the U.S. were making it a policy issue. It
showed too that environmentalism had "progressed from the limited aims of
nature protection and natural resource conservation to the more comprehensive
view of human mismanagement of the biosphere."[11] And perhaps most impor-
tantly, the Stockholm meeting brought less-developed nations into the discussion
of environmental policy. Perceptions of the problems and what should be done
about them were different in developed and developing nations. Developing
nations made it clear that their first priority was economic growth and if environmental degradation was a consequence, they would live with it. This was the
beginning of a developed-developing nation or "North-South" discussion of
what should be done for the global environment, who should do it, and who
should pay for it, that continues to the present.

Another piece of the story of environmentalism in the U.S. involves ideological fractures that occurred in the past several decades. Between 1969 and

---

11. John McCormick, *Reclaiming Paradise: The Global Environmental Movement* (Bloomington: Indiana
University Press, 1989), p. 104.

1980, Congress passed more major environmental legislation than it had in all previous U.S. history. This was a consequence of many factors, not the least of which was the presence of a powerful environmental lobby in Washington, D.C. The conservation movement evolved into environmentalism and a massive demonstration of public interest in the environment was staged as Earth Day in April 1970. Membership in environmental organizations increased rapidly allowing them, with increased budgets, to hire professional staff and build strong central offices in the nation's capitol. These NGOs worked the issues with lobbying and direct mail, monitored regulatory activity and compliance, increasingly used the courts, and became part of the environmental policy process.

A grassroots environmental movement, in many ways different from the "mainstream" movement, appeared at this time. Grassroots groups often responded to a specific problem or issue, organized to deal with it, and disappeared when the issue was resolved. They forced cleanups of environmental sites, pressured corporations to consider the environmental consequences of their actions, argued for prevention of environmental contamination, and helped communities with major problems, such as toxic contamination at Love Canal in New York and Times Beach, Missouri. Members of these groups included a broader cross-section of class and occupation, and a higher proportion of women than mainstream groups, and were comprised almost entirely of volunteers. They involved minority groups to a greater extent, and formed coalitions in order to attain expertise that individual groups often lacked. They believed in citizen participation, focused their attention on human health issues, tended to be suspicious of experts, and often challenged the conventional belief in the goodness of economic growth.[12]

Other cleavages occurred in the American environmental movement. Michael McCloskey has described the different "camps" that have appeared in the recent history of the movement.[13] The dominant camp, which has here been called "mainstream," McCloskey refers to as "pragmatic reformers." Believing that government action was the best path to environmental protection, this camp worked within the existing framework of government. They were challenged by the "lifestyle camp" which thought the best path to the environmental protection goal was through rejection of conventional values and lifestyles, reduction of con-

---

12. Nicholas Freudenberg and Carol Steinsapir, "Not in Our Backyards: The Grassroots Environmental Movement," in Riley E. Dunlap and Angela G. Mertig, ed., *American Environmentalism: The U.S. Environmental Movement, 1970–1990* (Washington, D.C.: Taylor & Francis, 1992), pp. 29–32.

13. Michael McCloskey, "Twenty Years of Change in the Environmental Movement: An Insider's View," in Dunlap and Mertig, *American Environmentalism*, pp. 77–88.

sumption, and reform of the entire economic and political system. This camp, according to McCloskey, peaked and faded in the early 1970s.

In the 1980s a "radical wing" of the movement emerged that again challenged the pragmatism of the mainstream movement. McCloskey writes of them that "... mainstream groups ... were attacked for being wrong-headed in placing their faith in a government that had betrayed them." Many radicals wanted to attack the basic system of industrialism and consumerism, and the mainstream groups did not. The mainstream groups were attacked for not getting the job done—for being complacent, co-opted, bureaucratic, distant, arrogant, interested only in professional "perks" and money, and for being too conservative.[14]

McCloskey characterizes this split in environmentalism between the *pragmatists* and the *radicals* as being comparable with that between Pinchot and Muir, between the *conservationists* and the *preservationists*. The basic perception of the problem and consequent goals were different in both historical periods. As Pinchot and the conservationists accepted the course of the modern age and sought to manage it, so the mainstream environmental groups seven decades later accepted the basic system of industrialism and consumerism. They sought to work within that system, incrementally influencing public policy. Muir and the preservationists, on the other hand, doubted the course of the modern age and attempted to challenge it with their advocacy of wilderness preservation. So, too, did the later radical environmentalists who attacked the basic system and called for sweeping changes in the very foundation and fabric of society. They argued not only for preservation of nature but for lifestyle change and reduction of consumption. Throughout its history the conservation/environmental movement has suffered its own ideological cleavages.

This historical sketch is intended to show that environmentalism is not a movement that appeared full-blown on Earth Day 1970. While it seemed to burst on the public interest screen, it had been building for a century in the U.S. While its development was most extensive in America, people in other parts of the world had not been ignoring environmental concerns, and the Stockholm meeting in 1972 proved a catalyst for rapid emergence of environmentalism worldwide.

Environmentalism was not simply a concern of a privileged few, as some have alleged. The conservation movement emerged originally from concerns of educated, middle-class and mostly white Americans, but the constituency of environmentalism was broader, and continues to broaden. As it has become global, its constituency has changed to encompass people of differing races, classes, and gender.

---

14. McCloskey, p. 79.

Environmentalism is not and has never been monolithic in its core values and goals. Conservationists have worked for more efficient use of natural resources. Gifford Pinchot once said that the first principle of conservation was development, by which he meant that letting forests grow old and die or allowing water to flow from mountain to sea unused was wasteful and inefficient. Nature could be improved upon. John Muir, on the other hand, thought nature was perfect as God made it and at least some of it should not be "used" in the instrumental way Pinchot thought it should. The highest use of some of nature, thought Muir, was to let it be. Since the days of Pinchot and Muir, one school of environmental thought has been developing an "anthropocentric" or "human-centered" basis for an environmental ethic. Another has been working toward an "ecocentric" ethic, an ethic in which humans are not the source of all value but, which postulates that value lies in the "integrity, stability, and beauty of the biotic community," as Aldo Leopold phrased it in his path-breaking book, *A Sand County Almanac* (1949).[15]

ENVIRONMENTALISM AND IDEOLOGY

So what does all of this have to do with ideology? Is environmentalism an ideology? It seems to be comprised of a coherent set of ideas about the nature of human life and culture. It has a distinguishable set of core beliefs, some of which are:

- Nature is the foundation upon which the human community is built and is finite in its capacity to support that community.
- The relationship of humans to nature is thus of central importance and nature should consequently be considered in guiding human conduct.
- Humans are a part of an interdependent nature, not separate from it.
- Nature is complex and valuable and thus should be conserved *and* preserved. This is captured in Leopold's comment that "the first principle of intelligent tinkering is to save all the parts."
- People alive today must care for the earth in order that generations to follow can meet their needs and enjoy a quality life experience.

As we have seen, these and other beliefs that comprise the ideology of environmentalism have led to movements to effect social change. So it may be argued that modern environmentalism is itself an ideology which has and will generate considerable political activity.

---

15. Aldo Leopold, *A Sand County Almanac* (New York: Oxford University Press, 1949), pp. 224–225.

The demonstrations at the 1999 ministerial level meeting of the World Trade Organization (WTO) in Seattle were motivated in part by environmentalist views that environmental protection must be a part of all discussions of globalization of trade. The WTO had largely ignored the environment in its deliberations, manifesting the assumption that the environment—nature—could adapt to whatever measures it approved to advance globalization of trade. Defenders of the WTO argue that development ultimately lowers population growth, increases environmental consciousness, and provides the technology to address environmental problems. Environmentalists, on the other hand, driven by the beliefs mentioned earlier and without a voice in the actual deliberations, took to the streets to make the point that the WTO had it wrong—trade policy should adapt to environmental constraints rather than nature adapting to trade policy.

Analysis of the origins of conservation and environmentalism reveal influences of elements of the ideological spectrum described earlier in this book. As noted in the historical analysis, there are ideological splits within the contemporary environmental movement that revolve in part around disagreements about what the goals of environmentalism should be and how they should be pursued strategically and tactically. The conservation movement in the U.S. rose to prominence in the progressive period of American politics. Concern had been growing for decades about the effect of greed and fraud upon the nation's forests. Land laws had been abused by speculators since the beginning of the republic, but after the Civil War the abuses became so vast and so blatant, the accumulation of once-public lands in the ownership of a few by fraudulent means so excessive, that a reform of land laws and protection of the people's resources became a part of the progressive reform movement.

This movement took the form of advocacy of government regulation of natural resources to eliminate abuses. The General Revision Act of 1891 allowed the President to remove portions of the public domain from entry under the much-abused land laws, and by the time Theodore Roosevelt left office 170,000,000 acres of such reserves had been established. The Forest Service was created and authorized in 1905 to regulate use of these lands. Under Gifford Pinchot's leadership, the Forest Service proceeded to manage the resources of these reserves using the expertise of technically trained foresters and other experts. The story of this reform of forest policy and use (paralleled at the time by reforms in use of other natural resources) seems a clear example of reform liberalism at work. Government was at the center of the reforms, aiming to remedy perceived abuses of power and consequent inequalities through the use of expertise and bureaucracy. The very origins of the environmental movement can thus be traced back, at least partly, to the rise of reform liberalism in the Progressive Era.

After WWI, the connection of conservation with liberalism weakened and it was taken over by the business-minded Republican Party of the 1920s. This is illustrated by the major forestry legislation of the period, the Clark-McNary Act of 1924, which "codified the new alliance of conservation and business by offering cooperation and incentives, not penalties and force, for the improvement of privately owned timber."[16] Pinchot, out of forestry and into politics by this time, advocated stricter regulation and opposed the legislation, but conservation had taken a more conservative tack. Forestry graduates were going into industry rather than public service, and even the Chief of the Forest Service, William B. Greeley, left to become general manager of the West Coast Lumbermen's Association.

The second President Roosevelt (1932–1945) returned conservation to its liberal roots with his programs. FDR, of course, had several mammoth problems to address. One of them was continued degradation of the environment, most dramatically illustrated by the infamous Dust Bowl of the mid-1930s. The New Deal used government power well beyond the level imagined by the progressives, and truly big-government conservation was a feature of this period. Critics saw these moves as socialism on the march. The Civilian Conservation Corps (CCC) was formed to give jobs to the unemployed by tackling forest improvement projects. Among other work, the "CCCs" planted more than 3 billion trees, the first major effort at reforestation in the nation's history. Roosevelt, in a 1935 speech, stated his general stance on conservation.

> In his struggle for selfish gain, man has often heedlessly tipped the scales so that nature's balance has been destroyed, and the public welfare has usually been on the short-weighted side. Such public necessities, therefore, must not be destroyed because there is profit for someone in their destruction. The preservation of forests must be lifted above mere dollars and cents consideration.[17]

In American politics, the New Deal, as Stephen Fox has noted, linked the conservation movement for the first time with both reform liberalism and the Democratic Party. This linkage continues to the present, though some Republicans have become interested in using private incentives, rather than public coercion, to achieve environmental goals.

Conservationists and environmentalists have, since the New Deal, regarded government as the principal enactor of environmental protection. Preservationists worked from the 1930s to the 1960s to set up a system of legal protection for wilderness, achieving it with passage of the Wilderness Act in 1964. Aldo Leopold was part of this effort, arguing that the highest use of some parts of the national forests was to protect them, to set them aside from development. Leopold also

---

16. Stephen Fox, *John Muir and His Legacy,* p. 187.

17. Quoted in T. H. Watkins, *Righteous Pilgrim: The Life and Times of Harold L. Ickes, 1874–1952* (New York: Henry Holt, 1990), p. 469.

argued as an ecologist for a new definition of community, one that reached beyond humans to embrace nature, creating an argument for the intrinsic value of other species. Government was the instrument for protecting nature. To preserve wild places and species diversity, government drew wilderness boundaries beginning in 1964, and set up species protection processes in the Endangered Species Act of 1973. Increasing numbers of Americans "were extending the limits of their nation's traditional liberalism to include nature."[18]

Our attention in this chapter has been focused primarily on American environmentalism, but at the beginning of this discussion the contemporary challenge of environmentalism was cast as global. Qualities of a sustainable environment, as described by contemporary environmentalists, were presented. The question arises as to whether the characterization of environmentalism in America as aligned with reform liberal ideologies applies to the emerging global environmentalism. The answer is yes. In 1987 the Brundtland Commission concluded that institutional and legal change would be necessary to achieve sustainable development. The Commission suggested that governments incorporate sustainable development objectives into national policy, that regional and subregional organizations within and outside the United Nations be strengthened, that the UN and governments "support the development of regional and subregional co-operative arrangements for the protection and sustained use of transboundary ecological systems with joint action programmes to combat common problems such as desertification and acidification."[19]

On June 14, 1992 all 172 nations attending the United Nations Conference on Environment and Development in Rio de Janeiro, Brazil, adopted a strategy called *AGENDA 21*.[20] This was a global plan, a blueprint for changes deemed necessary to achieve global development in the next century that would be sustainable and protect environmental quality and soundness. The strategy was extensive and detailed, and parts of it were contentious, especially those dealing with financing of recommended measures and with transfer of technology from developed to developing nations.

What is significant about AGENDA 21 is that it represents a new level of agreement on the nature and importance of environmental factors in the future of economic development globally. AGENDA 21 includes proposals that reflect the core principles of environmentalism identified earlier in this chapter. Consumption patterns that damage the environment, it argues, must be changed.

18. Roderick Frazier Nash, *The Rights of Nature: A History of Environmental Ethics* (Madison: The University of Wisconsin Press, 1989), p. 86.

19. World Commission on Environment and Development. *Our Common Future*, p. 316.

20. AGENDA 21, United Nations document E.92–38352; A/CONF.151/26 (Volumes I, II, and III).

More efficient and environmentally sound methods of using resources must be developed. Agreements must be reached regionally and globally to protect the global commons of the atmosphere and oceans. Human settlements must be made more livable and sustainable by pollution prevention at the source, waste minimization, and use of cleaner technologies. All levels of political and economic decision-making must incorporate consideration of sustainability and environmental soundness. Economic systems must be reoriented to reflect true costs of economic activity, including environmental costs. The legal and regulatory framework for development must be restructured.[21]

A reading of the programs and activities suggested for implementation of the agenda suggests that government action will be essential in all parts of the effort. Governments will regulate, cooperate with each other to address problems that transcend national boundaries, provide financing or incentives for nongovernmental financing of critical and expensive measures, and educate their people about the need for these actions and expenditures. AGENDA 21 is clear that governments should not impose solutions unilaterally on their people, but involve them in decisions about proposed measures. A theme of the agenda is that people will accept responsibility and participate in solutions, Approaches will be democratic, participatory, open, and cost-effective, and all parties will be accountable.

The major national and international statements of strategy for achieving sustainability, such as the Brundtland report, the Report of the National Commission on the Environment in the United States, and the agenda that came out of the 1992 Rio de Janiero meetings, suggest that governmental action will be necessary to achieve sustainability. While these reports do not specify, for obvious reasons, the political theories that should underlie this government action, the environmentalism reflected in them seems to be of reform liberal character. It would be best, they seem to say, if people could come to see that it is in their interest to do what is needed, and not need to be coerced overly much. But still, some coercion for the common good will be necessary.

CONCLUSION

David Orr, in his book *Ecological Literacy* (1992), has cast the challenge of global environmentalism very clearly. He writes:

> Can we manage planet earth? Don't bet on it. But we have a chance to manage ourselves by restoring a disciplined and loving relationship to our places, communities, and to the planet. Good sense is required to know what's manageable

---

21. David Sitarz, ed., *AGENDA 21: The Earth Summit Strategy to Save Our Planet* (Boulder, Colo.: Earthpress, 1993), pp. 1–23.

and what's not and to leave the latter to manage itself. The problem is not the planet. We are the problem. Throughout history, humans have steadily triumphed over all those things that managed us: myth, superstition, religion, taboo, and above all, technological incompetence. Our task now is to replace these constraints with some combination of law, culture, and a rekindled reverence for all life. Management is then more akin to child-proofing a day-care center than it is piloting "spaceship earth."[22]

Orr's view is that application of technical and managerial expertise will not be sufficient for the human community to successfully address the problems involving environmental degradation. Success will require deep examination of cultural assumptions, beliefs, and values. Only such self-examination by people across the world will lead to actions necessary and sufficient to confront the challenge.

In the mid-1970s, psychoanalyst and writer Erich Fromm stated the challenge even more emphatically:

> The need for profound human change emerges not only as an ethical or religious demand ... but also as a condition for the sheer survival of the human race. Right living is no longer only the fulfillment of an ethical or religious demand. For the first time in history the *physical survival of the human race depends on a radical change of the human heart.* However, a change of the human heart is possible only to the extent that drastic economic and social changes occur that give the human heart the chance for change and the courage and vision to achieve it.[23]

Fromm argues that a way of life based on "having" in which people define their value in terms of their possessions cannot be sustained. Thus, the physical threat to species survival. Fromm was principally concerned with surviving the Cold War, rather than with environmentalism. However, Fromm's studies of the human condition led him to conclude that the environment simply could not support a burgeoning human community basing its well-being on "having." So he cast the challenge in the same way as many environmentalists.

Whether environmentalism as ideology and social movement can produce sufficient changes remains to be seen. Some argue today that only an environmentalism that embraces justice and equity, as well as environmental conservation and preservation, will be sufficient to contribute significantly to addressing the challenges of sustainability. Some see signs that environmentalists are doing so.[24]

---

22. David Orr, *Ecological Library: Education and the Transition to a Postmodern World* (Albany: State University of New York Press, 1992), p. 162.

23. Erich Fromm, *To Have Or To Be?* (New York: Harper & Row, 1976), pp. 9–10.

24. See Mark Dowie, Losing Ground: American Environmentalism at the Close of the Twentieth Century (Cambridge, Mass.: The MIT Press, 1995), and Robert Gottlieb, *Forcing the Spring: The Transformation of the American Environmental Movement* (Washington, D.C.: Island Press, 1993).

The reports and agendas of the major national and international commissions we have reviewed suggest also that environmentalist influences on international consideration of development have resulted in a global environmentalism that involves consideration of justice and equity at its core.

We have seen that *global* environmentalism is a very new movement in international affairs, appearing in a significant way only in the late 1960s. Only recently has the global community recognized in any significant way that nature knows no borders, and that all peoples and nations depend on the same nature. Will this realization derived from recent global environmentalism make any difference in global politics? Reflecting on the image of earth from space, the poet Archibald MacLeish wrote in 1970: "To see the earth as we now see it, small and blue and beautiful in that eternal silence where it floats, is to see ourselves as riders on the earth together, brothers on that bright loveliness in the unending night— brothers who see now they are truly brothers."[25] And yet, three decades later, such an awareness of brotherhood seems elusive. Though the Cold War face off of superpowers, a consequence of ideological confrontation, has ended, a third of the world's 193 nations, according to one assessment in 1999, are engaged in "hot" if limited wars at the close of the century, driven by growing human population and competition for natural resources, among other factors.[26]

Will environmentalism as described in this chapter, a young, ill-defined, and evolving ideology and social movement, be of significance in the world of the next century? There is no doubt that issues of sustainability will receive ever more attention as more people compete for a limited resource base. It is likely that an ideology of environmentalism will permeate global politics, raising concerns about nature to new levels and affecting policy worldwide to an extent and in ways that we cannot clearly predict today.

---

25. Archibald MacLeish, quoted in *This Island Earth* (Washington, D.C.: National Aeronautics and Space Administration, 1970), p. 3.

26. National Defense Council Foundation, *World Conflict Report 1999*. Washington, D.C., December 1999. http://www.ndcf.org/World99.htm.

CHAPTER THIRTEEN

IDEOLOGY, IDENTITY, AND HUMAN DEVELOPMENT

". . . to be human is to be the product of a particular society and culture, which is the product of past history. Yet to be human is also to have a share in making history, transmitting, altering, and preserving culture, shaping society. It is we who enact the forces that shape us."

HANNAH PITKIN

We are entering a new millennium. The potential for a world free of the wars and political excesses of the twentieth century rests in part on how we can think through the meaning of this century's experience with ideology. The ideological spectrum we have analyzed centers on two questions: the relative importance of similarities and differences between people, and the relationship between individual freedom and the power of the community. We return to these questions in an effort to place them in a contemporary perspective.

To understand the first of these questions, the political implications of the similarities and differences between people, in a contemporary perspective, we need to consider how politics fits with the larger question of patterns of human development. With that in mind, we can address the second question, the issue of freedom, authority, and the power of the state.

Throughout Part One of this book, we have used a spectrum that presents individual freedom and government power as a trade-off. To have more of one, it seems, is to have less of the other. While this is a useful analytic device for understanding classical ideologies, it also may be misleading about what good politics requires.

In this second part of the book, we have seen that to have the *freedom* to enjoy living with nature, there must be *power* to prevent abuses of the environment. To enjoy the possibility of freedom that comes with breathing clean air, enjoying nature, fitting our lives to natural rhythms and processes, we have to work within limits about how the environment will be treated. Some agency of the community has to set those limits. The truth is that saving the environment will mean that freedom and power will be interdependent. We cannot have one without the other. Freedom and power depend upon each other.

The same is true for the politics of gender and race. There can't be justice in gender and racial matters without a particular chemistry between freedom and power. It took a powerful federal government to open up voting roles, public accommodations, and job opportunities for racial minorities. Their freedom, in a substantive sense, depended upon it.

Answering the question about what is to be done requires a knowledge of the inevitable limits of freedom, so that genuine liberty can be brought about through the admixture of the right amount of government power. Ah, but the phrase, the "right amount"—how do we know when we have it?

Political theorists, as opposed to ideologues, deal with these complexities. As we mentioned in the first chapter, Michael Freeden, in his comprehensive study of ideology and political theory, points out that ideology simplifies and "de-contests" inherently ambiguous and complex relations hidden within concepts such as freedom and power.[1] What separates ideologues from political theorists is that the latter try to explore the complex relations that are often hidden in ideologies.

The purpose of political theory is, as Hannah Pitkin stated so well, to separate out what can be changed about the human condition from what is given, what is inescapable, the latter being the province of philosophy. The political theorist " delineates ... 'what has to be accepted as given' from 'what is to be done.'" The task of political theory is, then, to answer the political question of "how and where and with whom we might take action, given our present circumstances."[2]

---

1. Michael Freeden, *Ideologies and Political Theory: A Conceptual Approach* (Oxford: Oxford University Press, 1996), p. 76.

2. Hannah Pitkin, *Fortune Is a Woman: Gender and Politics in the Thought of Niccoló Machiavelli, with a New Afterword* (Chicago: University of Chicago Press, 1999), p. 290.

The answer to this question, Michael Freeden would tell us, cannot be a simple "de-contestation" of a concept like freedom to mean that all power is bad, and all individual choice is good. To be free from the oppression of slavery, the power of government to legalize and defend it must be overthrown—but another kind of government power, the power to protect rights and restore citizenship, must be authorized to legitimate a government intent on more humane policies.

The sexism and racism that arise out of de-contesting simple classifications of gender or genes brings clarity, but confuses the issues of freedom and power, similarity, and difference. The theorists of gender and racial nationalism have struggled to find the connection between what is universal, such as conceptions of human rights, and what is particular, such as the cultures of nations and the variations among women as well as men. We have to uncover the essential similarities in all people and fit politics to these realities. We also have to find the differences that are critical to identity and developmental freedom for each group of people, and even for each particular person.

To undertake this task of separating out what can be done from what is inescapable, we need to have a sense of how identities are formed, how they interact with ideology, and how politics can best be fitted to the process of identity development. In search of answers to these questions, we will turn to some contemporary research on the phenomenon of human identity.

IDENTITY AND THE FUTURE OF IDEOLOGY

The study of ideologies teaches us that beliefs about politics are linked to the human quest for meaning and a sense of purpose in life. Ideology is tied to the personal need for identity, and the development of identity is as fundamental to life as physical survival. If ideas are to serve as a source of illumination for understanding the path to a better world, it is important to see the connection between ideology, the phenomenon of identity, and the larger process of human development.

Ideology and Human Development

Erik Erikson, the principal theorist of the formation of human identity, points out that all human beings seem to strive toward a sense of *competence* and a feeling of community with others. By competence Erikson means the capacity to perform tasks of personal development and economic production in a manner that is qualitatively pleasing. At the same time, people aspire to a sense of community, or wholeness, by which the pieces of life come together with a meaning and purpose that create a satisfying self-concept. When these drives are frustrated or diverted by environments and forces that exploit, oppress, and corrupt, people develop pseudoidentities based on racism, sexism, and other pathologies of personal and social destruction.[3]

With the development of an environment that fosters a humane process of identity formation, a just and equitable society becomes possible. Erikson's research is based on observations of both genders as well as several cultures. He places human development in a framework based on the following assumptions:

> (1) That the human personality in principle develops according to steps predetermined in the growing person's readiness to be driven toward, to be aware of, and to interact with, a widening social radius; and (2) that society, in principle, tends to be so constituted as to meet and invite this succession of potentialities for interaction and attempts to safeguard and to encourage the proper rate and the proper sequence of their unfolding. This is the "maintenance of the human world."[4]

Other theorists of human development such as Lillian Rubin and Carol Gilligan have made clear the inescapable consequences of personal relationships and commitments in understanding just how this environment must be constructed. Rubin's *Intimate Strangers* and Gilligan's *In a Different Voice,* along with Erikson's classic, *Childhood and Society,* are sources that shed light on this stream of thought.[5]

In this process of development, identity formation involves a set of relations—an inescapable set of relations—between self and society. It is neither a pure assertion of individual choice nor the wholly contrived product of a culture. Rather, it is an unfolding transaction between the initiative taken by the individual, and a society that, at its best, offers opportunity as well as support at each stage of life.

The empirical research done over the past three decades on the basis of these theoretical insights converges on a simple framework for understanding these

---

3. Erik Erikson, *Identity: Youth and Crisis* (New York: W. W. Norton, 1968), pp. 25, 246. Cf. Kenneth Hoover *et al.*, *The Power of Identity: Politics in a New Key,* Chaps. 1 and 2. Erikson was widely read by leaders of the black liberation movements. Cf. Erikson, *Identity,* Chap. 8.

4. Erik Erikson, *Childhood and Society,* 2nd ed. rev. (New York: W. W. Norton, [1950], 1963), p. 270. Erikson makes an important point about conformity and the formation of identity: "One may suspect that all identity is conformist, that a sense of identity is achieved primarily through the individual's complete surrender to social roles and through his unconditional adaptation to the demands of social change. No ego, it is true, can develop outside of social processes which offer workable prototypes and roles. The healthy and strong individual, however, adapts these roles to the further processes of his ego, thus doing his share in keeping the social processes alive" (p. 412n).

5. Lillian Rubin, *Intimate Strangers: Men and Women Together* (New York: Holt and Rinehart, 1983); Carol Gilligan, *In a Different Voice* (Cambridge, Mass.: Harvard University Press, 1982).

identity relations. Identities are formed out of relations having to do with a person's *competencies,* the *communities* they belong to, and their *commitments* to others.[6] When these elements are securely in place, individuals have achieved a sense of identity.

The striking finding of this research is that those who have consolidated a sense of identity are much *more* likely to be tolerant of differences, and much *less* likely to be authoritarian in their approach to politics.[7] The clear implication of this research is that, in a world of distinctive identities arising from differing racial, religious, gender, and ethnic backgrounds, the key to advancing toleration and democracy lies in securing the foundations of identity for as many people as possible.

The focus of this chapter is on how ideology can be understood in relation to the phenomenon of identity formation. Ideology clearly plays a role in de-contesting the ambiguities and complexities of life in society, and thereby contributes, for better or worse, to identity formation. In the next section, we will illustrate how this works by considering some contemporary political issues. These illustrations will show how political theorists can illuminate the issues behind these de-contestations and, hopefully, offer some insight about how identities might be secured without resorting to negative identity strategies, such as discrimination, intolerance, or victimization. With some illustrations in mind, we can better address the question of "What is to be done?"

Social Regulation: The Market, Government, and "Civil Society"

The need for social regulation is inescapable. The alternative is violence as a means of settling disputes between individuals and communities, and inequality of the kind that would recreate the situation that led to the political excesses of the last century. The means of social regulation require careful consideration. The market is one process of social regulation, which directs effort through a price system to the satisfaction of demand. It is far better at accomplishing this goal than any system of centralized bureaucratic planning. But the intersection of patterns of supply and demand with the requirements for a sustainable environment and for a coherent process for human development make further regulation necessary. The market will not distribute medical care, education, housing, or environmental protection in a manner that will preserve the basis for humane processes of human development.

---

6. For a summary of extensive research in this field, see James Marcia, "Ego Identity: Research Review," in Hoover *et al., The Power of Identity,* pp. 85–122.

7. *Ibid.,* pp. 35–37.

But what kind of regulation? Ultimately, this is a moral issue. There must be a moral dimension to political life. There needs to be room for the private expression of moral choice—and voluntarism has its great role—just as there must be means for a publicly expressed moral choice. Why? Because the market as a device for moral choice fails a simple test: the means of entry into the market are distributed on the basis of wealth and resources—that is, quite inequitably. In a democratic society, in contrast, citizenship is the basis for participation, and it is distributed in accord with the principle of an irreducible minimum of human dignity to which every person can lay claim. Absent that premise, we do not have a society but an auction block in which the vagaries of fortune rule.

Adam Smith thought he was addressing the moral basis of society. For Milton Friedman and Friedrich Hayek, Smith's contemporary interpreters, the root of morality in the marketplace is that it protects individual choice by avoiding coercion. This sort of reasoning may be lost on those who do not have the means to play the market game, or on those who find themselves in a condition where collective patterns of action have consequences for them beyond their power to respond, such as children, the homeless, those discriminated against, and those victimized by the exploitative use of private wealth and power.

Furthermore, it is obvious that just as governmental efforts to enforce material equality involve abuses of individual freedom, so also does unrestricted individual choice have entirely predictable social consequences: great inequality and the poverty, discrimination, and even violence. Consequently, morality cannot attach solely to individual freedom of choice, it must include a social term that recognizes our common humanity. It must be observed that political processes protect individual choice, too—through the ballot box, through due process of law, and through the very concepts of constitutionalism and the protection of civil rights.

The problem, of course, is how to constitute legitimate authority. In this respect, it is important to escape the trap of thinking that authority can be found only in government—or in the marketplace. The third term in this discussion is the private relations of individuals that are found in civil society.

In his provocative analysis of community intervention into questions of personal well-being, Alan Wolfe argues in *Whose Keeper?* that the principal responsibility for human development must be assigned neither to the market, as in the United States, nor to the government, as in Scandinavia, but rather to the moral and social relations of "civil society."[8] Where the market or the government ceases being the servant of civil society and begins to replace its essential functions, a

---

8. Alan Wolfe, *Whose Keeper?: Social Science and Moral Obligation* (Berkeley: University of California Press, 1989).

loss of moral agency occurs along with a weakening of the human ties that make life tolerable.[9] Although the relations that constitute civil society do not constitute an easily definable entity, they include the family, community customs, and rituals of friendship and mutual concern, among other elements.

Wolfe defends his thesis by citing the consequences for human development of the market orientation in the United States, and the governmental orientation in Scandinavia, for the treatment of people at various life stages. In the United States he finds a pattern of family breakdown due to the invasion of commercial values at the expense of mutual commitment.[10] In Scandinavia, he finds that both children and the elderly become wards of an increasingly impersonal bureaucracy.[11] Although the results of the latter system are preferable to the consequences of the former, in his view, the question of personal moral responsibility remains. So does the suspicion that something essential to society is being undermined through these forms of institutional appropriation.

Wolfe's investigation offers a potent reminder that civil society is indeed the third term in the equation of government and the market. The justification for action through government depends not only upon a shared understanding of the developmental needs of people but also upon a demonstration that action through government offers benefits that cannot be obtained by leaving the matter in private hands. Specifically, the question of the loss of individual agency and moral choice suggests the key element of the test. What Wolfe characterizes as moral agency finds an analogue in developmental theory as the psychological necessity for personal choice and commitment. This test is easier to meet when government provides options that can be chosen, rather than an enforced policy of conformity to a single standard.

The least burdensome threshold of justification for community action involves creating options that can be freely chosen by the community's members. Few people argue with the desirability of creating parks in a city, for example, because there is a general recognition of the value of having an alternative to the private monopolization of nature. More important is the provision of public schools so that education becomes a choice available to all rather than just to the rich. *The function of the community in relation to human development is primarily to create constructive choices rather than to compel conformity.*

In addition to providing choices where no satisfactory alternatives would otherwise exist, the creation of public options can serve a regulatory purpose. The public sector, by setting standards for employment practices such as

---

9. Wolfe, *Whose Keeper?* pp. 30, 107–109.

10. Wolfe, *Whose Keeper?* pp. 58–77.

11. Wolfe, *Whose Keeper?* pp. 162–167.

nondiscrimination by the armed services and other public employers, has set a benchmark for the private sector.

The next most coercive level of public action involves the monopolization of a service or commodity. In the case of utilities, including communication and transportation services, a case can often be made that the service can be provided at a nonprohibitive cost to all members of the community only if private operators are excluded from taking over the most profitable aspects.

Finally, when it comes to the protection of the lives of people and of their legitimate interest in property, coercive power can be justified by comparison with the alternative: the sort of "war of all against all" envisioned by Hobbes.

I have sketched this continuum of public options from the least to the most coercive for a purpose. It is to suggest a frame of reference consistent with a *human development perspective* on public policy. In the name of human development, inescapable functions must be performed by the community. The world is not so simple that all of the good is found in the market and all of the bad in the state. There are abuses of human values in the market, just as there are in the state—the two are fated to be interdependent. Corporations can trample human dignity every bit as ruthlessly as governments.

Where government is not effective, the market is a device of simple exploitation of the poor by the rich, of the law-abiding by the criminal, and of the environment by its destroyers. On the other hand, where the government controls too much of economic activity, exactly the same list of abuses can be identified—only with somewhat different players using another set of symbols as justification. And for all of the debate centering on these two institutions, neither of them— and maybe not even both of them together—can satisfy the deep human craving for meaning in life, for continuity in the developmental rhythms of personal existence, for a sense of community with others.

These are the realities that we must face in the new millennium. The effort to construct new ideologies must center on combinations of political economy and of social understanding that will make it possible to sustain our physical existence on this planet while assuring millions of people that there can be a place for them and their kind alongside others who have different rituals, languages, and beliefs. That is the task that awaits the best efforts of analysts of ideology.

FREEDOM, AUTHORITY, AND THE STATE

Power is an inescapable part of people's lives. Few aspects of our relations with others are more vexing. When the problem of power moves from the interpersonal level to the realm of communities and states, most people see its realities only indirectly. Their perceptions are too often shaped by the media and by what leaders would like them to think.

As for people's beliefs about politics, they are sometimes more a reflection of personal needs for reassurance, or outlets for aggression, than judgments based on careful thought and analysis. A casual understanding of ideology can amplify the risk of misjudgment. Yet for all these limitations, people solve problems of power and freedom every day in ways that generate creativity and improvement for themselves and others, whether personally or at the level of a community and even a nation.

The ideologies we have examined contain great wisdom about the uses of power, but the wisdom has to be rescued from simplifications and dangerous illusions. Ideologies begin from models of life that can too easily become stereotypes. In classical liberalism, the ideal of the autonomous, freely choosing individual carries with it none of the complexity of human interdependence with society and the environment. Taken at face value, it is an invitation to license and to the disintegration of society. C. B. Macpherson argues that the concept of "possessive individualism" at the heart of classical liberalism, and now of libertarian conservatism, takes us straight into a dilemma from which there is no escape:

> As soon as you make the essential human quality the striving for possessions rather than creative activity, you are caught up in an insoluble contradiction. Human beings are sufficiently unequal in strength and skill that if you put them into an unlimited contest for possessions, some will not only get more than others, but will get control of the means of labour to which the others must have access. The others then cannot be fully human even in the restricted sense of being able to get possessions, let alone in the original sense of being able to use their faculties in purposive creative activity. So in choosing to make the essence of man the striving for possessions, we make it impossible for many men to be fully human.[12]

If the starting point is a simple belief in individual freedom, and if this is followed through to the organization of a purely utilitarian state based on private property, then the path leads directly to the domination of some individuals by others— and to the destruction of the original ideal of freedom for all.

Similarly, communitarian ideologies depend upon conceptions of community that can be reduced to caricatures of harmony and cooperation. What Eugene Kamenka suggests about socialist conceptions of the general will could be said of

---

12. C. B. MacPherson, *The Real World of Democracy* (New York: Oxford University Press, 1965), p. 54.

any communitarian ideology, whether it be socialist, communist, traditional conservative, or fascist:

> Precisely because socialists can still give no coherent content to that central con-
> cept of the general will as a truly universal will or to the social interest as some-
> thing in which all individual interests can be reconciled and brought to agree-
> ment, the concept of community remains in socialism important but
> fundamentally incoherent. It operates usefully as a critical idea, like alienation,
> against which particular realities can be judged. But when it is treated as some-
> thing that can be brought into reality in a specific sense, sharply defined, it
> becomes brutal, oppressive and intolerable.[13]

Just as simple individualism can disguise a process of domination, so an illusory
"general will" can be made into a mask for tyranny.

The answers to these ideological simplifications and illusions lie in the future
as well as in the past. If classical liberalism is carefully examined, there is more to
be found than simple individualism. As we saw in Chapter 2, there is Jefferson's
notion that individuality carries with it the creator's intention that the real purpose of each person's unique talents should be to complement the talents of others in building a society. In that respect, the community has rights too, such as
the right to expect the best effort of all concerned, and the duty to provide what
is necessary for that to happen.

There are similar insights in Locke, Mill, and T. H. Green—and in contemporary thinkers who consider the classical and reform liberal traditions.[14] For
them, freedom is not simply a license for self-indulgence, it is a *means* to the
development of the potential of each individual to think, to be moral, and to do
good in her or his community. *Developmental freedom* is at the heart of classical
liberalism, not the freedom envisioned by the ideologues of *laissez-faire*. And
developmental freedom requires a properly constituted community so that identity formation may proceed in a life-affirming manner.

As for the communitarian image of the "general will," Rousseau never
argued that the general will could be imposed on any society. Rather, he suggested that individuals might be brought into harmony with others in circumstances where they felt free, secure, involved in making crucial decisions, and on
reasonably equal footing with others in a material sense. These conditions, not
the precise definition of an abstract general will, are the keys that open the door
to community. In the history of communitarian thought, there are manifold

---

13. Eugene Kamenka, *Community as a Social Ideal* (New York: St. Martin's Press, 1983), p. 26.

14. See, for example, Charles W. Anderson, *Pragmatic Liberalism* (Chicago: University of Chicago
Press, 1990); and David Spitz, *The Real World of Liberalism* (Chicago: University of Chicago Press,
1982).

speculations and reports of experimentation with these and other proposed conditions. To go beyond an introductory text and read these insights in the original is to participate in a great and fateful conversation that has been going on for centuries.

The history of political philosophy suggests that, in times of political crisis, powerful new systems of ideas can be created by theorists sensitive to developments around them, and original enough to synthesize ideas into terms that communicate new understandings for cultures in need of answers. Classical liberalism received its most powerful formulation in the century of England's great civil war, the seventeenth century. Both the Declaration of Independence and the *Communist Manifesto* were written in the midst of revolutionary fervor. As sweeping cultural and economic changes come to the surface of society, they are captured in the writings of great political theorists.

The future of ideology does not lie in the rehashing of old stereotypes packaged with appealing symbols for mass consumption. The future lies in escaping from these simple images toward a more mature and intelligent understanding of life, of power, and of the potential of politics to improve society. Although they are still in their formative stages, some of the liberation ideologies discussed in Chapters 9, 10, and 11 have tried to build bridges between individualist and communitarian ideologies through a new understanding of the social and political requirements for humane personal development.

Yet the creation of a society cannot be merely the work of its politicians or its scholars. All the hopeful ideals of political philosophy, whether individualist or communitarian, rest on the thoughtful engagement of the individual citizen. Those who command the greatest power in a society, whether through force or intellect, are usually nothing more than adept followers of the public will. The will of the people must be formed out of the common sense and careful thought of the citizens, or no amount of clever rationalizing, and no quantity of arms, will save society in the end. The alternative to humane understanding is the abdication of individual participation to manipulation and domination by others.

In the twentieth century, the state proved to be as dangerous to the cause of economic justice as it was in the service of nationalism and racial purity. But it is well to remember that the state was given these roles only when previous combinations of political economy failed to prevent the most outrageous forms of inequality, of ethnic strife, and of racial hatred. Russia under the czars was just as surely a tyranny as it was under communism; Germany in the 1930s could not sustain democracy in a time of massive economic crisis; and South Africa was itself a product of the introduction of European settlers into a continent inhabited by indigenous peoples of a vastly different racial and cultural background. In the United States, slavery and the racist institutions and practices it spawned are still the most important problems the nation faces.

Although we may identify strong government with ideological extremes, it is not so clear that government itself was the cause of fascism or of communism. It is more likely that tyrannical governments were the result of extreme conditions of inequity and insecurity that undermined identity formation and delivered the public into the hands of ideologues.

CONCLUSION

To end where we began: ideology is the means by which human beings try to link morality to action in the world. It is inescapable and essential to the human experience—and is linked with the process of identity itself. The search for meaning will be served by propaganda, stereotypes, and symbolic manipulation if it is not served by our best judgment.

As Morris Berman points out, "An idea is something you have; an ideology is something that has you."[15] To understand what is to be done, we need to turn from ideology to the world of ideas, to political theory. Citizens must have ideas, not just ideologies. Ideas are open to discussion, evidence, verification, and challenge. Ideologies too often are not.

The human quest for meaning will be served in one way or another. Whether consciously or not, ideology forms a part of every person's life. The question is whether we can form identities that rely more on ideas than ideology. Bettering the human condition in the twenty-first century requires the best application of knowledge, faith, and judgment in ways appropriate to the times and to our experience of society.

---

15. See http://www2.memes.com/meme/

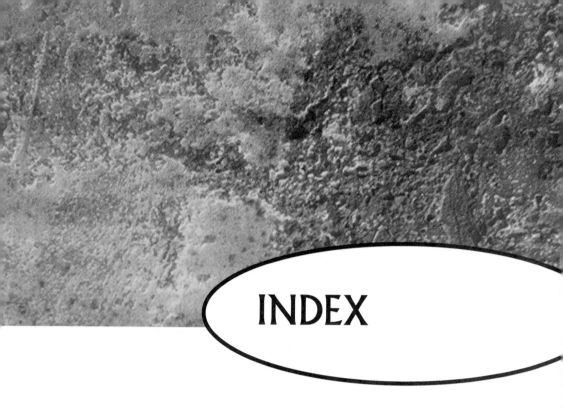

INDEX

Page numbers in *italics* denote figures; those followed by "n" denote footnotes

OF RELATED INTEREST

Contemporary Political Ideologies:
A Comparative Analysis, 9th edition—Lyman Tower Sargent

Contemporary Political Ideologies:
A Reader—Lyman Tower Sargent

Democratic Politics and Policy Analysis—
Hank C. Jenkins-Smith